COUNSELING WIDOWERS

Working with widowers can be one of the most challenging parts of a therapist's career. Despite the need for better research and professional guidance, therapists have often been left alone to confront a group struggling with high rates of suicide, mortality, physical health problems, and depression. *Counseling Widowers* builds from the latest developments in grief research and men's studies to bridge the gap between counseling practice and the needs of bereaved men. In these pages, therapists will find tools for adjusting their clinical strategies to work more effectively with these men. Through a more empathic understanding of widowers, therapists can help them build from their strengths as they face the loss of their partner.

Jason M. Troyer, PhD, is an associate professor of psychology at Maryville College in Maryville, Tennessee. Dr. Troyer has taught college courses on death and dying and has provided individual and group counseling for bereaved college students and older adults. His research focuses on the grief experiences of widowers.

The Routledge Series on Counseling and Psychotherapy With Boys and Men

SERIES EDITOR

Mark S. Kiselica
The College of New Jersey

ADVISORY BOARD

Deryl Bailey
University of Georgia

Chris Blazina
Tennessee State University

J. Manuel Casas
University of California—Santa Barbara

Matt Englar-Carlson
California State University—Fullerton

Ann Fischer
Southern Illinois University—Carbondale

David Lisak
University of Massachusetts—Boston

William M. Liu
University of Iowa

James O'Neil
University of Connecticut

Steve Wester
University of Wisconsin—Milwaukee

VOLUMES IN THIS SERIES

Volume 1: *Counseling Troubled Boys: A Guidebook for Professionals*
Mark S. Kiselica, Matt Englar-Carlson, and Arthur M. Horne, editors

Volume 2: *BAM! Boys Advocacy and Mentoring: A Leader's Guide to Facilitating Strengths-Based Groups for Boys—Helping Boys Make Better Contact by Making Better Contact with Them*
Peter Motorola, Howard Hiton, and Stephen Grant

Volume 3: *Counseling Fathers*
Chen Z. Oren and Dora Chase Oren, editors

Volume 4: *Counseling Boys and Men with ADHD*
George Kapalka

Volume 5: *Culturally Responsive Counseling with Asian American Men*
William M. Liu, Derek Kenji Iwamoto, and Mark H. Chae, editors

Volume 6: *Therapy with Young Men: 16–24 Year Olds in Treatment*
David A. Verhaagen

Volume 7: *An International Psychology of Men: Theoretical Advances, Case Studies, and Clinical Innovations*
Chris Blazina and David S. Shen Miller, editors

Volume 8: *Psychotherapy with Older Men*
Tammi Vacha-Haase, Stephen R. Wester, and Heidi Fowell Christianson

Volume 9: *Engaging Boys in Treatment: Creative Approaches to Formulating, Initiating, and Sustaining the Therapy Process*
Craig Haen, editor

Volume 10: *Dying to Be Men: Psychological, Social, and Behavioral Directions in Promoting Men's Health*
William Courtenay

Volume 11: *Engaging Men in Couples Therapy*
David S. Shepard and Michelle Harway, editors

Volume 12: *Gender in the Therapy Hour: Voices of Female Clinicians Working with Men*
Holly Barlow Sweet, editor

Volume 13: *Tough Guys and True Believers: Managing Authoritarian Men in the Psychotherapy Room*
John M. Robertson

Volume 14: *Men, Addiction, and Intimacy: Strengthening Recovery by Fostering the Emotional Development of Boys and Men*
Mark S. Woodford

Volume 15: *Breaking Barriers in Counseling Men: Insights and Innovations*
Aaron Rochlen and Fredric E. Rabinowitz, editors

Volume 16: *Counseling Widowers*
Jason M. Troyer

Volume 17: *Counseling Gay Men, Adolescents, and Boys: A Strength-Based Guide for Practitioners and Educators*
Michael M. Kocet

COUNSELING WIDOWERS

Jason M. Troyer

NEW YORK AND LONDON

First published 2014
by Routledge
711 Third Avenue, New York, NY 10017

and by Routledge
2 Park Square, Milton Park, Abingdon, Oxon, OX14 4RN

Routledge is an imprint of the Taylor & Francis Group, an informa business

© 2014 Taylor & Francis

The right of Jason Troyer to be identified as author of this work has been asserted by him in accordance with sections 77 and 78 of the Copyright, Designs and Patents Act 1988.

All rights reserved. No part of this book may be reprinted or reproduced or utilised in any form or by any electronic, mechanical, or other means, now known or hereafter invented, including photocopying and recording, or in any information storage or retrieval system, without permission in writing from the publishers.

Trademark notice: Product or corporate names may be trademarks or registered trademarks, and are used only for identification and explanation without intent to infringe.

Library of Congress Cataloging-in-Publication Data

Troyer, Jason.
　Counseling widowers / by Jason Troyer.
　　pages cm. — (The Routledge series on counseling and psychotherapy with boys and men)
　Includes bibliographical references and index.
　1. Widowers.　2. Widowers—Counseling of.　3. Widowers—Psychology.
4. Bereavement.　5. Grief therapy.　I. Title.
　HQ1058.T76　2014
　306.88'2—dc23　　　2013045384

ISBN: 978-0-415-89733-4 (hbk)
ISBN: 978-0-415-89734-1 (pbk)
ISBN: 978-0-203-80422-3 (ebk)

Typeset in Perpetua
by Apex CoVantage, LLC

Printed and bound in the United States of America by Publishers Graphics, LLC on sustainably sourced paper.

This is book is dedicated to my grandfathers, Lloyd John Troyer and Christian Burkholder—the two widowers who started me on this journey.

CONTENTS

	Series Editor's Foreword MARK S. KISELICA	xi
	Foreword KENNETH J. DOKA	xiii
	Acknowledgments	xvii
	Introduction	xix
1	Overview of Widowers	1
2	Male Gender Role and Widowers	17
3	Overview of Grief Theories	40
4	Mediators of Widowers' Grief	70
5	Men's Grief	93
6	Common and Complicated Grief Responses	111
7	Processes and Techniques of Counseling Widowers	131
8	Widowers in Groups	164
9	Understudied and Minority Widowers	178
	References	199
	Index	219

SERIES EDITOR'S FOREWORD

Boys and men form important connections with other people throughout their lives. Extensive research on attachment relationships suggests that most boys form secure attachments to their significant caregivers, and most men have secure attachment styles during adulthood (Kiselica & O'Brien, 2001). Males enjoy same-sex and cross-sex friendships throughout life (Canary & Emmers-Sommer, 1997; Rawlins, 2008), and most boys experience romantic attachments during adolescence (Carver, Joiner, & Udry, 2003). Although there has been a steady decline in the percentage of both men and women marrying since the 1940s, the majority of males age 15 years or older (55%) still marry at least once, and about one in five males between age 50–69 years have married twice (Kreider & Ellis, 2011). Thus, boys and men tend to seek out and are able to form strong bonds with others, even though the manner in which they express their closeness in relationships may be different from how women express intimacy.

Considering that intimate attachments are important to men and that men who marry do so out of love for their wife or partner, a desire to make a lifelong commitment, and because they value having a companion and want to have children within a supportive relationship (Cohn, 2013), the loss of a spouse or partner represents a significant loss for a man. Recognizing that this is the case, I had always hoped that this series would include a book devoted to addressing the challenge of helping men who become widowers. So, I was very pleased when Dr. Jason Troyer, associate professor of psychology at Maryville College, reached out to me with a proposal to write a book on counseling widowers.

Dr. Troyer is the ideal person to write *Counseling Widowers*, and his book is an important contribution to the mental health literature and The Routledge Series on Counseling and Psychotherapy with Boys and Men. Dr. Troyer is an authority on widowers and grief counseling. He has worked in numerous clinical settings facilitating grief groups and providing community-based death education, taught college courses on death and dying, and conducted numerous research projects focused on the grief experiences of widowers. In *Counseling Widowers*, Dr. Troyer has integrated findings from the psychology of men, the men's studies field, and thanatology to provide us with a compassionate and rich understanding about how widowers experience and express their grief and how we can help them. Accentuating the many developmental strengths of men, he explains how to adjust the process of counseling and psychotherapy to meet the needs of widowers in a gender-sensitive manner, accentuating active, cognitively oriented strategies of helping. Recognizing the cultural diversity of widowers, Dr. Troyer addresses variations in counseling and psychotherapy that are sensitive to widowers of different ages, sexual orientation, and religious, racial, and ethnic backgrounds. He discusses both individual and group work with widowers, and he provides vivid case examples and cites useful resources that can help any clinician understand how to proceed with the immensely fulfilling work of helping widowers to recover from the painful grief associated with losing a wife or partner.

I am grateful to Dr. Troyer for producing this much-needed volume, and I trust practitioners will treasure his fine work.

Mark S. Kiselica, Series Editor
The Routledge Series on Counseling and Psychotherapy With Boys and Men
The College of New Jersey
December 1, 2013

References

Canary, D. J., & Emmers-Sommer, T. M. (1997). *Sex and gender differences in personal relationships*. New York: Guilford.

Carver, K., Joyner, K., & Udry, J. R. (2003). National estimates of adolescent romantic relationships. In P. Florsheim (Ed.), *Adolescent romantic relations and sexual behavior: Theory, research and practical implications* (pp. 23–56). Mahwah, NJ: Erlbaum.

Cohn, D. (2013). *Love and marriage*. Washington, DC: Pew Research Center.

Kiselica, M. S., & O'Brien, S. (2001, August). Are attachment disorders and alexithymia characteristic of males? In M. S. Kiselica (Chair), *Are males really emotional mummies? What do the data indicate?* Symposium conducted at the Annual Convention of the American Psychological Association, San Francisco, CA.

Kreider, R. M., & Ellis, R. (2011). Number, timing, and duration of marriages and divorces: 2009. *Current Population Reports* (pp. 70–125). Washington, DC: United States Census Bureau. Retrieved on November 27, 2013 at www.census.gov/prod/2011pubs/p70–125.pdf

Rawlins, W. K. (2008). *Friendship matters: Communication, dialectics and the life course*. New Brunswick, NJ: Transaction Publishers.

FOREWORD

One of the criticisms of our earliest understandings of grief was that it was primarily based on the studies of women—particularly widows in the United States, the United Kingdom, Australia, and Canada. This is reasonable since there were so many more widows than widowers and many were amenable to participating in that early research. In many ways, this early research in grief reflected a general bias in the field of counseling. Sue and Sue (2013) have identified that an emphasis on emotional expression is a strong component of the culture of counseling. They note that such an emphasis may not be a good fit with many cultural groups where emotional expression is not always prized. Certainly it is not always a good fit with the contemporary Western culture of masculinity.

This is one of the reasons why Jason Troyer's *Counseling Widowers* is so warmly welcomed. It would be welcome if only to fill a void in our literature. However, Troyer offers much more than that. *Counseling Widowers* is apt to become a classic because of the five contributions that the book offers.

First, the book begins with a strong appreciation of the psychology of men. Some of the literature in this emergent field paints a very negative picture of the male experience. Males are often seen as emotionally constricted, solitary with their problems, and prone to anger and alcoholism. However, other literature—and Troyer's *Counseling Widowers* is very much part of this—notes the inherent strengths in the male role such as responsibility for others, carrying on despite difficulty, and being a team player. Troyer offers explicit techniques that recognize, validate, and build on these strengths. For example, in one case, Troyer offers a positive approach for a male client who deals with his grief by being immersed in his work. While commending the client for his devotion to caring for the financial needs of family, he sensitively assists the client in evaluating the cost of that approach, gradually helping the client develop a more balanced posture.

A second contribution is Troyer's mastery of contemporary theories of grief. If for no other reason, *Counseling Widowers* would be valued for its *tour de force* of the history of theory in grief. Troyer offers an excellent summary of current approaches acknowledging both their strengths and limitations. His work is comprehensive here reviewing Worden's Task Model as well as the continuing bonds approach and the dual process model. Throughout this discussion Troyer notes the limitations of models. Yet he also offers succinct advice on the value of these concepts and theories in counseling men.

That brings in a third strength of the book—his recognition of the particular grieving styles that males may use. Here I must begin with a disclosure. It is gratifying to see Troyer base much of his work here on the literature of grieving styles developed by Terry Martin and me (Doka & Martin, 2010). Yet Troyer puts it to good use—noting that while the relative newness of the work limits empirical support, we can acknowledge that many men may express their grief in more cognitive and behavioral—or what we term—*instrumental* approaches. Again, Troyer effectively develops the ways that clinicians can utilize these approaches both in individual and group counseling.

This is the fourth strength of the book. It is eminently practical. Throughout *Counseling Widowers,* there is a variety of case illustrations and just general tips about approaches toward counseling men from basic approaches to advertising services to the intricacies of counseling. Clinicians, both new and experienced, will find much of value here.

The last gift of *Counseling Widowers* is sensitivity to the disenfranchised male griever. Troyer acknowledges the many faces of male loss. The male experiencing the loss of a partner may be younger or older, with children or without. He may be cohabitating with a partner—in the nether status of widowhood—grieving a partner unacknowledged by others. He may be a gay male married or cohabitating with a partner of the same sex—again perhaps with a loss acknowledged by only some in his immediate circle. He may be grieving an ex-spouse or former partner.

One of the little tidbits that struck me as I read this book brought me to Sue and Sue (2013) once again. In Troyer's work one of his suggestions for making counseling male-friendly was to ensure that one has male-oriented magazines in the waiting room. In my course on Counseling the Culturally Diverse, I often stress the value of having ethnic magazines, relevant to the groups one is counseling, in the waiting room. Yet I have never really applied it to male clients. It should be so obvious—the culture of males often has a less-than-comfortable fit with the culture of counseling. Happily, *Counseling Widowers* narrows this gap.

Kenneth J. Doka, PhD
Professor, The Graduate School, The College of New Rochelle, New Rochelle, NY
Senior Consultant, Hospice Foundation of America, Washington, DC

References

Doka, K. J., & Martin, T. L. (2010). *Grieving beyond gender: Understanding the ways men and women mourn.* New York, NY: Routledge.

Sue, D.W., & Sue, D. (2013). *Counseling the culturally diverse: Theory and practice* (6th ed.). New York, NY: John Wiley & Sons.

ACKNOWLEDGMENTS

I would like to thank Mark Kiselica for guiding and supporting me through the writing of this book. Thank you for your kind words of encouragement and for your mentorship. I would never have started this book if Dana Bliss had not recognized its potential, and I would never have finished it without the guidance and patience of my editor, Anna Moore. Special thanks to Ken Doka for supporting this book from the very beginning. Thanks to all of you for your respective roles in this creating this book.

I would like to thank my colleagues at Maryville College for the institutional and personal support. Specifically I would like to acknowledge my psychology colleagues, Crystal Colter, Karen Beale, Arianne Schratter, Chad Schrock, and Kathie Shiba, for making my daily work so enjoyable. Thanks also go to my department chair, Lori Schmied, and my academic dean, Barbara Wells, for supporting my sabbatical—this book would never have been written without it. Special thanks to the library staff, including Roger Myers, Marina Jaffe, and Neena Teaster, for tracking down obscure journal articles and texts. I would also like to express my appreciation to the students who have assisted me with my research on widowers including Jill Copeland, Lauren Kidd, Jordan Sherrod, and Windsor Wall.

I have been blessed to be surrounded by exceptional men throughout my life. Virtually everything I know about friendship I have learned from my Tribe: Matt Hoffman, Keith Russell, Kevin Wheeler, Greg Schickler, Matt Yates, Jason Steingraber, and Dan Flynn. Thanks also to Lynn Gibson for his friendship and insightful discussions and to my brother, Trent, for his lifelong friendship.

To my parents, Omer and Mary Jane, thank you for your unending love and support. You have been a lifelong source of inspiration and the foundation for any success I have ever had. I would like to thank all of the widowers who have shared their lives with me. I am constantly amazed by your resilience and courage in the face of loss.

ACKNOWLEDGMENTS

To my daughters Gwendolyn and Juliana, thank you for your love and patience, especially when I was not available to spend more time with you. Finally, this book would not have been possible without my true companion and wife, Jenny. Your love and support has made all things possible and worthwhile.

INTRODUCTION

Researchers overlook widowers; practitioners are frustrated by them. This is troubling because widowers face higher rates of depression (Lieberman, 1996; van Grootheest, Beekman, Broese van Groenou, & Deeg, 1999), health problems, and overall mortality than widows (Mineau, Smith, & Bean, 2002). They are 5 to 12 times more likely than widows to commit suicide (Luoma & Pearson, 2002), and they seek and receive less social support (Lee, Willetts, & Seccombe, 1998; Stroebe & Schut, 2001). Widowers are shocked to have outlived their wives and are distraught when they realize they have also lost their closest confidante. Without someone to protect and provide for, widowers feel that life has become meaningless. Additionally, widowers are handcuffed by a culture that has taught them to remain stoic and never show pain. Despite this, widowers have distinctive strengths that can help them survive and thrive—yet most therapists tell them not to trust their instincts. This book brings together the view that men have strengths and weaknesses as a result of their psychological development and socialization with a new perspective on grief that is more action-oriented and cognitive in nature. Through an accurate understanding of the factors that shape men, therapists can more empathically understand grieving widowers and more effectively help them build from their natural strengths.

Over the past 20 years a new movement in the study of men and masculinity, generally referred to as the New Psychology of Men (NPM) (see Levant, 1996; Levant & Pollack, 1995), has outlined the distinctive challenges that men and boys face due to specific childhood experiences and socialization pressures as well as their unique strengths. Early works by Pleck (1981), O'Neal (1981) provided much of the foundation, while later works by Levant (1992, 1995 (with Pollack)), and Pollack (1998) and others have developed and advanced the model. Recently the positive psychology/positive masculinity (PPPM) perspective has further emphasized the process of building from men's strengths (Kiselica, 2011; Kiselica & Englar-Carlson, 2010; Kiselica, Englar-Carlson, Horne, &

Fisher, 2008). These perspectives have provided a foundation for many new ideas and applications for counseling boys and men; however, it has not been extensively applied to widowers.

Boys and men are pressured to conform to gender roles, and grieving widowers are no exception. Therapists must understand where widowers' ideas of what it means to "be a man" come from in order to empathize with them. Boys are instructed to turn away from mutually beneficial relationships in order to establish their independence and self-sufficiency (Bergman, 1995). It is not exactly clear to the boy what a "real man" does, other than refrain from being dependent on others. Some authors have suggested that the only clear rules boys have are to reject anything perceived to be feminine (Brooks, 1998). This creates a lifelong habit of compartmentalizing their lives. Thus, men avoid sharing information, concerns, doubts, or anything else that would lead to emotional vulnerability (Pollack, 1995). Although men seek to become autonomous, this is not actually what happens. For example, by turning over all matters of 'feminine' emotions to his wife a husband creates a dependence on her for interpreting and expressing emotions—what Pollack calls 'pseudoautonomy.' Practically speaking, this often takes the form of wives handling much of the communication within and between families, including observations of developmental milestones such as births, graduations, birthdays, marriages, divorces, and deaths. Men attempt to maintain their autonomy by abdicating all matters infused with emotion (except anger or frustration), but in reality create a critical dependency on their wives.

What effects does this have on widowers? For widowers, this social and intrapsychic pressure to live up to these vague, but strict standards of male gender socialization are combined with the pressure faced by the bereaved regarding socially and culturally determined 'rules' for grieving (Harris, 2010). Imagine an older widower who has just lost his wife. He was taught long ago that a man needs to be independent from others and be able to stand alone. He has learned to avoid anything feminine because it may impair his abilities or he may be viewed by others as gay. These rules have been continually reinforced from multiple sources throughout his life. In some ways, these characteristics have served him well. He is proud of the sacrifices he has made to provide the resources his family needs—he believes he has fulfilled his part of the deal. To accomplish this he has relinquished the 'emotional stuff' to his wife for the last 50 years. She dies. He never expected to outlive her. Upon her death he must now deal with his greatest loss without any practice or inclination for understanding or expressing emotions. He sets to work planning the funeral arrangements and completing the necessary tasks. After the formal rituals of death are complete, he is alone—but this is not the kind of autonomy he wanted. Although others see him as a strong, independent man, he is now trapped in a new land without his lifelong partner, his interpreter. Before now he has always gone off on his own to solve his difficult problems. But this problem doesn't have a solution.

What if he seeks counseling? Most therapists believe that expressing grief-based emotions are necessary for healing. This perspective, called the 'grief work hypothesis,' suggests that emotions must be openly expressed for grief to be resolved (see Stroebe, 1992). This model has dominated grief counseling for the past few decades and is still a prevalent model. It has been criticized for focusing only on affective responses to grief as the only effective methods (Doka & Martin, 2010; Rando, 1993; Wortman & Silver, 1989). Only recently has there been the introduction of a new grief model that expands the emotion-based model to include cognitive and action-based components. This model more accurately incorporates the effects of most men's psychological development and gender role socialization.

While several authors have discussed this new model (e.g., Golden, 2000; Levang, 1998), Doka and Martin (2010) have provided the most thorough description. Their thesis is that individuals will express different patterns of grief and these patterns exist on a continuum with 'intuitive' and 'instrumental' defining each pole. An intuitive grief pattern reflects the current paradigm; emotion-based grieving is necessary for healing. An instrumental pattern comprises cognitive and action-based grief. Therefore, instrumental grievers tend to use physical action and problem-solving as a means for expressing their grief. They tend to experience emotions in a more muted way and focus on using reasoning to deal with the new challenges that the loss has created. Doka and Martin suggest no one exemplifies just one style, thus the continuum model, and the two different patterns are not necessarily dictated by gender, although men tend to demonstrate a more instrumental pattern while women tend to exhibit a more intuitive pattern. Contrary to the grief work paradigm, which suggests that open expression of emotion is the only route to grief resolution, Doka and Martin do not hold one pattern to be more effective than the other.

Most therapists are unaware of grieving styles that include action-oriented and cognitive components; they believe the grief work perspective is the best theory for working with bereaved clients. Consequently, most therapists encourage men to express their feelings as the primary means to express grief even though most men tend to be more cognitive, action-oriented, and problem-solving focused. This mismatch between men's typical patterns and therapists' beliefs about the 'right' way to grieve leads to unproductive counseling sessions. Men leave counseling feeling incompetent and misunderstood—often giving up on counseling. Therapists wonder why their techniques and interventions are not working or believe their grieving male clients are just being 'resistant.'

INTRODUCTION

Widowers are hurting and most therapists are ill-equipped to help them. This book provides therapists with a clearer understanding of how the psychological development and gender role socialization of boys and men shape widowers' grief processes. As a result, therapists will develop a more accurate view of their grieving male clients and will learn counseling strategies that take advantage of most men's natural action-based and cognitive grieving style. Through a more empathic understanding and male-friendly counseling techniques, therapists can develop a more collaborative and productive counseling relationship with their widowed male clients.

1

OVERVIEW OF WIDOWERS

There is a paradox in this book that is shared with many books on counseling and therapy with men. If men do not seek counseling then why write a book about it? There is some truth to this—men, including widowers, are less likely to seek out a psychotherapist. But some do, and more and more are. While the stigma of counseling and asking for help still holds some men back from seeking assistance, this roadblock is fading. The more important question is: How can we best help men who *do* walk through the therapist's door?

This book, along with the other books in this series, provides a part of the answer to this question. Few would argue that men who have lost a spouse or partner are hurting; many of them could benefit from professional assistance. But unfortunately, most psychotherapists are poorly prepared to deal with grief *and* with male clients. Many psychotherapists use counseling techniques that work well for women and rely on outdated perspectives on grief. This is why I have heard many stories of widowers quickly leaving individual or group counseling because they felt misunderstood and out of place.

In 2006, Mark Kiselica (the editor of the Counseling and Psychotherapy with Boys and Men series), wrote, "If we really hope to help teen fathers to become caring, competent, and committed parents, then we must begin by thinking complexly about these young men" (p. 227). Similarly, I offer this paraphrase: If we really hope to help widowers heal, then we must begin by thinking complexly about these men. To do this we must learn about widowers and dispel the myths that surround them. Not every younger widower is Tom Hanks in *Sleepless in Seattle* nor is every older widower Walter Matthau or Jack Lemon in *Grumpy Old Men*. Not only must we reexamine what we know about men, but we must consider grief in all its forms—not just emotional grief, but also cognitive and physical aspects of grief. To counsel grieving men, your toolbox must be large and diverse. If it helps, think of me as your neighbor who has the biggest tool collection on the block, and this book is my effort to share my tools with you.

Throughout the book I share comments by widowers from various sources. Widowers interviewed or counseled by someone else have been cited according to the original publication. All uncited widower quotes are based on my personal research or work with widowers. In all cases the names of the widowers and details of their situation have been changed to protect their confidentiality. In some cases two or more widowers' experiences have been combined to highlight a particular concept and for the sake of brevity.

Definitions

Widower

My definition of a *widower* is broader than typical. It includes men who have experienced the death of a person with whom they shared a significant, committed, romantic relationship. The relationship might be classified as married, engaged, partnered, or divorced and includes female and male partners (married or unmarried). Although this book does not focus on the needs of men who are caregivers for their ailing partners, many of them could benefit from the information contained. Some of these caretaking husbands/partners may consider themselves to be 'widowers in waiting.' For example, men caring for a wife or partner who is suffering from dementia may reach the point where they feel that their partner has already 'died' psychologically.

Married/Partnered

Throughout the book I use both *married* and *partnered* almost interchangeably. The terms married and partners can be inferred to include those who are legally married, common-law married, consider themselves married (despite the choice or inability to legally marry), engaged, or are in a long-term cohabitating relationship. In short, any man who thinks of himself as being connected to another in a loving, exclusive relationship. However, when I summarize previous studies of widowers the term *married* will reflect individuals who are legally married as virtually all studies about widowed people involve legally married couples.

Challenges Facing Widowers

Grief research has focused almost exclusively on widows (Wortman & Boerner, 2011), making widowers an almost invisible group (Thompson, 1998). There are almost 3 million widowers in the United States including more than 21% of men over the age of 75 (US Census Bureau, 2010). Despite this, widowers are sometimes considered to be a 'forgotten' population (Rubinstein, 1986) because there are approximately four widows for every widower (US Census Bureau, 2010). However, the shrinking gap between the life expectancy of men and women, along with other factors, indicates that the ratio of older men to older women will likely become more equal and will result a larger number of widowers (Centers for Disease Control and Prevention (CDC), 2012; Thompson, 1998).

Being forgotten is a position that society does not often recognize for men since they, especially Caucasian men, are typically viewed as possessing most societal advantages. For example, widowers have frequently been left out or included only as a small minority in major studies of grief. For example, widowed men constituted less than 23% of the participants in Parkes's (1996) *Bereavement: Studies of Grief in Adult Life* and less than 15% of the Changing Lives of Older Couples (CLOC) survey (Carr, 2006). This means that in some major studies of widowed individuals results for widowers are being tabulated based on a few dozen participants while results for widows are based on a few hundred participants. Unlike situations where members of specific ethnic groups or other minorities in a given population are targeted for research, "there is no concerted effort to target [older men] as a special population" (Stelle & Uchida, 2004, p. 100).

Further complicating the picture is that widowed individuals participate in grief research for different reasons. Stroebe and Stroebe (1989) found that widowers who participate in bereavement research report less depression than widowers who refuse to participate, whereas widows had the opposite pattern. This sampling error based on self-selection could lead researchers studying spousal bereavement to *overestimate* widowers' coping while *underestimating* widows' coping.

Based on the studies of widowers thus far, researchers have discovered that widowers frequently have a difficult time dealing with the loss of their spouses. In fact, many researchers have reached the conclusion that, on average, widowers have a more difficult time than widows (Stroebe, Stroebe, & Schut, 2001; Umberson, Wortman, & Kessler, 1992). Most widowers and widows agree with this conclusion (Bennett, 2009; Bennett, Hughes, & Smith, 2003). The extent of their difficulties can be seen in smaller social networks, inadequate coping strategies, higher rates of depression, higher rates of substance use, poorer physical health and mortality rates, and dramatically higher suicide rates. Furthermore, the number and proportion of older widowers is expected to increase dramatically in the next few decades. When examined together, these concerns support further research on this understudied population.

Let me be clear—this chapter is not an effort to prove that widowed women have it easy. Loss of a partner is one of, if not *the* most, challenging event for most widowed men *and* women (Carr, 2006; Holmes & Rahe, 1967; Raphael, 1983; Rubinstein, 1986). Just like widowers, widowed women also suffer from inadequate social support, depression, substance abuse, poor health, higher mortality, and suicide. The goal of this chapter is simply to provide therapists with an overview of the various challenges facing widowed men.

Social Support and Social Engagement

The positive influence of social support in coping with stressful events has been well supported, although the relationship is complex. Less social support is associated with higher depression (Lee, Willetts, & Seccombe, 1998), higher mortality rates (Bennett, 2002), poorer coping (Bennett, Hughes, & Smith, 2005; Dimond, Lund, & Caserta, 1987; Levy, Martinkowski, & Derby, 1994), and lower life satisfaction (Bennett, 1998). Marriage is generally acknowledged to have more benefits for men (Coombs, 1991). For men, having a marriage partner is correlated with self-esteem (Carr, 2004c), better physical health (Courtenay, 2011), less binge drinking (Byrne, Raphael, & Arnold, 1999), lower depression (Lund, Caserta, & Dimond, 1989), and lower mortality rates (Helsing, Szklo, & Comstock, 1981). Furthermore, men have generally relied on their wives for maintaining connections to their extended family (sometimes called 'kin-keeping') and other social networks (McIntosh, Pearson, & Lebowitz, 1997).

Given that most married men rely on their wives as their primary source of social and emotional support (Umberson et al., 1992), the accessibility of supportive networks is an important consideration for widowers. The availability of social support is multifaceted. Most studies measure multiple aspects of social support including the number of close relationships, the frequency of contact, the perception of support, and the strength and structure of the relationships. Studies have shown that after their spouse dies widows have larger social networks, experience an increase in friends, and receive more support from their children than widowers (Lee et al., 1998; Stroebe & Schut, 2001; Stroebe, Stroebe, Abakoumkin, 1999; Umberson et al., 1992), as well as stronger ties within their social networks (Dimond et al., 1987). Furthermore, widows are more likely to have high self-efficacy regarding their interpersonal skills and ability to recruit social support (Fry, 2001a). Widowers are generally more likely to use various professional services, such as housekeepers, when caregiving prior to the loss of their spouse (Bennett, 2009) and following their partners' deaths (Moore & Stratton, 2002). However, these types of hired services are different than social support that emphasizes personal companionship.

Given the importance of social support as a mediating factor for so many risk factors, why are widowers offered less social support and less likely to seek social support? Reasons for this may include a desire to not be perceived as weak or out of control, a preference for being alone, lack of practice at maintaining social and family relationships, being perceived as a romantic threat, and if the widower is grieving 'appropriately.' Bennett, Hughes, and Smith (2003) suggest that widowers "may not request help, since it would threaten the ideals of capability and control. Or men may not be offered help, since they are viewed as strong, capable, and in control" (p. 411). Although more research is necessary, I would argue that both of these factors, and others, play a role in influencing social support for widowers.

Some widowers simply prefer to cut back on their social interactions following a loss. Bennett (1998) found that older widowers were less socially engaged when compared to their pre-loss levels and had lower levels of social engagement when compared with widows or married men. For example, John, an older widower, expressed his preference to be alone in the first few months after his loss:

> I just wanted to sit here in this house and just reflect on our life together and just get engrossed in my thoughts. I didn't want to talk to anybody, I just wanted to think and try to put things in perspective. . . . And some other people might have wanted everybody to come in you know, but I did not. [Not] ministers or anybody. I just wanted to be with myself for a while.

Many widowers report that later they seek out more opportunities for social interaction (Cleiren, Diekstra, Kerkhof, & van der Wal, 1994). This may explain why the level of social support for widowers may be at its lowest during the first 16 months of bereavement and then begins to increase (Balaswamy, Richardson, & Price, 2004). This goes against the common assumption that social support for most bereaved individuals is highest immediately following the loss and then progressively declines. The truth is likely somewhere in the middle. Widowed persons are typically well supported in the first few weeks after the loss, but this initial surge trails off quickly for widowers (Stelle & Uchida, 2004).

Social contact may also be limited because widowers are not used to maintaining connections and have relied on their wife as their primary relationship (Davidson, 2004; Umberson et al., 1992). Consequently, widowers' previous reliance on their wives for social interaction and kinship connections may impede their ability to seek it out once their wife has died (McIntosh et al., 1997).

Widowed persons (male and female) also report being rejected by former friends due to being perceived as a threat, either as a romantic rival or as a reminder that death is a reality that everyone must face eventually. One widower described it like this:

> When you lose your wife, you also lose other couples as friends. I think there are two reasons for it. One is the threat syndrome. I think you become a threat to the male. The other is the thank-God-it's-not-me thing. You are a reminder of the road we all travel someday. Your aloneness is a constant reminder of people's vulnerability, that they too may suffer that loss. And I don't think they want to be around you. So you learn to be alone. (Campbell & Silverman, 1987, p. 126)

Although being a threat to friends is frequently cited by widowed persons, little research exists on the frequency of this types of rejection.

Another factor influencing social support is how the widower's grief is interpreted by others. For example, research has supported the view that bereaved men and women are viewed more favorably and would receive more support if their grief behaviors matched the socially accepted view of how they 'should' be grieving (men in more emotionally muted and physical ways; women more expressively; Kubitz, Thornton, & Robertson, 1989). Despite the inconclusive research, it is clear that men who grieve in overly emotional ways eventually will drive away support from those who expect that he should be 'over it by now.' Conversely, widowers who 'slam the door' on supporters will also see their support diminish. Tragically, widowers who discourage support initially may find it difficult to reclaim later when they decide to engage in more social activities (Cleiren et al., 1994). For example, although John initially did not want anyone to visit him, by the time I interviewed him 14 months after his wife died he had changed his view: "[Wanting to be alone] has passed. I wish people would come by now."

It is important to remember that, despite its significant empirical support, social contact is not inherently beneficial for grieving persons. Professional researchers (Lund, Caserta, & Dimond, 1993) and popular authors (Kelly, 2000) have pointed out that many friends and family members can be, at best, unintentionally hurtful and, at worst, harmful in their social contact with widowed persons. Widowed persons can be subjected to blame, guilt, and interrogations concerning the deceased's possessions. If the death was stigmatized (e.g., suicide, homicide, etc.) in any way, the social contact can add a further burden.

The lower availability of social support for widowers and their hesitancy to reach out for social support is troubling not only because social support is positively related to so many mental and physical health factors, but also because two predictors of complications in grief include the inability to express one's thoughts and feelings and not keeping busy (Lund & Caserta, 1992). A lack of supportive social relationships would likely have a negative impact on both these factors. More research is needed to compare the outcomes of grieving men who isolate themselves compared to those who embrace social support. While it is possible that isolating himself is a normal part of grief and provides an opportunity for a time of reflecting on his loss and reconstructing his worldview (Sanders, 1999), current evidence suggests that taking advantage of social support and being more socially integrated into his immediate community has significant advantages.

Coping Strategies

Coping strategies (or what some call *adaptive strategies*, see Corr & Doka, 2001) are specific efforts to manage perceived stressors; these efforts change constantly as the stressful situation or conditions vary (Lazarus & Folkman, 1984; Corr & Doka, 2001). In examining the coping behaviors of widowers, it is common for them to focus on the practical problems that bereavement has created instead of the resulting emotions (Stroebe, 1998). When they do confront painful emotions, they tend to engage in solitary, physical activities (Brabant, Forsyth, & Melancon, 1992). In one study Stroebe and Stroebe (1991) found that widowers who avoided focusing on their grief-related emotions were more depressed later in comparison to those who confronted their grief. However, this may only apply to widowers who engaged in extreme avoidance.

There are many possible explanations why men do not seek to express their emotions. The most common reasons involve the socialization and societal expectations that men not grieve openly, avoid vulnerability and signs of weakness, and that they be self-sufficient (Campbell & Silverman, 1987; Robertson & Fitzgerald, 1992; Stroebe, 1998). These social and cultural influences will be explored more fully in Chapter 2.

The challenge of studying coping strategies with bereaved individuals is that some argue that grief is not something from which one should or could recover. When coping with an illness, such as cancer, or with depression or anxiety, it is generally agreed that effective coping results in the reduction or absence of symptoms. Unlike these other concerns, the death of a loved one cannot be changed by any coping mechanism (see Wortman & Boerner, 2011).

Several authors and researchers (e.g., Golden, 2000; Schaefer & Bekkers, 2010) have argued that grieving men may benefit most from cognitive and physical coping methods and strategies. The typical argument is that men are most comfortable focusing on problem-solving and achieving practical results (Doka & Martin, 2010), especially if they endorse some aspects of traditional masculinity (see Levant, 1995).

Depression

Researchers have struggled with attempting to measure depression in widowed individuals. Furthermore, there is often confusion regarding the differences between depression and grief. Although there is certainly a relationship between grief and depression and there are advantages to using depression scales with grieving individuals, "there is now growing evidence that depression and grief represent distinct, though related, clusters of reactions to bereavement" (Hansson & Stroebe, 2007, p. 14).

Both older widows and widowers score higher on depression scales than married controls (Lund et al., 1989). Moreover, several studies have found the majority of widows and widowers to have elevated depression levels well after their loss and argue that the process of adjustment may continue for years (Arbuckle & deVries, 1995). Wortman and Silver (2001) reported that differences in depression scores for widowed individuals remained significant for as long as 15 years when compared to married controls. Additionally, manifestations of complicated grief, including survivor guilt, bitterness, and difficulty accepting death, did not decline over a period of five years in widowers and did not decline for widows over a span of three years (Bierhals et al., 1995). These results contrast sharply with a smaller body of research that suggests the differences in well-being between widowed individuals and married controls are minimal or at least eventually decline (Umberson et al., 1992; Lund, Caserta, & Dimond, 1986).

When comparing widowers and widows, the research on depression is mixed. Some studies have found no differences between bereaved men and women (Lund et al., 1986). Others have found that widowers have higher depression scores (Lieberman, 1996; Umberson, et al., 1992; van Grootheest, Beekman, Broese van Groenou, & Deeg, 1999; Wisocki & Skowron, 2000) and lower overall psychological well-being (Fry, 2001b). In comparing married and widowed women and men, Lee et al. (1998) found that married men had the lowest depression scores and widowed men had the highest, while the married women and widows' scores were not significantly different. Although various sources of strain such as dealing with household tasks and concerns about finances have been found to influence post-loss depression in widowed men, these factors did not account for a sizeable portion of their depression; the simple fact of being widowed appears to be the largest factor in depression following spousal bereavement (van Grootheest et al.,

1999). Overall, research provides tentative support for the view that widowed men experience more depression than widows and married men (Stroebe et al., 2001).

Health and Health Behaviors

Even before their loss widowers start off at a disadvantage in terms of physical health given that men in the United States die five years younger than women. Furthermore,

> men's adjusted death rates for heart disease and cancer—the two leading causes of death, which account for more than half of all deaths—are 50 and 80% higher, respectively than women's rates (DHHS, 2009a; Jama et al., 2008), and one in two men—compared with one in three women—will develop cancer in his lifetime (American Cancer Society, 2008). (Courtenay, 2011, p. 4)

Married men tend to have better health than unmarried men. There are several possible explanations for this. One is that men who are healthier are more likely to be married. The other explanation is that marriage partners help moderate each other's health behaviors. Umberson (1987, 1992) compared married, widowed, and divorced individuals and their rates of various negative health-related behaviors, including substance abuse, drinking and driving, marijuana use, and having a 'disorderly lifestyle.' Widowed and divorced individuals were more likely to be engaged in all of these behaviors except marijuana use. She also found that women provide more health monitoring for their husbands than vice versa.

Typically, widowed individuals experience a great deal of stress at the time of bereavement and as they transition to widowhood. A classic example of this is that the death of a spouse is rated as the most stressful event for adults on Holmes and Rahe (1967) classic *Social Readjustment Rating Scale*. As an acute and chronic stressor, bereavement can disregulate various neuroendocrine systems and result in impaired immune responses and poorer physical health (for a review, see Goodkin et al., 2001).

Health behaviors can be moderated by a variety of factors. Cooking experience and skill are related to having a healthy diet. One study of older men who lived alone (approximately half were widowers) found that men with better cooking skills reported better overall health and eating more vegetables (Hughes, Bennett, & Hetherington, 2004). The researchers concluded that cooking classes and updated information about healthy diets could benefit men who lived alone. Unfortunately, other researchers have found that, overall, widowed men decrease their consumption of vegetables (Fry, 2001a) and increased their consumption of fried food at restaurants (Eng, Kawachi, Fitzmaurice, & Rimm, 2005). Limited research has shown that older widowers often rely on extended family or friends for acquiring and cooking food. Furthermore, financial ability, ability and means of driving, sources of informal and formal support, and physical ability may significantly influence widowers' ability to acquire healthy food and prepare it (McDonald, Quandt, Arcury, Bell, & Vitolins, 2000).

The vast majority of research on the health behaviors of spousally bereaved individuals has used older persons. This dearth of research on health behaviors with younger widowers is concerning; although older age and poorer health are strongly related, when widowed persons are compared to age-matched still-married individuals, bereavement is related to more health problems in *younger* widowed persons (Stroebe & Schut, 2001).

Alcohol and Substance Abuse

Most studies of widowers find some increase in the use of alcohol following their loss (e.g., Barusch & Peak, 1997; Eng et al., 2005; Shuchter & Zisook, 1993). In a study in Australia Byrne, Raphael, and Arnold (1999) compared older widowed men's alcohol use to similar married men at 6 weeks, 6 months, and 13 months post-loss. Widowers were found to engage in significantly more binge drinking (5 or more drinks) and greater frequency of alcohol consumption. However, widowers who were non-drinkers before their partner's death did not begin drinking.

Another study found that widowed persons who were judged to have poor adjustment one year after their partners' deaths used more alcohol and drugs (prescribed and non-prescribed). Tolle, Bascom, Hickam, & Benson (1986) interviewed widowed spouses approximately one year after the death of their partner at a medical facility. Overall, 23% of the participants (these were mostly the widowed men) reported that alcohol helped them fall sleep and with their loneliness. The researchers found that 42% of the participants used drugs other than alcohol to help cope with post-loss challenges. Of those who used drugs, approximately 8% used non-prescribed drugs; these drugs could either be prescribed for someone else or illicit drugs.

More research on the use of alcohol, medications, and prescription drugs by widowed persons is needed given their influence on a variety of coping mechanisms and health variables. Limited research has found that widowers use more medications for the same medical problems than single, divorced, or married men (Sanfelix et al., 2008), but research in this area is limited. Taking into consideration that almost 9% of the US population uses an illegal substance (or misused or abused a prescription medication) at least monthly (NIDA InfoFacts, 2012), the lack of research on the use of illicit or unprescribed drugs while grieving is troubling.

Mortality Rates

When I tell people that I study widowers I frequently receive questions about the sudden deaths of surviving partners—commonly referred to as 'dying of a broken heart.' At times it seems that almost everyone knows a widowed person who died shortly after his or her partner died. (This includes me—both of my grandfathers died within three months of their respective wives.) So, is it possible to die of a broken heart? While the specific mechanisms are still being studied, researchers have consistently found that widowers have a higher mortality rate when compared to married men (Elwert & Christakis, 2008) and widows (Mineau, Smith, & Bean, 2002; Skulason, Jonsdottir, Sigurdardottir, & Helgason, 2012; Stroebe & Stroebe, 1993).

Most studies show the most dramatic differences in mortality rates for widowed persons (compared to those still married) immediately following the loss and up to six months (Bowling & Windsor, 1995; Stroebe & Stroebe, 1993). Parkes, Benjamin, and Fitzgerald (1969) found that older widowers had a higher mortality rate over the first four years post-loss, but the rate was much higher in the first six months. Other studies have found widowed men's mortality rates could be increased for more than a decade after their partner's death, especially if the widower had pre-existing health concerns (Schaefer, Quesenberry, & Wi, 1995).

The specific relationship between spousal bereavement, health factors, and mortality rates is not known and is likely to be complex (Parkes, 1996). Various theories examine the role of psychosocial stress during bereavement and the adjustment to widowhood as well as differences in health behaviors and coping strategies between widows and widowers. However, given that widowers engage in a variety of unhealthy behaviors such as having a poor diet, increased binge drinking, and increased substance use and these health behaviors are accompanied by higher rates of depressive symptoms and social isolation, it seems quite likely that these are significant factors.

Suicide

One of the biggest differences when comparing widowers to widows or married men is the disparity in suicide rates. Even before bereavement, men have a higher rate of suicide. In 2010, men's suicide rate in the United States was 19.9 per 100,000 per year compared to women's rates of 5.2. Furthermore, Caucasian males (25.7) had higher suicide rates than men from other racial groups including American Indian (16.1), Asian American (9.3), African American (9.1), and Hispanic (8.5) (Murphy, Xu, & Kochanek, 2013).

After losing a partner, the statistics are even bleaker. Widowed men commit suicide at a rate of more than three times the rate of married men. After adjusting for housing level, amount of education, smoking, and church attendance, the risk of suicide for widowed men rose to more than five times the rate of married men. For comparison, the risk for widows is not significantly higher than married women even when adjusted for demographic factors (Li, 1995). According to a Swiss study, the rate of widowers committing suicide is the greatest (approximately 6 times higher) during the first week post-loss and gradually improves throughout the first year (Ajdacic-Gross et al., 2008).

Younger Widowers and Suicide

Younger widowers experience an especially high rate of risk of suicide compared to married men and widows. Luoma and Pearson (2002) found that the youngest age group of white widowers (20–34 years old) had a suicide rate 17 times higher than married controls (and 4 times the rate of divorced men); their rate was at least 5 times higher than married counterparts through age 54. African American widowers in the same age group had a rate 9 times higher than married counterparts and was approximately 5 times as high through age 44. Given the significant increase in cohabitating unmarried couples, it is important to see if this trend is comparable for men who lose an unmarried partner.

Older Widowers and Suicide

Older widowers, especially those over the age of 75, are particularly likely to resort to suicide; they have a suicide rate greater than 80 per 100,000 per year. This is even more notable when compared to the older widows' rate of less than 8 per 100,000 per year (Luoma & Pearson, 2002). Unfortunately the high suicide rate of older men is likely to continue based on recent research that found the suicide rates of middle-aged men increased 27% between 1999 and 2010 (Sullivan, Annest, Luo, Simon, & Dahlberg, 2013). Overall, older widowers commit suicide at a rate that is quite disparate compared to older widows. This tendency, in combination with the fact that older adults are underserved in suicide prevention programs (Blando, 2011), suggests that additional outreach and research is essential.

Factors of Suicide

There are several factors that may be responsible for the higher rates of suicide by men and in particular widowed men (for a historical review see Canetto, 1992). These factors include the methods of suicide most frequently used by men, the effects of men's gender role socialization and psychological development, and the loss of the work role for men who have retired. Most completed suicides involve firearms, and men are even more likely to use them. In 2002, men were approximately seven times more likely than a woman to use a firearm to commit suicide (CDC, 2004). Older men (65+) use guns for suicide at a rate (76.5%) even higher than the rate for all men (McIntosh et al., 1997). Men, especially older men, are less likely to seek psychological help (Canetto, 1992) and this may result in higher rates of suicide than women. Furthermore, men may be less flexible in their coping as a result of deeply engrained gender role socialization. Specifically, men are likely to be more comfortable with violence (even toward themselves) and used to being in control. This may leave men, especially older men, with fewer coping strategies.

McIntosh, Pearson, and Lebowitz (1997) argue that suicide for older men is not purely a result of being widowed, but is primarily an interaction between marital status (older divorced men and unmarried men also have much higher suicide rates than the general population), social isolation, and social support. For most men, employment provides a significant portion of their social contact with others; furthermore, the importance of their workplace as a source of social connections and structure may be fully appreciated after retirement (Russell, 2004). Consequently, the loss of the work role for older, retired men may result in a view of having lower social status and less direction and purpose in life. This shift from feeling useful, powerful, and independent while working to feeling useless, weak, and dependent is often a significant loss for men upon retirement. The loss of the work role and the loss of a partner creates a 'double loss' for the widower. Upon retirement, a widower "may rely more heavily on his wife to derive personal social status and worth. Her death, therefore, takes on personal and social importance, under such circumstances, that exceeds the losses of either retirement or widowhood alone" (McIntosh et al., 1997, p. 206).

Research by Lund and Caserta (2001) provides some support for the challenge of having a double loss (work and wife). They found that men in their 70s had the poorest coping and inferred that the added stress of a recent retirement worsened their coping. Howell (2013) describes how important his multiple roles were after his wife died in midlife:

> Certain roles/identities become so central to us, so integrated into our everyday life that they can be described as master roles/identities. For

me, those were husband, father, teacher. These were no longer 'just' roles, they were at the core of my identity, my self. With the death of Diane, I ceased to be a husband, but remained a father and a teacher. It was these other roles/identities, these other selves, which helped me to maintain some kind of continuity and meaning in the chaos of loss and grief. . . . These continuities helped me to keep going and to strive to makes sense of that which made no sense. (p. 8)

Given the importance of these multiple roles in maintaining some aspects of one's identity and meaning-making, it raises the question of how widowers who no longer have these roles/identities will manage during a difficult time.

It is important to remember that even though the rate of suicide for widowers is higher than almost any other group, it is still a small minority of all widowers. Most widowers are not suicidal, although some express less fear of death believing they will join their partner some day. Andrew, an 86-year-old widower who had been married for 63 years before his wife died, told me that he was not afraid of death and was looking forward to joining his wife. His response is one that I'll always remember:

Well, I don't dread it. I'm like this little boy that was in some kind of class, in church I guess, and the teacher wanted everybody to hold up their hand that wanted to go to heaven. Everybody held up their hand except this one little boy. She said, "Johnny, don't you want to go to heaven when you die?" He said, "Oh yeah, when I die. I thought you was trying to get up a load to go right now." (chuckles) That's kind of the way that I see it, I'm not in no hurry to go, but I don't dread it.

Expectation of Death Before Partner

While it is crucial to have a thorough understanding of the various challenges facing widowed men, not all of these challenges are easily quantifiable. One significant, yet difficult to measure concept is the general unexpectedness of being a widower. Quite simply, men do not expect to outlive their wives. When there are almost four times as many widows as widowers (US Census Bureau, 2010), it is reasonable for husbands to assume that their female partner will outlive them. Men are frequently reminded of this; most men witness their fathers die before their mothers and their male friends die before their wives.

In their in-depth interviews with 51 widowers, Moore and Stratton (2002) found that virtually all of them were surprised to outlive their wives. "While the widowhood came as shockingly off time to the younger men in our study, it seemed to be unexpected for most of the men, whatever their age and whatever the situation with the wife's health" (p. 89). They found that even some of the widowers who were caregivers for wives with terminal illnesses still felt that they would die before their wives. "We suggest that widowed men, as a group, are less likely to think that they will be widowed and that leaves them disadvantaged in adjustment to widowhood whatever their age" (p. 90).

While more research is needed, it is difficult to underscore how important this expectation is. I would argue that this general expectation by widowers to outlive their wives plays a role in many of the challenges outlined in this chapter. After all, why should a husband worry about developing social contacts beyond his wife or worry about developing self-care skills such as cooking healthy meals if he never expects to need these skills? Or considering this from the perspective of their wives, is it possible or even likely that women may work harder to develop a strong social support network after seeing many of their female peers outlive their husbands?

Financial Concerns

Widowers tend to have better financial resources than widows (Utz, 2006). This is an important consideration because adequate financial resources are positively correlated with so many other aspects of physical and mental health (Kaslow, 2004). While research suggests, on average, widowers are more likely than widows to have enough financial resources to maintain their standard of living, this does not mean they will be free from all types of financial concerns. A study of older married couples found that more than 50% of the wives performed the day-to-day financial matters (Assar & Bobinski, 1991). This suggests that when his wife dies, the widower will be faced with learning to conduct day-to-day financial tasks. Another study of 17,000 Americans found in almost half the couples the wife was the partner who had the greatest knowledge of the couple's finances (Lindamood & Hanna, 2005). The assumption that husbands handle all the financial matters and therefore will not be required to learn new skills appears to be outdated. Furthermore, as more and more wives work full-time and outearn their husbands, this disparity in financial security in widowhood may eventually balance out (Utz, 2006).

Limitations on Research With Widowers

In this chapter I have provided a summary of the challenges facing widowers. There are several limitations inherent in the current body of research on widowers. These include limited samples of widowers when comparing widowed men and women and that virtually all of the research with widowers focuses on older widowers. Furthermore, most studies only follow widowed persons over the course of months or a year, while most agree that the adaptation to the loss of a partner lasts at least two years (Sanders, 1999; Worden, 2009). Another limitation is that the majority of studies examine only married couples. Given that there were 7.7 million households with unmarried couples (6.6% of all households) in 2010 in the United States (Lofquist, Lugaila, O'Connell, & Feliz, 2012), these studies have excluded a sizeable portion of future widowed persons including same-sex couples and unmarried couples.

2

MALE GENDER ROLE AND WIDOWERS

When I tell people that I study widowers, their comments and questions often relate to the influence of gender: "Men grieve differently—don't they?" "Men seem to move on so quickly," and "That's just how men are." The popular perception is that being a man will affect his grief experience. I agree with this viewpoint; a widower's grief is influenced by his sense of what it means to be a man. However, I do not believe that a widower's experience of being a man is the only influence, nor does it affect all widowers the same way. The interaction between a widower's grief and his view of himself as a man is complex; furthermore, it evolves throughout his lifespan and is influenced by his losses.

In this chapter I will briefly outline the process of male gender role socialization including both the positive and negative effects on men. This will set the stage to examine how gender role socialization and male gender norms influence widowers' grief experiences. Given that adherence to traditional masculine norms can isolate widowers and frustrate therapists, a positive and empathic approach to counseling widowers will be introduced. Finally, I will offer specific strategies for welcoming widowers to counseling from a gender-aware perspective.

The last 20 years have brought about significant changes in the way researchers and therapists view men and grief. Consequently, both fields are still wrestling with many competing assumptions and models. As a result of being a relatively new field of study, major written works and shifts in perspectives in men's studies are still occurring frequently. I have written this book with a focus on the contributions from writers associated with the New Psychology of Men (Levant & Pollack, 1995) and Positive Psychology/Positive Masculinity (Kiselica & Englar-Carlson, 2010) perspectives. There are other perspectives, including the mythopoetic (Bly, 1990; Keen, 1991), men's rights (Farrell, 1993) and conservative, which also contribute to a new understanding of men (for an overview, see Kilmartin, 2000). I believe the NPM and PPPM perspectives provide a middle ground between recognizing the strengths of traditional masculinity, yet seeking to reduce its negative outcomes, and always seeking to validate feminist perspectives.

Male Gender Roles

"A gender role is a generalized social role, one that cuts across many situations. A gender role is a set of expectations for behaving, thinking, and feeling that is based on a person's biological sex" (Kilmartin, 2000, p. 20). Therefore, gender roles are a result of an interaction between biological sex and socialization. Gender roles comprise gender stereotypes and gender norms. *Gender stereotypes* are "culturally based overgeneralizations about the characteristics of people who belong to the biological categories of male or female" while *gender norms* are "beliefs about how males and females should be (prescriptive) and about how they should *not* be (proscriptive)" (p. 21). Although gender norms and stereotypes make up gender roles, they are often in conflict. For example, the stereotype that men do not cry often conflicts with the proscriptive norm that men should be caring. Furthermore, gender-based norms may conflict with other types of norms. A common discrepancy for widowers is the conflict between the norm of showing respect to his wife (even after death) and the norm that men should be self-sufficient; engaging in one can violate the other.

Male Gender Role Strain Paradigm

Theorists have put forth several different explanations for the development of gender roles. The *gender identity model* was the most prevalent throughout much of the 20th century. It suggests that men and women are genetically programmed to act in 'gender-appropriate' ways and that there are unique standards for masculinity and femininity. Adherents of this perspective believed masculinity was clearly distinguished from femininity and there was a historical standard of masculinity (Kilmartin, 2000; Levant, 1996). This standard is sometimes referred to as *masculinity ideology* (Pleck, 1995). Supporters of the gender identity model generally believe that modern men have had too little contact with male role models and have spent too much time with their mothers (Pleck, 1995).

Pleck (1981, 1995) introduced the *gender role strain paradigm* as an alternative to the gender identity model. He argues that male gender roles are socially constructed and largely defined by norms and stereotypes. Because male gender roles are contradictory and inconsistent, most men violate some gender norms at some point in their lives. Upon violating gender norms, men experience condemnation (either from others or internally), which influences them to conform. While some gender norms are positive and beneficial, others are psychologically and physical dysfunctional.

Men may experience one or more of the following three negative reactions: gender role discrepancy, gender role trauma, and/or gender role dysfunction (Pleck, 1995). Gender role discrepancy refers to the incongruity a man feels when he is unable to live up to the expectations of the traditional male gender role. For example, a widower who finds himself crying in front of others may experience a sense of failure to live up to traditional masculine norms. Cognitive dissonance theory would suggest that the man must either change his behavior or his view of gender roles (or perhaps distract himself from or deny the discrepancy) in order to relieve that anxiety caused by the sense of incongruity. Even if a man is able to achieve his view of traditional masculinity, he will continue to feel strain because his status can always be lost. This ongoing attempt to achieve and maintain their status as 'real men' causes men to experience strain and trauma (Pleck, 1995). This strain may be especially difficult during times of crisis and loss—as when a man becomes a widower. Finally, Pleck maintains that if a man is able to achieve the ideals of a traditional gender role, the consequences are often negative and will result in dysfunction in his life. For example, men who embody traditional male norms must give up the ability to identify and express emotions including loss, hurt, and powerlessness. They are forced to tackle problems alone. They are forced to work to maintain their psychological and financial independence, often in exchange for time spent for those for whom he is providing the resources.

The sum of the negative consequences of restrictive gender roles is called *gender role conflict*. James O'Neil and his colleagues (for a summary, see O'Neil, 2008) have been studying the concept and implications of gender role conflict in men for over 25 years. Research has supported four patterns of gender role conflict including: (1) conflict between work and family relations; (2) restrictive emotionality; (3) restrictive affectionate behavior between men; and (4) success/power/competition. The implications of gender role conflict are far reaching. These four patterns of gender role conflict can significantly influence a man's view of himself, his thoughts, his actions, and how he views and treats others (O'Neil, 2008).

What creates gender role strain and conflict? As mentioned, proponents of gender *identity* theory suggest that modern boys and men may not fully be masculine because of a lack of time with male role models. Conversely, Pleck (1995) argues that men are uncomfortable with their gender identity not because it is an innate drive that has been thwarted by modern society, but because they have been presented with a socially constructed standard that is nearly unattainable. This results in men either trying to achieve an impossible standard of masculinity and experiencing the negative effects (gender strain), or they are left feeling like they are not men because they recognize they do not match the standards (gender discrepancy).

A benefit of using the gender role strain lens to examine gender norms is that it can explain the individual differences seen in boys and men because each male experiences gender socialization differently (e.g., some parents endorse and reinforce very traditional male gender norms while others endorse flexible and non-traditional norms, etc.) (Addis & Mahalik, 2003). Unfortunately some researchers and therapists mistakenly assume that gender role socialization is an unchanging trait of the individual man. In other words, it can be easy to make the mistake that boys and men are passively "stuffed like a turkey" by social and cultural forces (Kilmartin, 2000), when in reality the process is a complex and ongoing interaction.

Development of Male Gender Norms

If traditional male gender norms are so harmful, then why are they being taught to our boys? First, not all traditional gender norms are harmful. Later in the chapter I will present a more thorough examination of how some traditional gender norms are beneficial for men. Second, while many people do not endorse traditional and inflexible gender norms, these norms are still reflected in many aspects of society and culture. Multiple sources, such as parents, siblings, teachers, and other role models, instruct boys and men about acceptable masculine thoughts and behaviors. Movies, books, television, the Internet, and other culturally relevant media also provide examples of masculinity. Not all of these examples are negative, and I believe many of these messages are becoming healthier and more adaptive examples of masculinity. However, boys and men still receive many messages that promote a highly sexualized, aggressive, self-reliant, and authoritarian view of masculinity.

It is important to remember that boys and men are not simply passive recipients of cultural messages about masculinity. Instead, boys and men interact with their families and larger social groups; this interaction is what influences how gender role norms are understood and either accepted or rejected. Boys and men are exposed to various examples of masculinity and, based on those models, try out different behaviors. Based on their preconceived notions of what masculinity is and reactions by others, the actions and thoughts of boys and men are molded. These preconceived notions are influenced by culture, role models, and the individual's physical and cognitive abilities, among other factors.

The Four Injunctions

One of the most difficult parts of being socialized as boys is that traditional male gender norms are not clear or consistent. In fact, boys often receive conflicting messages about what they 'should' be doing. However, there are several 'rules' for boys and men that have been generally consistent in Western cultures over the past several generations. Brannon (1976) described four themes regarding traditional masculinity; they have become known as the 'Four Injunctions' (a term used by Pollack, 1998).

Brannon's Four Injunctions

1. Sturdy Oak: Men and boys should be stoic, independent, and not show weakness.
2. Give 'em Hell: Men and boys are wired to be brave and fearless; 'boys will be boys.'
3. The Big Wheel: Men and boys should achieve status and dominance over others.
4. No Sissy Stuff: Men and boys should avoid anything feminine and should especially avoid expressing tender emotions (lest he appear to be homosexual).

Brannon (1976) described the Four Injunctions as a set of general rules that boys and men must follow in order to be viewed as a 'real man.' He acknowledged that there are multiple versions of 'real men': the successful athlete, the rich businessman, the hard-working blue-collar man, and the gregarious and handsome playboy, among others. However, these four themes are generally present in all versions of the idealized man. Without a doubt there has been a shift in American culture toward greater tolerance for various behaviors and attitudes in boys and especially in adulthood; however, these four rules still play a significant role in the life and development of boys and men (Pollack, 1998).

There are four reasons why trying to uphold traditional masculine norms are particularly problematic for men: (1) the standards are unclear; (2) the standards are impossible to attain; (3) the status of 'real man' is impermanent; and (4) the result of not living up to the ideal is shame.

Standards Are Unclear

At first glance Brannon's (1976) injunctions appear to be clear. In practice, however, the rules regarding masculinity are vague and virtually indiscernible. Brannon specifically lists "No Sissy Stuff" as the first injunction because it is the first lesson most boys are taught. Boys are not provided a set of rules to follow; instead, they are only told to avoid anything feminine (Kilmartin, 2000). It is no wonder that a boy can feel anxiety when he is "surrounded by adult females, offered few positive images of what he is expected to be, but chastised and sometimes shamed for being a 'sissy' if he emulates girls and women" (Brannon, 1976, p. 14). Therefore to not risk violating gender role norms (which are poorly defined), some boys and men will respond by adhering strongly to traditional male gender norms—sometimes to an exaggerated degree (Pleck, 1981). To further confuse the issue, there is diversity in rules associated with masculinity based on geographic location, culture, race, level of acculturation, and other factors. This has led many (e.g., Pleck, 1995; Kilmartin, 2000) to use the term *masculinities* to reflect the multiple forms of masculinity. Given the ambiguity in the standards and forms of masculinity, it is inevitable that boys and men will experience gender role discrepancy (see Pleck, 1981, 1995).

Standards Are Impossible to Maintain

Based on traditional standards, masculinity is an impossible standard, and gender role trauma (Pleck, 1981, 1995) is inevitable. Brannon (1976) described out how mythical a 'real man' who faithfully meets all of the standards is:

> All together and in its purest form, the male sex role depicts a rather remarkable creature. This hypothetical man never feels anxious, depressed, or vulnerable, has never known the taste of tears, is devoid of any trace or hint of femininity. He is looked up to by all who know him, is a tower of strength both physically and emotionally, and exudes an unshakeable confidence and determination that sets him apart from lesser beings. He's also aggressive, forceful, and daring, a barely controlled volcano of primal force. (pp. 35–36)

More recently this version of the ideal man has become unattainable for another reason. Boys and men are receiving mixed messages. The more recent standards of masculinity ask boys and men to be sensitive, yet still largely be independent and strong (Pollack, 1998). One man in McGill's (1985) study on men and relationships voiced a common reaction to these mixed messages:

> Women may say they want men to be more open and honest, to show their feelings more, and the whole bit. But when men are that way, women can't handle it. They don't know what to do. Nine times out of ten, they end up falling apart. . . . She doesn't have the slightest idea how to handle my emotions. No woman does, and if they don't know that, they find out. I guarantee you that once a woman has been with a guy who has been really honest, has really opened himself up to her, she'll never want him to do it again. (p. 225)

Critics may argue that men never really give themselves or their partners a chance for change—there may be some truth to that. Given that most men have little practice in sharing their feelings, it is not surprising that it may happen awkwardly. However, my main point is that many men continue to feel as though they cannot take a chance on violating the original rules of masculinity. Boys and men quickly learn that they are never shamed when they keep their feelings to themselves whereas sharing involves great risk.

Masculinity Is Impermanent

Not only is traditional masculinity a vague and unattainable goal, but even if a man could achieve such a status he would not be able to maintain it. This is because being a 'real man' is an impermanent status (Krugman, 1995). Therefore, boys and men must stay hypervigilant to violating any of the 'rules' in an attempt to sustain their sense of masculinity. Certainly both men and women have socially driven gender roles to live up to, yet men's status appears to be in constant jeopardy. For example, a financially and professionally successful man who is viewed to be self-sufficient and in control of his emotions would seem to meet all of Brannon's requirements. However, his status as a 'real man' could always be lost. For example, he could fail in his business endeavors and become financially destitute (violating the Big Wheel injunction). He could come out of the closet as a homosexual (violating the No Sissy Stuff injunction). His partner could die and he could fall apart emotionally (violating the Sturdy Oak injunction).

Shame

What is the result of breaking the Four Injunctions? What do men and boys experience when they have been told that they have broken 'the rules' of manhood? Shame. Shame is a powerful motivator for boys and men; shame involves emotional disconnection, rejection, disparagement, and a direct fear of one's sense of self (Krugman, 1995; Osherson & Krugman, 1990). Girls and women also experience shame as part of their gender socialization and personal development. But as Pollack (1998) says, "while girls may be shame-sensitive, boys are shame-phobic: they are exquisitely yet unconsciously attuned to any signal of 'loss of face' and will do just about whatever it takes to avoid shame" (p. 33). Furthermore, shame is often internalized so boys and men can experience it without the scrutiny of others (Krugman, 1995). To avoid shame, a man typically believes that he must follow the Four Injunctions and fulfill other roles he believes are part of being a 'real man.' The problem, as mentioned, is that the injunctions are not specific or attainable, and are impermanent.

The Injunctions Today

Are Brannon's (1976) injunctions still relevant today? I would argue that they are an imperfect, yet still useful way of viewing gender norms for boys and men. Undoubtedly the rigidity of the injunctions has moderated in the last 35+ years, but I believe boys and men are still held to the core features of the injunctions. In fact, when I introduce the injunctions in counseling, they have tremendous face validity with men. Virtually all men can remember specific experiences which relate to the various injunctions and how they were affected by them. In my opinion, they provide a quick way to connect with men and begin the process of examining their gender socialization and development. Furthermore, I think these standards are often felt acutely by middle-aged and older men—who happen to be the most likely demographic group to become widowers.

It is worth noting that Brannon's injunctions continue to be reflected in more recent descriptions of male behaviors. For example, Mahalik, Good, and Englar-Carlson (2003) have provided a more updated description of types of male behaviors by describing seven different, but related, 'scripts' of masculine behaviors. These scripts correspond to the endorsement of various aspects of traditional masculinity as they demonstrated by male clients. The scripts include aspects of Brannon's injunctions, but are more specific. The seven scripts are: Strong-and-Silent, Tough Guy, Give 'em Hell, Playboy, Homophobic, Winner, and Independent.

Male Gender Roles and Widowers

Gender role socialization has a powerful impact on widowers and their grief; of course, the degree to which a man adopts and attempts to live up to the traditional male gender role will influence his individual reaction. Using Brannon's (1976) injunctions as a general guide, I will review various ways bereaved men's reactions to a loss may be negatively influenced by their attempts to maintain the standards of traditional masculinity. These influences can be traced back to Brannon's (1976) injunctions as well as the various ways men become dependent upon their partners.

Four Injunctions and Widowers

I believe the most damaging injunction for widowers is attempting to live up to the standards of a Sturdy Oak. By trying to present himself as tough, independent, and confident, a widower dooms himself to endure his grief alone. By trying to live up to this ideal, widowers avoid assistance from others and shun professional counseling or grief groups. Furthermore, he tries to convince himself and others that he is not hurting at all or needs no support. After his wife died, Darren Humphries (2012) wanted to be able to present an image of resilience to others.

> There's no one for me to talk to about this. I have to show a strong face, to show that I'm coping, to show that everything's fine, so that people don't have to worry about me. People aren't supposed to have to worry about me. And so I have nobody to share all this with. The one person that I could have been open and vulnerable enough with is the one person who isn't here anymore. I am utterly, utterly alone. And I will be for a long time to come.

Almost as harmful as the Sturdy Oak mentality is when a widower believes that he must avoid any behaviors or attitudes that could be misconstrued as feminine. In adopting a No Sissy Stuff stance, the widower denies himself any opportunity to cry, express longing, or demonstrate any other signs of vulnerability. The only acceptable emotions a widower could express are anger or revenge. While male gender norms have shifted over the last several decades, these injunctions still play a powerful role in men's grief.

> Despite verbalizations that today's male is more able and willing to express feelings, there is still tremendous discomfort in our culture when a man openly admits to painful emotions of hurt and loss, weeps outwardly, admits being disoriented, or shudders with fear. . . . Unfortunately, today's male actually continues to exist in a cultural atmosphere that has little real tolerance for the emotional pain of grief. The result is that many men either grieve in isolation or attempt to run away from their grief through various means. (Wolfelt, 1990, p. 20)

Furthermore, men are especially hesitant to share their personal reactions and emotions with other men because they fear that others will question their sexual orientation.

When a man focuses on being self-sufficient (Sturdy Oak) and in control of his emotional reactions (No Sissy Stuff), he tends to compartmentalize his life. A common form of this compartmentalization is when a man separates his work life from his personal life (Krugman, 1995). This compartmentalization also includes a man's emotional response to difficult events. This may be what allows some men to witness horrible events and limit their sadness or fear. For example, Lamers (2002) describes how pilots on missions during the Vietnam War would intentionally suppress their grief despite learning that a fellow airman had been killed. Grief was held in until the completion of flight operations. While this ability can be advantageous in specific circumstances (e.g., war, natural disasters, etc.), it can also create a psychological distance between the man and others if he maintains this compartmentalization.

A widower can make his grief more difficult by attempting to live up to the other two injunctions, although the previous two create the most problems. By struggling to continue to be the Big Wheel, a widower can convince himself that he should continue to be someone that others can depend on. This may be especially true in situations when a widower has dependent children and believes he must appear to be in control and have all the answers, but may also apply with adult children as well. Furthermore, the widower may return to work as quickly as possible partially because working may be one reaction that he views as masculine. The Give 'em Hell perspective may influence a widower who believes he must act macho and project a sense of dangerousness. These widowers may be more likely to respond to extreme grief reactions through risk-taking or suicide. As mentioned in Chapter 1, widowers have a suicide rate at least five times higher than married men (Luoma & Pearson, 2002).

To further complicate matters, a widower is likely to have internalized these unrealistic standards. Consequently, his personal ideal of a 'real man' (e.g., I can't show any weakness so I'll act like I'm fine) and his assumptions about what others believe (e.g., I'll lose all respect from my friends if I start crying in the middle of a round of golf) may control his behaviors even more than his actual violations of traditional male behavior (Krugman, 1995). As he likely learned when he was a boy, it is safer not to do anything that may even remotely be viewed as unmanly—better to simply hide his reactions from others.

Husbands' Reliance on Wives

Despite the pressure to become self-sufficient and independent, paradoxically there are several ways in which men become reliant or dependent on their wives (what Pollack (1995) calls *pseudoautonomy*). Husbands frequently rely on their wives for the expression of their emotions and for validation of their masculinity. Pleck (1980) argued that "men experience their emotions vicariously through women" and "depend on women to help them express their emotions" (p. 420). For example, who writes the cards for significant events such as weddings, birthdays, and funerals—is it the husband or the wife? Another vivid example is a widower who admitted that he had never attended a funeral before his wife's funeral because he had relied on her to attend them as a representative for both of them. In this way his wife acted as a 'surrogate mourner' (Sanders, 1999). Only after understanding the benefit of the social support he received at his wife's funeral did he realize how important it was for him to be there for others in the future.

Pleck (1980) also maintained that women have a unique power to validate a man's masculinity. For a traditional man to feel masculine, his role must be endorsed by a woman. Brannon (1976) provided the example of his father (who he says epitomized traditional masculinity) being shamed by his mother. After his father had been out extremely late with his friends, Brannon's mother locked him out of the house. After banging on the door his father eventually left to return the next morning. Years later in an argument his mother said, "If you were a *real man*, you'd have chopped down my front door that night I locked you out!" (as a neighbor had done years earlier) (p. 35). While men (and boys) may present themselves as not caring about what others think of them, in reality their intimate partners have great power over whether or not they feel like a 'real man.'

The power held by women to help their husbands express their emotions and to validate their masculinity is strengthened by the tendency of men to rely exclusively on their wives or intimate partners for this assistance (Umberson et al., 1992). In his study of several hundred men and their relationships McGill (1985) found that:

> most men disclose the intimate details of their lives to only one special woman. Few men, however, were found to have anything remotely similar with another man. As a result, almost all men become highly dependent upon a woman to provide intimacy and support that is so integral to their emotional well-being. (pp. 38–39)

So what happens when she dies? The widower had invested extraordinary power in one person. For many men she was the sole confidante of his emotions, and he likely relied on her to express his emotions for him. Furthermore, she had the ability to help him feel masculine. So in his grief, a widower may now be left without an emotional translator and correspondent—a tough spot to be in when he is facing his greatest loss.

Positive Aspects of Traditional Masculinity

While it is easy to point out the ways that traditional male gender roles can limit and hurt boys and men (and those with whom they interact), it is critical to examine how these gender roles can also be a positive influence. Men, in general, do not need a complete overhaul. Traditional aspects of masculinity are not inherently bad except when men adhere to them in an inflexible and exaggerated manner (Mahalik et al., 2003; Pollack, 1995). Levant (1995) lists several strengths of traditional male gender norms.

Positive Aspects of Traditional Masculinity (Levant, 1995, p. 232)

1. Self-sacrifice for family
2. Ability to withstand hardships
3. Tendency to care for others
4. Loyalty, dedication, commitment
5. Stick-to-it until problem is corrected
6. Problem-solving ability
7. Think logically
8. Self-reliance
9. Stay calm in danger
10. Assert himself

All of these positive qualities of traditional masculinity are based on the assumption that the individual is using them in a flexible and accommodating manner. All gender norms become problematic when used dogmatically. Furthermore, many of these characteristics can also be applied to traditional femininity.

More recently, Mark Kiselica, Matt Englar-Carlson, and colleagues (Kiselica, 2011; Kiselica & Englar-Carlson, 2010; Kiselica, Englar-Carlson, Horne, & Fisher, 2008) have proposed and described a positive psychology/positive masculinity (PPPM) model. Building from the robust literature on positive psychology (for an overview, see Snyder, Lopez, & Pedrotti, 2011), the PPPM emphasizes the strengths of male development, male socialization, and masculinity. The PPPM was introduced based on a concern that the New Psychology of Men (NPM), while often acknowledging some strengths of traditional masculinity, nonetheless emphasized the deficits of male development. This emphasis has led some mental health professionals to approach counseling with boys and men from a biased perspective that impedes therapeutic assistance (Kiselica, 2011). Conversely, the PPPM model allows therapists to focus on what male clients are doing right and use these as 'building blocks' for building a therapeutic relationship and as a foundation for the client's positive changes (Kiselica et al., 2008). Furthermore, the PPPM framework is useful because it can be combined with a variety of other perspectives including the NPM perspective, the gender role conflict perspective, as well as psycho-educational and cognitive perspectives (Kiselica, 2011).

Kiselica and Englar-Carlson (2010) present 10 aspects of traditional masculinity that can be viewed positively and improve counselors' effectiveness with boys and men.

Positive Aspects of Traditional Masculinity (Kiselica & Englar-Carlson, 2010, pp. 277–278)

1. Male relational styles—tendency to "have fun and develop friendships and intimacy with each other through shared activities"
2. Male ways of caring—"expectation that they must care for and protect their loved one and friends" and "take action based on how a person sees things from another's point of view"
3. Generative fatherhood—responding "consistently and readily to his child's developmental needs over time with an eye toward helping the next generation lead a better life"
4. Male self-reliance—a boy or man "considers the input of others with regard to problems, yet remains 'his own man' and does not allow others to force their decisions on him"
5. The worker/provider tradition of men—"engaging in work helps a man to feel that he has achieved one of society's criteria for manhood" and "provides men with a sense of purpose and meaning"
6. Male courage, daring, and risk-taking—"boys and men display many forms of daring, and the courage they muster while taking worthwhile risks—such as facing peril to protect others, completing dangerous but necessary jobs, or pushing themselves to their limits during athletic competitions—is admirable"
7. Group orientation of boys and men—"boys and men are oriented toward banding together to achieve a common purpose"
8. The humanitarian service of fraternal organizations—men have a long history of developing humanitarian groups which provide an opportunity for "a sense of belonging and participating with others for the common good"
9. Men's use of humor—"many boys and men use humor as a vehicle to *attain* intimacy"
10. Male heroism—boys and men use all of these qualities "to demonstrate exceptional nobility in the way they lead their lives, overcoming great obstacles and making great contributions to others through extraordinary efforts"

The culture in which the man lives will influence the emphasis and level of endorsement he gives to each of these 10 male strengths. Furthermore, these strengths are social constructions that are neither exclusive to men nor biologically or genetically determined. However, the positive aspects of masculinity are gender-specific as such that boys and men typically learn them from other boys and men and will exhibit them differently than girls and women will exhibit them (Kiselica, 2011).

An Empathic and Affirming Approach to Helping Widowers

Therapists can help widowers by approaching them from an empathic and affirming point of view. Professionals in both men's studies and grief counseling have identified a lack of empathic understanding as central concerns to helping men and the bereaved. Pollack (1995) said this about men: "If we truly want men to become more empathic, *we need to become more empathic to men*" (p. 35, italics in original). Neimeyer and Jordan (2002) suggested a similar approach for the bereaved:

> As we contend with the subtle difficulties experienced by the bereaved clients who consult us in grief therapy, we have come to understand many of these problems as an expression of empathic failure—the failure of one part of a system to understand the meaning and experience of another. (p. 96)

A critical part of developing empathy for men (and consequently, widowers) is recognizing the challenges and strengths they develop through male socialization and development. While empathy for widowers is larger than constraints based on gender socialization, I believe widowers' behaviors and attitudes related to gender roles are the primary force impeding others from viewing them empathically. For example, because male gender role socialization encourages men to neither express their pain (No Sissy Stuff) nor seek assistance (Sturdy Oak), men often hide or minimize their concerns (Zinner, 2000). This can make it especially difficult for therapists (as well as a widower's loved ones) to feel empathy toward a widower. After all, if a widower is presenting himself as being all right, then it may seem as if he does not need any empathy. Furthermore, a widower may be deprived of empathy by behaving in ways that others interpret as callous or uncaring. Examples of widower's behaviors that might be viewed as insensitive by others include not crying, returning to work quickly, removing all of his partner's pictures and personal items, going on dates, and avoiding discussions about his deceased partner.

It is easier for therapists and loved ones to be empathic toward widowers if these behaviors are viewed in terms of male gender socialization and traditional gender norms. If he endorses restrictive gender norms, the widower may simply be doing the best he can. Furthermore, it would be helpful if the therapist could begin with an understanding of how a widower's gender-related behaviors and attitudes have been useful in the past. Two previously mentioned approaches can help therapists view widowers more empathically: Kiselica, Englar-Carlson's, and others (Kiselica, 2011; Kiselica & Englar-Carlson, 2010; Kiselica et al.,

2008) PPPM perspective and Mahalik, Good, and Englar-Carlson's (2003) masculinity scripts.

Using the Positive Psychology/Positive Masculinity Approach

As mentioned, the PPPM perspective emphasizes the recognition and promotion of healthy aspects of masculinity. This does not mean that therapists using the PPPM perspective ignore ways in which men are hurting themselves or others. Instead, it means the therapist begins with recognizing and validating what the client is doing right. Examples of this include reaffirming and reinforcing a widower's disclosures and desire to seek help (as in therapy), recognizing situations when he has sacrificed to help loved ones and provided for others, and acknowledging when he has been self-reliant, among others. The therapist can create opportunities to recognize and validate a widower's healthy aspects of masculinity through these types of questions: [I have included several potential positive aspects of masculinity (see p. 29) (Kiselica & Englar-Carlson, 2010) that may relate to the widower's answer].

- **What are some of the ways you cared for your partner before and after her or his death?**
  [Male relational styles; Male ways of caring; Worker/provider tradition; Male courage, daring, and risk-taking; Male heroism]

- **How have you taken care of your loved ones before and after your partner's death?**
  [Male relational styles; Male ways of caring; Generative fathering; Worker/provider tradition; Male courage, daring, and risk-taking; Male heroism]

- **What challenges have you had to overcome before and after your partner's death?**
  [Male relational styles; Male ways of caring; Generative fathering; Male self-reliance; Worker/provider tradition; Male courage, daring, and risk-taking; Male heroism]

- **Do you have a group of men in which you find support?**
  [Male ways of caring; Group orientation of boys and men; Humanitarian service of fraternal organization; Men's use of humor]

- **Do you belong to any groups that help others? (e.g., fraternal/service organizations, community or faith-based groups)**
  [Male ways of caring; Group orientation of boys and men; Humanitarian service of fraternal organization; Men's use of humor]

The PPPM perspective emphasizes building from strengths and establishing a trusting relationship before delving into the harmful patterns associated with gender role conflict. In these situations it is often best to immediately express empathy, but wait to directly intervene until a trusting therapeutic relationship has been established. For example, if a therapist criticizes a widower's reluctance to show his grief to his children without considering that it could also be an expression of caring for his family, the widower will assume the therapist does not understand. It is possible that the widower is avoiding his own grief reaction or is denying the reality of his partner's death. However, by immediately assuming a negative interpretation of the widower's actions, a therapist will likely harm the relationship and will impair future work (see Kiselica & Englar-Carlson (2010) for a description of a case example).

Recognizing Masculinity Scripts

Mahalik, Good, and Englar-Carlson (2003) have outlined a similar perspective for working with men; they discuss the process of intervention as related to seven categories of masculine behaviors or 'scripts.' Perhaps more important than describing the various scripts (e.g., Playboy, Strong-and-Silent, etc.) is their explanation for how a therapist can help a male client identify the scripts he endorses and how they can be a benefit and detriment to his current concerns. Their primary proposal is that all scripts can be adaptive if men use them adaptively instead of unbendingly.

Therefore, Mahalik and his colleagues (2003) suggest that an important part of working with male clients is identifying if a particular script (or multiple scripts) are applicable to a client. Upon identifying it, the therapist and client examine how it has been useful for the client in the past. This helps reinforce why the client has previously used this script and why he is likely to continue to use it now. However, if the client is using the script in an inflexible or overzealous manner, then it likely comes with various costs. For example, a widower may be proud of his role as a 'Provider.' Financially providing for his children after the loss of his partner is an admirable pursuit and the therapist should acknowledge and reinforce this positive sacrifice. However, if he is working 80 hours a week, never taking vacations, and neglecting his emotional connection with his children, then his strict commitment to the script comes with costs such as a poor relationship with them, poor physical and psychological health, and so on. The next step is to help the client examine how these costs may be related to the concerns that brought him to counseling. Finally, the therapist can help work with the client to moderate his views and behaviors that allow him to respond to his current concerns in a more flexible manner.

A significant benefit of both the PPPM and masculinity scripts perspectives is that they allow the therapist to begin with admiring and affirming the client's use of positive aspects of traditional masculinity. Continuing the previous example, the first step is not to tell the widower how foolish he is for neglecting his children. Instead it is to congratulate him on continuing to be able to provide for his children during a difficult transition. Only after a genuine recognition of his accomplishment should the therapist explore the sacrifices he has had to make to fulfill this role. In this way, the therapist can begin by focusing on qualities that most men prize. Then the therapist can take the stance of helping the client reframe his previous attempts to solve his problems as strategies that need to be 'tweaked' or 'dialed back' instead of the stronger, more condemning message of: 'You're doing it wrong.' Men, who often worry about the lack of clear goals or expectations in therapy, are likely to identify with this process because it is affirming, concrete, and goal-directed. By beginning with affirming the client's attempts to solve the problem, the therapist can help build hope and establish a positive, collaborative relationship. Furthermore, therapists can use this approach in conjunction with almost any theoretical orientation.

Therapists can easily adapt this affirming, male-friendly approach to working with widowers. A key part of the process is working with the widower to identify the positive traits that may be at the core of his current problems. In Table 2.1 I have outlined some potential positive reframes for various attitudes or behaviors that are concerning to the widower.

This approach may not be useful for all bereaved male clients, nor is it a panacea; many widowers will have complex problems that will require the use of additional techniques and counseling processes. However, I believe that using the PPPM and masculine scripts perspectives can be immensely useful in examining the widowers' grief reactions, building collaborative relationships, instilling hope, affirming the clients' strengths, and creating counseling goals.

Following their losses, widowers are often forced to make changes including their assumptions about gender norms. These changes can be healthy, adaptive, and necessary. Furthermore, the widower may be particularly open to change and to new examples of masculinity that can be more adaptive. For example, Parkes (1996) relates the story of a widower who had avoided any outward expression of his emotions until the funeral.

> [The widower] saw his father weeping at the funeral. He had always regarded his father as 'tough' and his first reaction was one of shocked surprise. Then it dawned on him that perhaps there was nothing wrong with weeping at a funeral and he too began to cry. Subsequently he viewed this event as a valuable lesson which had helped him over a difficult hurdle. (p. 173)

Table 2.1 Positive Reframes of Widowers

Widowers' Attitudes or Behaviors of Concern*	Positive Reframe of Concern
Avoidance of other people; unable to be around other couples, etc.	Commitment, loyalty, dedication to partner
Avoidance of assistance (family, friends, group support, or professional assistance)	Focus on self-reliance; pride in ability to solve problems and think logically; ability to withstand hardship
Guilt related to feeling happy or enjoying life	Desire to please partner; focus on putting partner's needs before his own; self-sacrifice for partner/family
Inability to change maladaptive routines	Commitment to tradition; commitment to patterns co-established with partner; stick-to-it mentality
Avoidance of situations, topics, places that would evoke emotions	Desire to appear in control; desire to provide a sense of strength and stability for others; focus on staying calm in the face of danger
Overly quick adjustment and/or removal of reminders	Adjust to new circumstances quickly (e.g., work changes, etc.); ability to let go of things beyond his control
Quick development of new romantic relationships	Ability to let go of things beyond his control

* These 'attitudes or behaviors of concern' are only concerning if they are maladaptive for the widower or significant people in his life.

Throughout this book I will provide more examples where psychotherapists can do both. They can help widowers recognize and use their strengths while also learning to make adjustments that help them adapt to their losses.

Widowers' Avoidance of Counseling

In the final section of this chapter I will briefly review the reasons why men tend to avoid seeking counseling. Specifically, I will review the ways in which traditional masculinity conflicts with the values associated with counseling, and I will present several strategies for psychotherapists to be more welcoming to men.

Gender Role Socialization and Help-Seeking

Many of the reasons men avoid seeking psychological help can be traced back to traditional gender norms. Researchers have found several traits and beliefs that are associated with negative attitudes toward seeking counseling including endorsement of traditional masculinity, concerns related to expressing emotions to others (especially other men) (Good, Dell, & Mintz, 1989), power, success, and competition (Robertson & Fitzgerald, 1992). I believe these factors are the primary reason why bereaved men are less likely to seek professional help for their concerns (see Parkes, 1996).

"I believe that men's aversion to therapy is so powerful that it's wise to assume that most male clients, at some level, don't want to be there" (Brooks, 1998, p. 42). Although we could interpret Brooks's comment as pessimistic, I believe it simply reinforces the importance of understanding how male gender norms and socialization influence men's views of professional psychological help. There are several reasons why men who identify with traditional masculinity resist seeking psychotherapy. One reason is that the prevailing stereotypes popular in various media include detached traditional psychoanalysts and therapists who focus exclusively on emotions (and particularly, pushing the client toward strong displays of emotions) (Brooks, 1998). Another reason is that the social construction of masculinity is at direct odds with many of values and demands of modern psychotherapy. For example, a man violates the injunction to be self-sufficient (Sturdy Oak) if he has to ask for help. Consequently a male client may fear that his therapist will attempt to coerce him into becoming a 'sensitive' man, thereby giving up aspects of his masculinity that he values highly (Mahalik et al., 2003). Furthermore, men often have difficulty identifying and describing their emotional reactions (Levant, 1990), which is typically the focus of traditional counseling (Sue & Sue, 2013). A final factor that may impede men's use of psychotherapy is their fear of dependence and emotional intimacy. Men, in general, are less comfortable with emotional intimacy and this may be especially difficult in therapy. Levant (1990) suggests that "with a female therapist, the transference may be eroticized; with a male therapist, it can lead to fears of homosexuality" (p. 310).

Addis and Mahalik (2003) describe several key social factors that can decrease a man's tendency to seek psychological help, including: if the problem is viewed as unusual, if the problem reflects key aspects of his identity, if he believes he cannot reciprocate in some way, if his peers emphasize values of self-sufficiency, and if seeking assistance is viewed as being more costly than any benefits it may provide. Each of these factors can be mediated by social forces that counteract these factors. For example, the ideal social perspective that would be most favorable for a widower to seek counseling is a scenario where he believes his concerns are common, his problems are not viewed as an innate reflection of his identity, he believes he can return the favor in the future, he is encouraged by his peers, and he predicts that the rewards of counseling will far outweigh any disadvantages. Unfortunately, widowers are clearly in the minority (when compared to widows), as they tend to view the loss of their partner as egocentral (i.e., it threatens core qualities such as remaining self-sufficient, ability to protect loved ones, etc.), assume that therapy is not reciprocal (i.e., he can't return the assistance he receives to the therapist), are rarely encouraged to seek help by their peers, and are highly suspicious of the benefits of therapy.

At first glance it would seem likely that encouragement from loved ones to seek assistance may be a simple and effective way to increase the chances that a widower would seek help. However, for some widowers (and men with other concerns), the opposite is true. So why do some men seem to be especially resistant to counseling despite encouragement from loved ones? Addis and Mahalik (2003) propose that 'reactance theory' may provide part of the answer. Reactance theory suggests that people will tend to choose actions that allow them to regain a sense of autonomy after experiences that they perceive as threatening to their freedom. Therefore, if a widower interprets his partner's death as a danger to his autonomy, then he will be less likely to do anything else that he would judge as being threatening to his autonomy. Given that most men view seeking professional psychological help as giving up their sense of self-sufficiency, it follows that widowers with these views would also be less likely to seek assistance. Furthermore, if the widower's loved ones are encouraging him to seek counseling (even with the best of intentions), this may also be viewed as a loss of control and may cause him to be especially resistant to following through.

It is important to remember that it is not simply the fact of being male or female that dictates whether or not an individual is more or less likely to seek psychological help. Instead, a more likely connection is the degree to which an individual endorses socially constructed traditional male gender norms that are incompatible with help-seeking (Addis & Mahalik, 2003; Good et al., 1989). This is critical because the influence of these norms can be moderated. As Robertson (2001) states hopefully, "If counseling does not require men to set aside their sense of independence, their comfort with goals, tasks, and activities, or their preference of developing an understanding of the situation, then the idea of seeking help may be more appealing" (p. 156).

Counseling Widowers From a Gender-Aware Perspective

Psychotherapists can take several actions to increase the likelihood that widowers will feel welcome in counseling and that counseling will be successful. First, therapists should be aware of their views of masculinity and male gender norms. Therapists can view counseling with male clients as a cross-cultural process. Finally, therapists can take specific steps to make the entire help-seeking process more welcoming.

Therapists must understand how gender roles and stereotypes influence widowers' desire to seek counseling and how they behave in counseling. The most important preparation a therapist can undertake is to examine his or her own assumptions about male gender norms (Brooks, 1998; Mahalik et al., 2003). To what degree do you endorse specific behaviors by men? Is it ok for men to cry? How do you react to men that strike you as 'needy'? Is anger a healthy emotion? For example, some counselors may respond to male clients' desires for clear answers to their problems as resistance to the therapy process or to developing a therapeutic relationship. Other therapists may espouse the benefits of expressing emotion, but consciously or unconsciously discourage male clients from expressing anger. A mindset that may help therapists adjust to the different style and expectations of male clients (especially those who strongly identify with traditional masculinity) is to view counseling with them as a cross-cultural experience.

Counseling Men as a Multicultural Process

Several clinicians and researchers (e.g., Liu, 2005; McCarthy & Holliday, 2004) have advocated for conceptualizing therapy with men as a cross cultural experience. Therapists may find that counseling men, especially those who endorse traditional masculinity and have an authoritarian personality style (see Robertson, 2012), may be frustrating. This may be particularly true if a therapist's caseload is largely made up of female clients or male clients who are a good fit with the practice and philosophy of traditional counseling. It can help therapists be more empathic with their male clients if they view them as another multicultural group. Jolliff and Horne (1996) provide this critical reminder:

> Interestingly, when the question is raised about low use of counseling services by minorities and those who ethnically and culturally differ from European ancestry, it is with the assumption that something is wrong with the counseling service that makes it unamenable to the needs of minorities. When it comes to working with male clients, however, the tendency has been to blame men for not being open to the counseling experience. Rather than chiding men for not using the services, it may be useful to ask how therapy can be more relevant for men. (p. 56)

Some may argue that this shift in perspective is unnecessary given that psychotherapy was historically developed by men and men continue to benefit from greater social and political power (see Brooks, 1998). However, this viewpoint forgets that psychotherapy has largely been designed using female clients. Furthermore, while it is true that much of the original foundation of psychology was developed using male participants, men were typically studied as a stand-in for a generic human. This is vastly different than studying men as 'gendered beings' (Kilmartin, 2000). Just as counseling with individuals from different cultural backgrounds requires more than a cursory reading of a textbook; it takes a shift in perspective and an examination of the therapist's cultural assumptions. Brooks (1998) suggests that the same shift is necessary when working with men: "I have come to believe that psychotherapy with traditional men is much more complicated than simply adding a few new techniques to one's therapy repertoire. . . . We are agents of a gendered culture and must be gender-aware therapists" (p. xiv).

Psychotherapists can approach widowers (and all male clients) in a more empathic way by remembering that they are similar to individuals from other groups who generally have less experience with psychotherapy. After all, therapists do not work with Mexican Americans, or gay men, or Deaf clients without acknowledging that adjustments may be necessary. Therapists have been educated to be sensitive to their clients' ethnic backgrounds, social pressures, and other factors that may influence their work with them. This is as it should be. Simply add men to the list. After all, they also experience social pressures that run counter to the practices of traditional psychotherapy and have little experience with seeking professional psychological assistance.

Welcoming Men to Counseling

Brooks (1998) suggests that for traditional men "a visit to the therapist's office is a psychic equivalent to the dentist—without the assurance that anything as practical as pain relief will be accomplished" (p. 71). However, there are several things therapists can do to be more welcoming to widowers and other male clients. First, therapists can be aware of their physical environment. Small things can help make widowers more comfortable including having male-friendly magazines in the waiting area (Sweet, 2006) and having men pictured on advertisements and websites (Barusch & Peak, 1997).

As with other male clients, widowers may be more likely to approach psychotherapy with specific questions including concerns about the value of therapy (Levant, 1995). This can be frustrating for therapists who operate from a theoretical orientation that emphasizes the counseling process and a thorough exploration of the client's background and concerns. Consequently, therapists can help male clients feel more comfortable by being specific about their counseling methods, be clear about an estimated time frame for the counseling process, and engage in problem-solving strategies when appropriate. Men may be especially responsive to psychotherapy that has a significant psycho-educational focus (Brooks, 1998; Levant, 1990).

Gender Role as One of Many Factors

Although I have focused on the influences of gender role socialization and men's views on masculinity in this chapter, it is critical to remember that this is one of several important factors for widowers. Therefore, his individual gender norms may not fit the patterns of traditional masculinity. Furthermore, it is easy to slip into the assumption that a widower's masculinity is a fixed trait. It is important to avoid this fallacy. It is common for a widower to change his attitudes and behaviors in regard to grief and masculinity following his partner's death. In fact, the reason he is entering counseling, the loss of his partner, may be the event that has the largest influence on his views about what it means to be a man.

At first glance the behaviors and attitudes of some widowers may cause others to assume that the widower is callous, uncaring, or incapable of expressing emotions. Therapists must be willing to look deeper than the surface and collaborate with the widower to determine if his assumptions about what it means to be a 'real man' may be influencing his grief. Through an approach that reinforces the benefits of traditional masculinity, therapists can help the widower see where his gender based attitudes may be limiting and harming him. Furthermore, if therapists can approach widowers from a gender-aware perspective, therapists can be more welcoming and more effective with widowers.

3

OVERVIEW OF GRIEF THEORIES

Theories and conceptualizations of grief have shifted dramatically over the last 50 years. In this chapter I will outline common grief reactions, the major theories of grief, and recent research on grief (i.e., Stroebe & Schut, 1999; Worden, 2009). A portion of the chapter will examine shifts in conceptualizing grief including challenges to the 'grief work' hypothesis—the view that a man must be emotionally expressive to resolve his grief—and shifting perspectives on ongoing connections with the deceased. It is critical that psychotherapists have a thorough understanding of common grief reactions and recent grief research and theory in order to not perpetuate grief myths.

Definitions

One might expect that there would be wide agreement in the field of thanatology on the definitions of terms such as *grief*, *bereavement*, and *mourning*. Unfortunately that is not the case. The term *grief* has more agreement than the other terms. I agree with Worden's (2009) definition: grief is "the *experience* of one who has lost a loved one to death" (p. 17). Rando (1993) describes four aspects to experiencing grief: "psychologically (through affects, cognitions, perceptions, attitudes, and philosophy/spirituality), behaviorally (through personal action, conduct, and demeanor), socially (through reactions to and interactions with others), and physically (through bodily symptoms and physical health)" (p. 22). Worden (2009) and Doka (1993) also point out that grief can challenge an individual's spiritual beliefs as well. Therefore, a comprehensive view of grief goes beyond focusing exclusively on the affect of the griever and recognizes the cognitive, physical, spiritual, and social aspects of grief.

Loss is frequently used to represent any significant death or change which causes grief including a person, animal, or role. Using this definition the death of a spouse, as well as the death of one's favorite dog, being fired from a valued job, and finalizing a divorce, would all be considered losses. In this book I will almost always use loss to refer to the death of a loved one, but it could also mean the psychological loss of a living person, as in the case of severe dementia (see Boss, 2006). *Secondary losses* are a frequently mentioned concept in thanatology. A secondary loss refers to psychological, physical, psychosocial changes that result from a loss. For example, for a widower the death of his wife may also result in the secondary losses of a co-parent, confidante, chef, best friend, financial planner, family organizer, and so on. Bill, a 55-year-old widower, described it this way:

> It's very simple to say I lost my wife, but that's not true. That's not true of anyone. In no significant sequence, in no particular order of importance, I say I lost a friend, I lost a lover, I lost a mother, I lost a sister, I lost a doctor, a nurse, a teacher, a finance expert, a fighter, I lost many, many people when I lost this one person. That's a lot. A lot of people think it's just . . . a wife, just a person, just one person. But unless you've walked that path, it's hard to imagine all the things you have to do for yourself all of a sudden. (Campbell & Silverman, 1987, p. 124)

While grief refers to the individual's reactions to a loss, the terms *bereaved* or *bereavement* refer to the status of experiencing a loss (usually a death) regardless of whether or not grief reactions are present (Rando, 1993; Worden, 2009). This is the most common distinction between grief and bereavement, but some writers have used grief and bereavement almost interchangeably (e.g., Fitzgerald, 1994; Sanders, 1999). The term *conjugal bereavement* refers to the death of a partner; someone who is *conjugally bereaved* is a widowed man or woman. Most of the research on conjugal bereavement has examined only married couples (for an exception see Lund, Caserta, Utz, & deVries, 2010).

Mourning is the term related to death and loss that has the least amount of agreement (Brabant, 2002). Generally speaking there are two related, but different uses for *mourning*. Mourning can refer to the individual's adaptive process in response to the loss (Rando, 1993; Worden, 2009), or to the socially and culturally sanctioned acts and rituals associated with the public expression of grief (Sanders, 1999; Stroebe, Hansson, Stroebe, & Schut, 2001; Wolfelt, 2006) or both (Rando et al., 2012). Rando (1993) has differentiated between grief and mourning in that mourning involves the individual's active (physical and psychological) steps in his or her grief process while grief is a more passive experiencing of the loss. This distinction between active and passive aspects of loss reactions is not widely used in the grief literature. In fact more recently authors have downplayed the differences between the terms and argue for using them as interchangeable synonyms (e.g., Granek, 2010).

Manifestations of Grief

It is common for grievers to wonder if their experience of grief is typical or abnormal. Various researchers have compiled lists of common grief reactions; some of these are based on clinical experience while others are based on empirical studies using symptom checklists. I have combined an extensive list of reactions based on two sources (see "Common Emotional, Physical, Behavioral, Cognitive Grief Reactions" box). These reactions are common in grievers and their mere presence does not imply abnormal grief; however, almost any reaction (or more likely, group of reactions), if severe enough, can be a signal that the bereaved's experience is atypical. Just as men and older adults struggling with depression tend to focus on their physical and cognitive symptoms (Courtenay, 2011), widowers will also tend to focus on the physical and cognitive grief reactions. Therefore, it is important to inquire beyond the affective reactions when working with widowers.

Common Emotional, Physical, Behavioral, and Cognitive Grief Reactions

* = From Worden, 2009
\# = From Stroebe & Stroebe, 1987
^ = From Rando, 1993

Emotional/Affective
Sadness*^
Anger*#^
Guilt*#^
Anxiety*#^
Loneliness*#^
Fatigue*^
Helplessness*#^
Shock*#^
Yearning*#^
Emancipation*
Relief*^
Numbness*#^
Depression#^

Despair#^
Dejection#^
Distress#^
Fears#^
Dread#
Self-blame#
Self-accusation#
Hostility#^
Irritability#^
Anhedonia#^ (loss of pleasure)
Longing#^
Pining#^

Physical
Tightness in chest or throat*^
Hollowness in the stomach*^
Oversensitivity to noise*
Sense of depersonalization*^
Short of breath*^
Muscle weakness*^
Lack of energy*^
Dry mouth*^
Physical complaints similar to deceased#
Immunologic/endocrine changes#^
Susceptibility to illness/disease#

Cognitive
Disbelief*^
Confusion*^
Preoccupation*#^
Sense of presence*#^
Hallucinations*^
Suppression#^
Denial#^
Lowered self-esteem#
Self-reproach#
Hopelessness#
Sense of unreality/depersonalization#^
Memory/concentration problems#^

Behavioral
Sleep disturbances*#^
Appetite disturbances*#^

Absentminded behavior*^
Social withdrawal*#^
Dreams of deceased*^
Avoiding reminders of deceased*^
Searching and calling out*#^
Sighing*^
Restless hyperactivity*#^
Crying*#^
Visiting places/carrying objects that remind the survivor of the deceased*^
Treasuring objects that belonged to the deceased*
Agitation#^
Tenseness#^
Fatigue/lethargy#^
Exhaustion#^
Somatic complaints#^

Metaphors for Grief

The benefit of listing each individual grief reaction is so that clients and therapists can quickly review them. However, this practice presents grief in a very artificial way because reactions to loss are rarely experienced individually nor are they stable. Often the bereaved will use metaphors to describe the depth and changing nature of his experience. Here are a few common metaphors for grief.

Grief as a Wound or Amputation

Although grief is often described as a psychological wound, Golden (2000) argues that an amputation metaphor is more accurate:

> [Significant] loss leaves behind the old metaphor for grief which is that of a wound, and brings forth a different image: that of an amputation. Dealing with a loss . . . is more like learning how to live after a part of you has been cut off than it is like healing from a wound. (p. 17)

Upon his wife's death C. S. Lewis (1961) described grief similarly, especially in terms of how one heals from the injury:

> To say the patient is getting over it after an operation for appendicitis is one thing; after he's had his leg off it is quite another. After that operation either the wound stump heals or the man dies. If it heals, the fierce, continuous pain will stop. Presently he'll get back his strength

and be able to stump about on his wooden leg. He has "got over it." But he will probably have recurrent pains in the stump all his life, and perhaps pretty bad ones; and he will always be a one-legged man. There will be hardly any moment he forgets it. Bathing, dressing, sitting down and getting up again, even lying in bed, will all be different. His whole way of life will be changed. (pp. 52–53)

Grief as World Being Shattered

Partners often serve as the most important referent for one another. After Winston Wilde's (1997) partner died, he realized how important this was:

Being in a loving relationship with a reflecting companion gives one a window into his own soul. My pane has been shattered. Dutifully I've swept up the shards and put them in the recycling bin. But a great wind has scattered the slivers about, ten thousand invisible land mines from a war now long lost, lying in wait for unpredictable moments of fresh blood. My lover is gone, and with him I lost my point of reference, the reliable reassurance of unconditional love and adoration. Our *pas de deux* [dance for two]—that anchor of our counterbalance—has ended. (p. 43)

The use of metaphor can be very helpful in grief counseling (Worden, 2009). Men, who are more likely to have trouble verbally describing their grief reaction, especially, may benefit from its use. A well-developed metaphor can help make the intangible reactions more real and can make it much easier to describe interrelated aspects of grief. Just as a blueprint can make a future building more real and accessible, so can a well-constructed metaphor make it easier for the widower to understand his own reaction and express it to a therapist.

Grief as a Spiral or Roller Coaster

Another common metaphor, especially in terms of the capricious course of grief, is of a roller coaster or spiral (e.g., Doka & Martin, 2010). For example, C. S. Lewis (1961) described his course of grief as a spiral:

For in grief nothing "stays put." One keeps on emerging from a phase but it always recurs. Round and round. Everything repeats. Am I going in circles, or dare I hope I am on a spiral? But if a spiral, am I going up or down it? (p. 56)

Researchers Zisook and Shear (2009) suggest that grief is especially disconcerting because it is unlike any other experience: "Healthy, generally adaptive people likely have not experienced such an emotional roller coaster, and typically find the intense, uncontrollable emotionality of acute grief disconcerting or even shameful and frightening" (p. 68).

Post-Death Encounters

Most manifestations of grief, such as crying and loneliness, are self-explanatory, but grief-related hallucinations and other post-death encounters are commonly misunderstood by the public (and some therapists) and therefore deserve further explanation. A variety of terms has been used to describe these phenomena including *extra-ordinary experiences* (LaGrand, 2005), *sensing the presence* (Simon-Buller, Christopherson, & Jones, 1998), *post-death encounters* (Nowatzki & Grant Kalischuk, 2009), *post death contact* (Klugman, 2006), and *after death communications* (Guggenheim & Guggenheim, 1995). I use the term *post-death encounters* to include sensory experiences (hearing, seeing, being touched by, or smelling something directly related to the deceased) and sense of presence experiences (Troyer, in press).

Prevalence rates of post-death encounters (PDEs) by the conjugally bereaved have varied from over 80% (Grimby, 1998) to 35% (Byrne & Raphael, 1994). A significant majority of widowed individuals have reported PDEs to be pleasant or beneficial; typically fewer than 15% of a sample report being frightened by the PDE, although many participants report being initially surprised or confused (e.g., Grimby, 1998; Olson, Suddeth, Peterson, & Egelhoff, 1985; Rees, 1971). Participants have generally reported being hesitant to share their PDEs with other individuals (Olson et al., 1985; Rees, 1971). Most important, widowers report that their PDEs can be very important grief experiences (Troyer, in press).

Overview of Grief Theories and Controversies

A recent surge in research has taken aim at many of the long-held assumptions regarding grief (for an overview see Corr & Doka, 2001; Wortman & Boerner, 2011). Several of the major controversies in grief studies include: (1) a shift from older stage or phase models of grief such as Kübler-Ross's Stages of Grief (1969; Kübler-Ross & Kessler, 2005) and Parkes's (1996) Phases of Grief to more recent grief models including the Dual Process Model (Stroebe & Schut, 1999) and Two-Track Model (Rubin, 1999); (2) cutting ties (Freud, 1917; Lindemann, 1944) versus continuing bonds with the deceased (Klass, Silverman, & Nickman, 1996) as the eventual goal of grief; (3) the view that 'grief work' must be accomplished (Sanders, 1999) versus a perspective that most bereaved are generally resilient and extensive grief work is unnecessary (Bonanno, 2004; Stroebe & Stroebe, 1991); (4) the focus on emotional expression (Staudacher, 1991) versus a valuing of cognitive and physical expression of grief (Doka & Martin, 2010); and (5) grief counseling as beneficial (Allumbaugh & Hoyt, 1999; Larson & Hoyt, 2007a) versus grief counseling as potentially harmful (Jordan & Neimeyer, 2003; Neimeyer, 2000).

Many suppositions about death have become entrenched in the field despite having limited or no empirical support. Most of these perceptions can be traced back to Freud or interpretations of Freud's work (Archer, 1999; Wortman & Boerner, 2011; Wortman & Silver, 1989), although several authors (e.g., Granek, 2010) have argued that Freud's views on mourning have been grossly misrepresented. Only recently have many assumptions about the goals, length, and treatment of grief been challenged. In this chapter, I will briefly review the assumptions and recent criticisms regarding the grief work assumption, 'cutting ties' versus continuing bonds, and stage models versus contemporary grief theories. Furthermore, the important concept of disenfranchised grief is examined.

Grief Work

The perspective that a bereaved person must 'work through' his loss in order to successfully resolve it has a long history. This process is known as *grief work* and the assumption that it must be completed prior to healthy resolution is called the *grief work hypothesis* (Stroebe, 1992; Stroebe & Stroebe, 1991). Freud (1917) is recognized as providing the foundation for this perspective while subsequent clinicians, including Lindemann (1944), are credited with advancing the perspective until it was virtually unquestioned in grief counseling (Granek, 2010; Stroebe, Schut, & Stroebe, 2005; Wortman & Boerner, 2011; Wortman & Silver, 1989).

There is no single agreed upon definition of grief work. The most commonly cited components of grief work include a preoccupation with the deceased, frequent reflection on the death and the preceding events related to it, an absence of positive reactions or personal growth, and an emphasis on experiencing and expressing emotions during the reflection. The eventual goal of grief work was the detachment from the deceased (Parkes, 1996; Stroebe, 1992; Wortman & Boerner, 2011). It was also assumed that the avoidance of grief work was pathological and would lead to delayed or complicated grief (Parkes, 1996; Stroebe,

Schut, & Stroebe, 2005). Here are two examples of how the grief work assumption has been described in popular grief books:

> In order to mourn completely, we must realize our needs. We need, first of all, to take the time to grieve. We need to talk and to cry as much as we can. (Tatelbaum, 1984, p. 24)

> Simply put, there is really only one way to grieve. That way is to go through the core of grief. Only by experiencing the necessary emotional effects of your loved one's death is it possible for you to eventually resolve the loss. If you try to walk around the perimeter of loss, that loss will remain unresolved, and you will be more likely to endure painful emotional, psychological, or physical consequences. (Staudacher, 1991, p. 3)

The grief work hypothesis has been criticized on several grounds. Its biggest flaw is the lack of empirical support for bereaved persons benefitting from grief work. Wortman and Silver (1989) were among the first to challenge the grief work assumption and reported there was little empirical evidence to support it; likewise, later researchers have found no support for grief work as necessary for most bereaved persons (Bonanno & Keltner, 1999; Stroebe & Stroebe, 1991; Stroebe, Stroebe, Schut, Zech, & van den Bout, 2002; for a review see Wortman & Boerner, 2011). Another critique stems from examples of cross-cultural and historical groups that have violated the grief work assumption, yet not experienced the negative consequences that were expected (Stroebe, 1992; Stroebe & Schut, 1999). Furthermore, theorists had not clearly distinguished grief work from other concepts such as rumination, yearning, and searching for meaning (Stroebe, 1992). Finally, grief researchers who endorsed the grief work assumption undervalued the protective benefits of some degree of repression and avoidance (Bonanno & Field, 2001; Stroebe & Stroebe, 1991), the benefits of positive emotions soon after loss (Elison & McGonigle, 2003), as well as the potential positive effects of maintaining a continuing bond with the deceased (Stroebe & Schut, 2005).

Perhaps the most harmful aspects of the grief work hypothesis have been its comprehensive application and narrow focus on affective responses. For many decades the grief work hypothesis has been universally and rigidly prescribed; all individuals suffering a significant loss were expected to 'work through' their grief (Larson & Hoyt, 2007b). Winokuer and Harris (2012) admonish grief therapists who might assume that grief work was required of all bereaved individuals: "This type of theory-bound, cookie-cutter approach to grief counseling can cause more harm than good, completely undermining the unique needs and personal characteristics of the bereaved individual who may seek assistance through grief counseling" (p. 221). The single-minded emphasis on emotional catharsis and, consequently, the neglect of other components of grief, including cognitive and physical aspects, has been another harmful result. Larson provides an extreme example of this when he recalls "health professionals informally charting the number of hours bereaved family members had cried as an index of progress in their grieving progress and hearing admonitions to grievers that they must 'empty their pools of pain'" (Larson & Hoyt, 2007b, p. 167). In regard to widowers, the grief work assumption has devalued less emotionally expressive methods of grieving that tend to be more frequently used by men (Stroebe & Schut, 1999).

This challenge to the grief work assumption leaves psychotherapists in a tough position. Does this mean that it is not useful to have clients express negative emotions regarding their losses? Is it better to help clients distract themselves than to focus on working through a loss? The short answer is: not necessarily. Only a few researchers assert, based on empirical findings, that any significant exploration of emotional reactions may be harmful. For example, based on their study that does not support the grief work hypothesis, Bonanno, Papa, Lalande, Zhang, and Noll (2005) suggest that "it may be inadvisable under any circumstances, even those in which a bereaved person appears to be suffering greatly, to encourage intensive processing of a loss" (p. 96). Other researchers argue that this is an example of going too far in rejecting the grief work assumption and providing equally inadvisable counterassumptions: that no one needs to go through grief work and it is inherently harmful (Larson & Hoyt, 2007a).

In summary, researchers have examined a variety of different components of the grief work hypothesis including support for emotionally working through a loss, the benefits of avoidance, and the impact of talking or writing about negative reactions to a death (see Wortman & Boerner, 2011 for a review). What they have found is that, generally speaking, working through grief is not the *only* way for *everyone* to cope or adapt to a loss. In other words, the empirical research has moved the field from the unconditional acceptance of the grief work hypothesis to the more difficult, yet more accurate, question of "what kind of grief processing may be beneficial for whom, and under what circumstances" (Wortman & Boerner, 2011, p. 453). *Let me be clear*—helping bereaved individuals express negative emotions and explore troubling memories can be immensely helpful, and psychotherapists may be in a unique position to help widowers because they may not feel comfortable expressing this with anyone else. But psychotherapists must remember that there is not one right way to grieve.

The challenge to the grief work hypothesis has validated the need for more research on resilience, positive emotions, and the potential benefits of distraction and avoidance. Furthermore, the reconsideration of the role of grief work has opened the door to examine another previously unquestioned assumption: the need to 'cut ties' with the deceased.

Cutting Ties

Around the same time that the grief work assumption was being challenged, theorists were also critically examining another core assumption in grief counseling—the importance of 'cutting ties' or disengagement from the deceased. Historically, grief models have focused on disengaging from, and perhaps even forgetting, the deceased as the goal of grief. Silverman and Klass (1996) suggest that the concept of 'letting go' has resonated with individuals in modern Western cultures because it matches the cultural emphasis on individualism and autonomy. Furthermore, the concept of a continued relationship with the deceased has been viewed as pathological because it is analogous to dependency—which is typically viewed negatively in Western cultures. Studies of various cultures have shown aspects both of cutting ties (e.g., 'tie-breaking' ceremonies for spousal bereavement) and continued relationships (Rosenblatt, Walsh, & Jackson, 1976). For example, Shinto and Buddhist traditions focus on a continued connection to the deceased while the Hopi (Native Americans) focus on forgetting the deceased as quickly as possible (Stroebe, Gergen, Gergen, & Stroebe, 1992).

The focus on disengagement from the deceased has a long tradition in recent grief theories and can be traced from Freud's (1917) early *Mourning and Melancholia*. Prior to this most Western cultures recognized an ongoing attachment with the deceased as a normal reaction (Klass & Chow, 2011). Drawing originally from a psychoanalytic perspective, the cutting ties perspective suggests that there is a limited amount of psychic energy to be investing in relationships. Therefore, if the griever is investing a significant amount of energy in the deceased, less is available for relationships with the living or future relationships (Boerner & Heckhausen, 2003; Wortman & Boerner, 2011). Despite his connection with cutting ties, when Freud wrote and talked about the deaths of his daughter and grandson he talked about grief never being completed and the deceased being irreplaceable (Freud, 1963; see Silverman & Klass, 1996; Worden, 2009). Despite these personal writings about his own experience with grief, later analysts interpreted Freud's perspective to be that any continuing relationship with the deceased should be eventually severed so the individual's psychic energy could be turned toward the living. To not sever ties has often been considered to be a sign that the bereaved was denying the reality of the loss (Silverman & Klass, 1996).

More recently, some grief researchers (e.g., Sanders, 1999) and authors of popular books about grief have continued to endorse cutting ties with the deceased. For example, Colgrove, Bloomfield, and McWilliams (1976/1991) in *How to Survive the Loss of a Love* reinforce the view of severing bonds with the deceased. One of their 94 lessons on grieving is "Don't Try to Rekindle the Old Relationship" which they equate to "a waste of valuable energy," "anti-healing," and "stupid" (p. 80). Thankfully, an alternative to this approach has received considerable attention and research: continuing bonds.

Continuing Bonds

In the book *Continuing Bonds: New Understandings of Grief*, Dennis Klass, Phyllis Silverman, and Steven Nickman (1996) summarized various counterperspectives to cutting ties and created a flood of discourse and research on the topic of ongoing relationships with the deceased. Although the concept of continued bonds had been discussed previously, this book provided an initial definition and summary of the research. The term *continuing bonds* refers to the view that "survivors hold the deceased in loving memory for long periods, often forever, and that maintaining an inner representation of the deceased is normal rather than abnormal" (Silverman & Nickman, 1996, p. 349).

The continuing bonds perspective builds from the view that the process of grief does not have a clear end, nor should there be an emphasis on cutting ties. Silverman and Klass (1996) summed up their perspective:

> We cannot look at bereavement as a psychological state that ends and from which one recovers. The intensity of feelings may lessen and the mourner become more future- rather than past-oriented; however, a concept of closure, requiring a determination of when the bereavement process ends, does not seem compatible with the model suggested by these findings. We propose that rather than emphasizing letting go, the emphasis should be on negotiating and renegotiating the meaning of the loss over time. While the death is permanent and unchanging, the process is not. (pp. 18–19)

This process is analogous to a new baby being born. The birth of the child changes his or her relationship with the mother, but it certainly does not end the relationship (Klass et al., 1996). Similarly, death changes our relationship to the deceased, but death does not cause the relationship to end.

Research has confirmed that the view of a continued connection to the deceased is a common experience of bereaved persons including children who have lost a parent (Silverman & Worden, 1992; Worden, 1996a), adopted children (Nickman, 1996), and widowed persons (Shuchter & Zisook, 1993). In fact, we frequently see the expression of continued connections to the deceased in our society. Most prominently are the ongoing ties that individuals feel with deceased public figures such as Elvis Presley, John F. Kennedy, Marilyn Monroe, James Dean, John Lennon, and Princess Diana (Rando, 1993).

Types of Continuing Bonds

Continuing bonds can take a variety of forms. The perception that the deceased are protecting or watching over the survivor is one form of continued bond (Klass et al., 1996). This perception can include a general sense of the deceased being aware of the survivor's life or the deceased serving as guardian angel. Another form of a continued bond is for the bereaved to sustain and promote the values and priorities of the deceased. In this way the deceased is viewed as living on through the survivor and the deceased may be seen as a role model. Furthermore, the ongoing relationship may be simply continued communication with the deceased. This commonly takes the form of talking (out loud or to oneself) to the deceased (Shuchter & Zisook, 1993). Sometimes this is a way for a widower to inform his partner on what is going on in his life (see Francis, Kellaher, and Neophytou, 2005). These characteristics show how continuing bonds are often adaptive and dynamic (Silverman & Nickman, 1996).

Harmful Continuing Bonds

A common misperception is that continuing bonds with the deceased are *always* healthy and beneficial to the bereaved. Klass and his colleagues (2006; Klass et al., 1996) are careful to point out that continued bonds with the deceased are not necessarily helpful to the survivor. What would make a continuing bond unhealthy or maladaptive? Klass (2006) states that "the criteria for the health of an interpersonal bond are the same whether the bond is between living people or between living people and dead people" (p. 845). In other words, if the continuing bond has aspects of negative relationships (contempt, hostility, rigid judgment, etc.) then it should viewed as unhealthy just as if those qualities described a relationship with a living person. A few examples of negative ongoing relationships include situations where there was a miserable or ambivalent partnership with the deceased, traumatic conditions related to the partner's death, or painful reminders of the partner. For example, the deceased partner may have belittled and disparaged the widower and left him with an ongoing sense that he will never live up to his deceased partner's expectations. The widower could feel an ongoing sense of guilt (however irrational) because he was unable to protect her from an auto accident. He may feel angry that a partner who committed suicide left him to talk care of three children on his own. Thus, some ongoing connections to the deceased are marked primarily by their painful associations and the resulting emotions such as guilt, regret, shame, anger, and fear.

Consequently, continuing bonds are not inherently beneficial or harmful, nor are they constantly experienced. Silverman and Nickman (1996) described the evolving nature of the ongoing connections and explained the fundamental paradox of continuing bonds:

> We hope that by talking about the value of bonds to the deceased, it does not seem we are advocating living in the past. The gratification that was available when the deceased lived is no longer available in the same way. Yet as mourners move on with their lives to find new roles, new directions, and new sources of gratification, they experience the past as very much a part of who they are. The deceased are both present and not present at the same time. It is possible to be bereft and not bereft simultaneously, to have a sense of continuity and yet to know that nothing will ever be the same. (p. 351)

Continuing Bonds and Grief Outcome

What about empirical studies on continuing bonds? Are continuing bonds helpful or not? Given the complexity of different types of and reactions to continuing bonds, it is too simplistic to ask if they are healthy or harmful (Klass, 2006). At this point, research is still limited (Wortman & Boerner, 2011). Some research has suggested a relationship with negative outcomes (e.g., Field, Gal-Oz, & Bonanno, 2003) while other studies have found more positive results (Stroebe & Stroebe, 1989). Most of the research that has found negative relationships has examined correlations between grief reactions and various types of continuing bonds. Thus, the directional causality between specific grief responses and continuing bonds cannot be determined (Wortman & Boerner, 2011). Or put another way, we cannot determine if depression or anxiety are a result of continuing bonds or vice versa. Furthermore, the immense range of behaviors, cognitions, and reaction subsumed under the umbrella of 'continuing bonds' (e.g., reminiscing with others about the deceased, seeing a vision of the deceased, acting on behalf of the deceased, etc.) make it impossible to reach any definitive empirical conclusions about their benefits or harmfulness at this time.

Continuing bonds are the antithesis to the previously unquestioned view of cutting ties with the deceased. While ongoing relationships with the deceased can be associated with negative grief reactions, continued bonds are not inherently harmful. In fact, bereaved persons often cherish ongoing connections to the deceased and will, understandably, object to the suggestion that they sever these ties; furthermore, these ties can often be used by the bereaved person (and psychotherapists) to aid their grief. Psychotherapists and other professionals who work with the bereaved should be aware of the prevalence and normality/normalness of continued bonds with the deceased (Silverman & Nickman, 1996).

Relationships With the Deceased and Grief Counseling

As with the 'grief work' hypothesis, this shift away from cutting ties with the deceased has challenged clinicians to surrender a common assumption about grief. Does this mean that it is never useful to help grieving clients cut some ties with the deceased? What about a client whose life appears to be thoroughly enmeshed with the deceased? Similar to the grief work perspective, we should be careful not to throw the baby out with the bathwater.

There are two ways to integrate these opposing viewpoints. One way is to avoid viewing this issue as dichotomous. I believe it is more useful and accurate to view the processes of cutting ties versus a continued relationship as being on a continuum (see Boerner & Heckhausen, 2003). Without question, there are some ties that must be cut, specifically those that require the bereaved to deny the physical reality of the death (Rubin, 1999). For example, preparing food each day to serve as if the deceased partner would magically show up to eat it is not a useful connection to maintain. Conversely, there are many ties that are well worth keeping. It would be foolish to try to convince a bereaved widower to deny or delete the positive changes in himself that he attributes to his deceased wife. He may see his generosity, compassion, and devotion to his family as traits he learned from his wife, and furthermore, view his commitment to these values as a way to honor his wife. Why would a counselor ever try to convince him otherwise?

Another way to help practitioners make sense of this debate is to avoid the dichotomy of cutting ties or a continued relationship and instead focus on *reconceptualizing* or *transforming the connection* to the deceased in a way that would be helpful to the bereaved (Boerner & Heckhausen, 2003). For instance, if a widower had relied on his wife to make healthy dietary choices, this aspect of their relationship could be continued but in a different format. Upon her death, the widower may choose healthier diet options not because his wife tells him to do so, but because he knows that it would be important to her to see him healthy.

A focus on transforming the relationship has several benefits. Bereaved clients are much more comfortable with the idea of maintaining a relationship, although in a new way, to the abandonment of the relationship to the deceased. Clients often erroneously believe that feeling better requires cutting all ties with the deceased and forgetting them. For example, one widower asked during his first visit to his therapist, "You're going to make me forget about my wife, aren't you?" (Elison & McGonigle, 2003, p. 151). This common myth that the goal of grief counseling is to disengage from the deceased to the extent of forgetting is one of the most harmful misconceptions in the field.

Some of the clinicians and researchers that have endorsed disengaging from the deceased have argued that their perspective has been misinterpreted and taken to the extreme. They suggest that the terms forgetting or closure do not reflect the absence of reminders. For instance, Sanders (1999) states that "letting go refers to the act of turning to new encounters, trusting the future" (p. 100) and "forgetting does not mean either that the bereaved will not experience poignant memories from time to time, or that anniversary reactions will be erased" (pp. 99–100). It is likely that this distinction is primarily a difference in emphasis. But unfortunately when grief theorists and writers use the terms 'letting go' and 'forgetting,' it can be all too easy for both the bereaved and therapists to take them literally. Given that most grief assistance is provided by self-help groups, layperson volunteers, and psychotherapists with limited training in modern grief models, it is common for grievers to be given a 'stripped down' version of a grief model. Consequently, it is easy for these caretakers to endorse the forgetting and letting go even if it is an oversimplification of a more complex model. Assuming that the views of theorists and clinicians, such as Sanders, that endorse cutting ties have been overexaggerated, this perspective still conceals the potential benefits of continued relationships with the deceased.

Rando (1993) argues that the view of 'cutting ties' with the deceased is the one aspect of grief in which both professionals and clients have been equally misinformed. As this assumption has received more attention, the questions being asked have changed. "The question should not be, Is wanting to maintain a connection with a deceased loved one wrong? But rather, What is an appropriate connection and what conditions promote it?" (Rando, 1993, p. 54).

Models of Grief

Kübler-Ross's Stage Model of Grief

Kübler-Ross's stage model of grief is easily the most recognized theory of grieving. In fact, it is difficult to overestimate its impact on Western culture. For example, it has been mentioned in episodes of popular television programs including *The Simpsons, The Office, Law & Order,* and *Monk*. Based on her interviews with terminally ill patients, Kübler-Ross described five stages that the dying person would go through: denial, anger, bargaining, depression, and acceptance. She reported her findings in her famous book *On Death and Dying* (1969).

Although her stage model was initially based on the experiences of terminally ill patients, and not those who were grieving the loss of a loved one, her stage theory was quickly used as a template for the expected reactions to the death of a loved one. Later, Kübler-Ross applied her theory directly to grieving people, but admitted that each person may not go through all the stages, nor follow them in any particular order (see Kübler-Ross & Kessler, 2005). Kübler-Ross should always be recognized as a pioneer in the field of thanatology; her courage to talk candidly with the terminally ill and express genuine concern about their dignity and right to accurate information was ground-breaking (Corr, 1993). However, her original stage theory has not been supported by research (see Wortman & Silver, 1989 for a review), and most experts agree that neither her stage model nor any other stage model of grief is a useful foundation for assisting the bereaved (see Attig, 1996).

Stage models of grief have been criticized on several grounds. Wortman and Boerner (2011) succinctly summarize the primary concerns with stage models of grief:

> First, they [stage models] cannot account for the variability in response that follows a major loss. Second, they place grievers in a passive role. Third, such models fail to consider the social or cultural factors that influence the process. Fourth, stage models focus too much attention on emotional responses to the loss and not enough on cognitions and behaviors. Finally, stage models tend to pathologize people who do not pass through the stages (Neimeyer, 1998). If people do not reach a state of acceptance, for example, they may be led to believe that they are not coping appropriately with the loss. (p. 288)

These are the most frequently cited criticisms of stage models of grief and provide the primary reasons why grief researchers and psychotherapists who specialize in grief generally do not use them.

Other critics have focused specifically on Kübler-Ross's Stages of Grief. For example, Corr (1993), in referring to Kübler-Ross's five stages, notes that "there is no reason to think that there are in fact only five ways in which human beings cope with anything as fundamental as dying" (p. 73). Another criticism is that the uniform progression of the stages has not generally been empirically supported (Bonanno & Boerner, 2007) (cf. Maciejewski, Zhang, Block, & Prigerson, 2007). Most grief research suggests a high degree of individuality in grief reactions (Rando, 1993; Stroebe, 1992; Worden, 2009; Wortman & Boerner, 2011). The view that the stage model is based entirely on Kübler-Ross's clinical impressions and not on empirical evidence is another criticism (Corr, 1993).

In her defense, Kübler-Ross said that she never intended for her stages to be interpreted this way. In her original book Kübler-Ross (1969) stated that the stages were not necessarily a stair-step process and the stages and other psychological defenses "will last for different periods of time and will replace each other or exist at times side by side" (pp. 147–148). In her last book before she died, she said,

> The stages have evolved ever since their introduction, and they have been very misunderstood over the past three decades. They were never meant to help tuck messy emotions into neat packages. They are responses to loss that many people have, but there is not a typical response to loss, as there is no typical loss. Our grief is as individual as our lives. (Kübler-Ross & Kessler, 2005, p. 7)

Furthermore, she describes the stages as "tools to help us frame and identify what we may be feeling. But they are not stops on some linear timeline in grief. Not everyone goes through all of them or goes in a prescribed order" (Kübler-Ross & Kessler, 2005, p. 7). Although not her original focus, Kübler-Ross (Kübler-Ross & Kessler, 2005) later argued that her description of grief could be applied to the bereaved and not just the dying (her theory had been widely applied to the bereaved for several decades by this point).

Contemporary Models of Grief

Many theories of grief and mourning have been developed since Kübler-Ross's stages of grief with most being developed in the last 20 years. While it is beyond the scope of this book to review all of the different models, I have chosen two to describe in detail: Worden's (2009) Tasks of Mourning and Stroebe and Schut's (1999) Dual Process Model (DPM). Although there several other well-studied theories of grief (e.g., Neimeyer's (2001) Meaning Making model, Parkes's (1996) Phases of Grief, Sander's (1999) Integrative Theory of Bereavement, Rando's (1984, 1993) Process of Mourning, and Rubin's (1999) Two-Track Model), I believe these two models are particularly well suited to widowers.

Worden's Tasks of Mourning

Worden (2009) believes the griever should play an active role in his or her grief and developed his model of grief as a set of tasks that the bereaved individual completes. This is a contrast to phase or stage models that imply the mourner moves passively through each stage or phase. Worden (2009) recognizes that the mourner does not have complete control of his grief recovery, but states that:

> mourning creates tasks that need to be accomplished, and although this may seem overwhelming to the person in the throes of acute grief, it can, with the facilitation of a counselor, offer hope that something can be done and that there is a way through it. This can be a powerful antidote to the feelings of helplessness that most mourners experience. (p. 38)

To be clear, this focus on being 'active' is not exclusive to physical activity. Instead it is a mindset that entails being engaged with one's own recovery. This can include a wide range of physical actions including physical activity, rituals, and working. But it also includes cognitive aspects (such as cognitive restructuring and self-efficacy) and spiritual aspects (e.g., reconstructing meaning) (see Attig, 1991).

The view of being an active participant in one's grief has received empirical support. Over the course of several studies, Lund, Caserta, and Dimond (1993) found that being active in one's life after the death of a spouse was critical to overall bereavement adjustment. Bereaved persons were able to maintain and improve their well-being when they took control of their life. They found that "taking control requires motivation, pride, skill, flexibility, some help from others, and the passage of time. The five best predictors of spousal bereavement that have emerged from our studies emphasize these requirements" (p. 252).

This focus on being active in one's grief is a big reason why I find myself drawn to Worden's task model. And while I know that many women identify with Worden's model, I believe that it especially resonates with bereaved men. Men, when faced with a challenging situation, want to have a clear goal and focus on 'doing something.' Grief is no exception. To be clear, Worden's tasks are not so prescriptive as to provide a detailed blueprint for grief resolution. But they do provide a starting point and allow the bereaved and therapists to tailor how the tasks are accomplished to each widower's specific needs and circumstances.

Unfortunately, many works published after the year 2000 continue to cite Worden's original edition and focus on the concept of cutting ties (e.g., Klicker, 2007). This inaccurately presents Worden's original version of his task model as his most recent position and leads readers to assume that he continues to endorse the cutting ties perspective. Furthermore, his model is often confused with being a stage model or being a linear process (e.g., Sabar, 2000). Worden (2009) ardently argues against this conceptualization of his model. However, just because it is task-based instead of stage-based does not mean the tasks are presented haphazardly. Worden states that the bereaved person may initially encounter the tasks in the order they are presented. For example, it is difficult, if not impossible, to 'embark on a new life' if one has not 'accepted the reality of the loss.' However, each task has multiple aspects and the bereaved should expect to revisit each task from multiple perspectives.

TASK 1: TO ACCEPT THE REALITY OF THE LOSS

Dan, a younger widower, described learning of his wife's death a few days after she had survived a stroke:

> The doctor was standing [outside her hospital room] with my father-in-law and he said we need to go in private. We went into a room and he told me she had passed away. That didn't register. We kept talking and had some conversation, and finally, he just had to grip me by the shoulders and say, "Your wife is deceased!" . . . it finally got through.

This is often what most people think of when discussing the denial of death—the disbelief that the loved one has died. But this is not the full extent of denying death. There is a wide range of cognitions and behaviors that signify a lack of acceptance of death. Some common and normal denial reactions include mistakenly seeing the deceased in crowds or other public places, expecting phone calls or visits, or other communication from the deceased. More extreme reactions such as not reporting the death to authorities and attempting to preserve the body at home or in another private setting are quite rare and typically reflect serious psychological disorders (Worden, 2009).

Kübler-Ross, who popularized the concept of denial in her stages of grief, recognized that symbolic denial is more common than literal denial (Kübler-Ross & Kessler, 2005). For example, men may be more likely to deny the meaning of the loss instead of the actual occurrence of the loss. Men may be more likely to rely on thoughts such as 'I can't do anything about it' or 'There is no use crying over what can't be changed.' In some cases, the widower may tell himself that the loss is presented as less significant than it really is. For example, he may say, "She wasn't a good mother," "We weren't really close," or "I don't miss her" (adapted from Worden, 2009, p. 40). Signs that the bereaved person may want to maintain the denial include removing items that remind him of the deceased partner. For example, getting rid of pictures and her clothes quickly and without regard to forethought and planning may be a sign of symbolic denial. Although in some cases, this might be a sign that the relationship may have been troubled and the surviving spouse may be relieved to remove the painful reminders from their home (Elison & McGonigle, 2003). Widowers may be more likely to use these types of denial because they are less comfortable feeling emotionally vulnerable. However, therapists should not be too quick to interpret various behaviors without a clear understanding of the circumstances of the loss and the bereaved person's intentions. In the majority of cases, widowed persons will naturally acknowledge the physical reality of the loss. If denial is an ongoing concern, it is likely to be related to not acknowledging the personal significance of the loss.

TASK II: TO PROCESS THE PAIN OF GRIEF

The pain that Worden (2009) refers to is more than just sadness; it also includes "anxiety, anger, guilt, depression, and loneliness" (p. 46). The mourner may have more difficulty with this stage because members of society may be uncomfortable with outward expressions of grief-related pain. In my opinion, this has gotten better in the last few decades, but can still be a significant concern. Sometimes others will attempt to provide support through trying to minimize the loss or by attempting to distract the mourner, or by trying to rush the griever back to a non-grieving state. For example, well-intentioned friends or family members may suggest that the widower will be all right without his wife ('you can learn to cook and take care of the children'), or may try to engage him in activities to take his mind off his loss, or try to rush him toward new relationships. Worden points out that these actions, which are intended to help the bereaved, may inadvertently inhibit Task I: Accepting the reality of the loss.

Widowers may try to avoid the pain of grief through a variety of methods. The use of 'thought-stopping procedures' is one way they might avoid the pain associated with the loss. Similarly, individuals may avoid people, locations, activities, and situations that are associated with the deceased. Another common method of avoiding the pain of the loss is using and abusing alcohol and drugs.

TASK III: TO ADJUST TO A WORLD WITHOUT THE DECEASED

Worden (2009) points to three areas of adjustment for the bereaved: external adjustments, internal adjustments, and spiritual adjustments. External adjustments relate to the changing nature of the world around the widower including different patterns of daily living and adjusting to all of the roles that the deceased provided. For example, the spouse was not only a wife, but also the facilitator of social contacts, the family event planner, the financial manager, the cook, the housekeeper, and other roles. Widowers find that they will need to step into these roles, find someone else to perform them, or do without.

Internal adjustments can include a new sense of self. This includes their new roles, as well as "how death affects self-definition, self-esteem, and sense of self-efficacy" (Worden, 2009, p. 47). Some argue that husbands have a more difficult time regarding loss because they define themselves in terms of being a provider and protector (Martin & Doka, 1996). While both parents typically share a protective role regarding children, men often view their role in a marriage relationship to be the financial provider and physical protector for the children and partner (Golden, 2000). The death of his wife, even when he was unable to protect her (e.g., from a random car accident, dementia, cancer, etc.), can cause a widower to feel anger and guilt. Some of this anger and guilt may come from his perception of failing in his protective role.

Spiritual adjustments include challenges to an individual's perceptions about how the world works, fairness, justice, and meaning. Spiritual adjustments are more likely in losses with circumstances that challenge our assumptions: the death of young children, innocent victims of accidents or homicides, suicides, etc. Worden (2009) describes failure in Task III as "failure to adapt to the loss" (p. 49). Some examples of failing to adapt include not adapting to fill new roles, not reconceptualizing their sense of self without the deceased, and not adapting to a new perception of the world.

TASK IV: TO FIND AN ENDURING CONNECTION WITH THE DECEASED IN THE MIDST OF EMBARKING ON A NEW LIFE

Worden's fourth task has evolved over the last four editions of his book (the first written in 1982). The first version of the fourth task was "withdrawing emotional energy from the deceased and reinvesting it in another relationship" (Worden, 1982, p. 15). This task was rephrased to "emotionally relocate the deceased and move on with life" in the second and third editions (Worden, 1996b, 2002). In the most recent edition, Worden (2009) has settled on "to find an enduring connection with the deceased in the midst of embarking on a new life" (p. 50). This revision represents a clearer recognition of the potential benefits of continuing bonds with the deceased. (Klass et al., 1996). As Worden (2009) says,

> The counselor's task then becomes not to help the bereaved give up their relationship with the deceased, but to help them find an

appropriate place for the dead in their emotional lives—a place that will enable them to go on living effectively in the world. (p. 51)

This shift has mirrored the evolution in the larger field from focusing on cutting ties to a perspective that understands that many forms of ongoing connections with the deceased can be healthy and adaptive. I find it commendable that Worden has been willing to make adjustments to this foundational aspect of his task theory. It is common to see researchers and clinicians cling to their original perspectives despite new evidence from research and clients suggesting otherwise.

Overall, I find Worden's task model immensely helpful because it can easily be explained to clients, it matches their grief experiences, and recognizes the natural variability and individuality in the grieving process. Furthermore, perhaps one of the best things about the model is that it is set up as an active process. Worden recognizes that the griever does not have complete control over his recovery and is influenced by outside forces, yet the task model provides the bereaved with a sense that specific actions can be taken to help oneself during grief. I think this is especially helpful for the average man who eschews the idea that grief can only be dealt with through emotional expression and would like to know the practical steps he can take to improve his situation.

Stroebe and Schut's Dual Process Model of Coping With Bereavement

Stroebe and Schut (1999) developed the Dual Process Model of Coping with Bereavement (DPM) in light of challenges to the grief work assumption and to better describe effective and poor adaptation to loss (Stroebe & Schut, 2010; Stroebe et al., 2005). The DPM suggests that the griever alternates between *loss-oriented* stressors and *restoration-oriented* stressors. Loss-orientated stressors are concerns related to dealing with the loss of the loved one including the recognition of the loss, dealing with the emotional pain of the loss, and developing a new, ongoing relationship with the deceased. The restoration-oriented stressors include developing new skills and fulfilling new roles (that were left by the deceased), distraction from grieving, and dealing with ongoing life responsibilities and challenges that are unrelated to the loss (paying bills, continuing to work, etc.). As might be expected, bereaved men tend to be more restoration-oriented than women and vice versa (Schut, Stroebe, van den Bout, & de Keijser, 1997; Stroebe, 1998). Although more research is necessary, initial studies have found that loss-oriented coping is particularly important immediately following the loss while restoration-oriented coping is more important later (Richardson & Balaswamy, 2001).

Oscillation is a key aspect of the DPM. It refers to shifting back and forth between loss-oriented and restoration-oriented needs.

> The principle underlying oscillation is that at times the bereaved will confront aspects of loss, at other times avoid them, and the same applies to the tasks of restoration. . . . Coping with bereavement according the DPM is thus a complex regulatory process of confrontation and avoidance. An important postulation of the model is that oscillation between the two types of stressors is necessary for adaptive coping. (Stroebe & Schut, 2010, p. 278)

The DPM states that the bereaved individual will frequently oscillate between loss-oriented and restoration-oriented coping and that these two coping methods cannot be performed at the same time. This reflects the natural process of alternating one's focus from the realities and challenges of grief to daily tasks and distraction of grief. Various forms of complicated grief (see Chapter 6) may arise when a bereaved individual does not oscillate between the two forms of coping. Some individuals may act almost as if the loss has not occurred (extremely restoration-focused) while others may focus exclusively on the loss and its emotional consequences (extreme loss-orientation) without facing the ongoing tasks of living (Stroebe & Schut, 1999).

There is a misperception that the Dual Process Model is the same as problem- versus emotion-focused coping (see Lazarus & Folkman, 1984). Specifically, loss-oriented coping can be erroneously viewed as being entirely emotion-focused, while restoration-orientated coping is believed to be only problem-focused. Actually either loss-orientation or restoration-oriented coping can be accomplished in an emotion- or problem-focused way (Stroebe & Schut, 2010). For example, a widower could use emotion-focused coping as part of his restoration process by sharing his feelings about being a suddenly single parent. Conversely a widower could use problem-focused strategies to create a memory book that helps him remain connected to his deceased wife (loss-oriented).

I believe the Dual Process Model is well suited to be paired with an empathic view of widowed men and a strengths-based approach. For example, the DPM can help widowers identify ways that aspects of traditional masculinity have been useful before and after his partner's death. Widowers (and all bereaved men) often tackle the practical problems associated with a death. These problems include making funeral arrangements, managing financial and legal concerns related to the death, continuing to work, and so on. Previous grief models largely ignored these efforts while the DPM recognizes that these restoration-oriented coping strategies are an important part of a larger coping process. Furthermore, previous stage and phase models did not account for the benefits of dosing emotions or occasional avoidance of grief (Stroebe et al., 2005).

Bereaved men who endorse traditional gender schemas may avoid loss-oriented coping processes (e.g., focusing on the loss, remembering/reminiscing about the deceased, and examining the changes that have resulted) because they often evoke feelings of sadness, lack of control, and emotional pain. However, the DPM recognizes that cognitive and physically active strategies can be used to cope emotionally. For example, writing a personal memoir of one's grief could be a primarily cognitive and behavioral loss-oriented coping strategy. Many rituals, including their planning and reflection, can also involve cognitive, physical, and problem-solving characteristics and be used to cope with the loss.

Benefits and Limitations of Using Grief Models in Psychotherapy

Introducing widowers to grief models can be helpful because they provide a general template for their grief reactions and hope for the future. Teaching clients about one or two grief models can be helpful for clients to provide a framework for their grief. A key aspect of therapy is providing clients with a framework or rationale for why they are experiencing their particular challenges and how to work toward positive change. Clients also benefit from learning about specific concepts related to their grief. For example, if a widower had assumed that he must forget his partner to feel better he will likely find great relief in learning about benefits of continuing bonds. Counselors frequently hear clients express relief after hearing that their particular concern or reaction has a specific term associated with it. This seems to make the concern less threatening and more concrete.

Introducing widowed clients to grief models can also provide hope in terms of a path through grief. I am not suggesting that grief models provide 'the answer' to grief, but they can serve to remind clients that their reaction to their loss will change over time. For example, clients can use Worden's (2009) tasks as a framework for understanding challenges to come. Although Worden clearly states that the tasks are not to be mistaken for stages or steps to grief resolution, they can still provide a general template for future steps.

There are several cautions to using grief models in grief counseling and therapy. The most important is to not state or imply that grief models are a lock-step path to grief resolution.

> Models are useful when they provide structure; summarize knowledge in a field; and offer a sense of direction for assessment, analysis, and intervention. However, when models of grief *become* the reality, there is a danger. The model then offers a *prescription* for how people ought to grieve rather than a *description* of the ways many people do grieve.
> (Doka & Martin, 2002, p. 345)

Counselors and concerned loved ones can intentionally or unintentionally create this misconception. When grief theories are misapplied bereaved clients "concerns about grieving correctly actually become a stressor in and of themselves" (Servaty-Seib, 2004, p. 127).

Stage models of grief, especially Kübler-Ross's model, are especially prone to misuse and misunderstanding. For example, a grief therapist reported a client who

> asked her to do something to make her mad. "Why would you want me to do that?" [the counselor] asked her, mystified. "My neighbor told me that at this stage, I should be angry, and I'm not," she confessed. "I'm afraid I'm not doing this right." (Elison & McGonigle, 2003, p. xxiii)

In this case, it appears that Kübler-Ross's model had been inappropriately explained by the neighbor as an intransigent path to grief resolution. Virtually all grief researchers argue that Kübler-Ross's (1969) Stages of Grief should not be used to demonstrate a typical grieving process to clients because they provide an overly simplistic perspective (e.g., Neimeyer, 2006; Winokuer & Harris, 2012). Furthermore, I would argue that since her model is so pervasive in Western culture, the therapist should introduce the topic early in the counseling process and dispel any myths or misconceptions related to stages of grief.

Models should always be presented tentatively and clients should always be reminded that models of grief and mourning are based on studies of large groups and are not predictive of how any individual must deal with his grief. Ideally, the counselor should learn something about the widower's loss and reaction to the loss in order to introduce models that have some relevance to the client's current reactions. There are enough contemporary models of grief (e.g., Worden's (2009) Task model, Stroebe and Schut's (1999) Dual Process Model, Rubin's (1999) Two-Track Model, etc.) for the therapist to choose from and ensure some relevance to the client's immediate reactions. Finally, therapists should be careful to limit the time spent discussing grief models. Rarely are bereaved individuals interested in the minutiae of meta-analytic findings and multiple regression-based studies to evaluate grief models. For the rare clients who are interested in delving into the details of a particular theory, it is best to provide some suggested readings and use the time together more productively.

Psychotherapists' Outdated Views of Grief Models

Although mental health professionals will frequently encounter clients who are experiencing grief and loss, most have inadequate training in modern theories and techniques of grief counseling (Freeman & Ward, 1998; Winokuer & Harris, 2012). According to Rando (1993), mental health professionals are poorly trained regarding grief and, therefore, perpetuate some of the same myths and misconceptions that the general public endorses. A study of 369 practicing counselors in the US found that more than 90% of the sample reported at least some familiarity with Kübler-Ross's stage theory, but only 28% were somewhat familiar with Worden's (2009) Task model (Ober, Granello, & Wheaton, 2012).

Perhaps these results should not be surprising given that none of the accrediting bodies of the typical paths to becoming a licensed mental health professional, including clinical or counseling psychology doctoral programs (APA), masters-level social work programs (CSWE), masters-level counseling programs (CACREP; Doughty & Hoskins, 2011), or masters-level marriage and family therapy programs (COAMFTE), require coverage of grief counseling. Unfortunately, the level of training and knowledge are not significantly better for physicians, nurses, and funeral directors (see Dickinson, 2007; Downe-Wambolt & Tamlyn, 1997; Wass, 2004; Wortman & Boerner, 2011).

Disenfranchised Grief

The concept of *disenfranchised grief* is critical for understanding the grief process of bereaved individuals. Over the course of two books, Doka and his contributors (1989a, 2002a) have introduced and developed this important concept. Doka (1989a) defined disenfranchised grief as "the grief that persons experience when they incur a loss that is not or cannot be openly acknowledged, publicly mourned, or socially supported" (p. 4). Consequently, disenfranchised grievers are denied the recognized status as a bereaved individual and the support that typically goes with it. Doka (1989a, 2002a) outlined five different ways grief could be disenfranchised. The original three (Doka, 1989a) include when the relationship is not recognized, the loss is not recognized, and the griever is not recognized. Doka (2002a, 2002b) later added two more types of disenfranchisement: the circumstances of the death and the ways individuals grieve. It is important to examine each type as it may apply to widowers because disenfranchisement is a common reason for seeking additional assistance.

The Relationship Is Not Recognized

This type of disenfranchisement occurs when the relationship is not recognized by broader society as being significant enough to warrant being grieved. Examples of this type of disenfranchisement include non-family losses (e.g., death of a close family friend known as 'Uncle' Bill), partners from extramarital affairs, cohabitators, homosexual relationships, and engaged couples. In each case, the significance of the relationship between the griever and the deceased is questioned as being strong enough or significant enough to acknowledge the right of the survivor to grieve. A widower may experience this form of disenfranchisement if he was divorced or separated from his partner, if he had been married a short time, or if he was not legally married to his partner. This type of disenfranchisement is one reason why my definition of a widower is so broad. I acknowledge all men who lose a romantic partner the right to grieve and to have their relationship be recognized as significant regardless of the legal status, current relationship status, or social recognition of their relationship.

The Loss Is Not Recognized

In this form of disenfranchised grief, the griever is not recognized because the loss is not acknowledged. Examples of this type of disenfranchisement include prenatal and perinatal losses (i.e., miscarriage, stillbirth, abortion), pet death, individuals who are in a coma, dementia, and 'psychosocial deaths.' The most common way that a widower's loss would not be recognized is in terms of a psychosocial death. Doka and Aber (2002) refer to psychosocial death as "cases in which the psychological essence, individual personality, or self is perceived as dead, though the person physically remains alive" (p. 219). This is similar to Boss's (1999, 2006) description of one form of an *ambiguous loss* where the deceased is psychologically absent, but physically present. Situations that may cause a psychosocial death include dementia, severe mental illness, conversion and indoctrination into a cult, and the addiction to substances among others. Because a physical death has not occurred, the husband/partner may not consider himself to be a widower, despite the fact that he may experience many of the same grief reactions.

A recent, prominent example of this type of loss was when it was reported that former Supreme Court Justice Sandra Day O'Connor's husband, who suffered from Alzheimer's disease, had a girlfriend at the assisted living facility where he lived. His dementia had reached a point where he no longer recognized his wife of 55 years. O'Connor was acknowledged for the grace she showed in accepting and supporting her husband, even continuing to visit him while he held hands with his new girlfriend on the facility's porch swing (Zernike, 2007). While the focus of the media was on O'Connor's graciousness, and without question her reaction is laudable, relatively little attention was given to her loss. While her husband had not died, her marriage had certainly changed, if not ended. One can only guess that grief must have been a part of this transition.

The Griever Is Not Recognized

A third form of disenfranchised grief involves ignoring the individual's ability to grieve. In these situations the bereaved individual is not recognized as someone capable of expressing grief (Doka, 1989a). Examples of groups affected by this form of disenfranchised grief include the very old, young children, and the cognitively or developmentally disabled. This type of disenfranchisement will most likely affect a widower who is cognitively disabled, is very old, or both. For example, if a man with dementia is widowed, his family and friends may assume (without good evidence) that he will not experience grief due to his impaired cognitive abilities.

Circumstances of the Death

This type of disenfranchised grief expands the idea of 'the loss not being recognized' to include aspects of the death that make others less likely to support the bereaved. Circumstances that might cause this type of disenfranchisement include losses that may cause the bereaved to feel shame or judgment (e.g., when the death is a result of suicide, homicide, AIDS-related death, autoerotic asphyxiation, etc.), losses that may induce common fears most want to avoid (e.g., death of a young partner, the death of a child, etc.), and losses that are subject to widespread societal and media scrutiny (e.g., suicide, homicide, etc.). For example, widowers whose partners die from suicide tend to receive less social support (Stillion, 1996). At a time when the widower is struggling with grief, anger, and guilt, he may be shunned by those he would typically rely upon.

Ways Individuals Grieve

The final type of disenfranchisement occurs when the bereaved individual is marginalized based on his grief response. Western culture generally expects some type of affective reaction or at least some outer sign that the loss has caused pain, yet dramatic displays of grief that are customary in other societies, are also generally unacceptable. Doka and Martin (2002) suggest that bereaved persons that experience their grief primarily in cognitive and physical ways (i.e., *instrumental grief*) may be more likely to be disenfranchised, especially soon after the loss. Individuals who express their grief in almost exclusively instrumental ways may show little to no affective expression of their grief, despite painfully experiencing the loss cognitively, physically, and spiritually. For example, a widower may be viewed as avoiding or denying his grief if he does not show some affective response (i.e., crying, sadness, etc.) shortly after the loss.

Disenfranchised Grief and Grief Counseling

Although the concept of disenfranchised grief has been criticized for being overly categorical (i.e., grief is either disenfranchised or it isn't; Robson & Walter, 2012–13), it is still an immensely useful concept for psychotherapists. If a widower is experiencing poor social support or is in a situation where his status as a legitimate griever is questioned (e.g., as an ex-spouse), it is likely that one or more forms of disenfranchisement is at work. Furthermore, the source of the disenfranchisement may come from the widower himself; this is known as *self-disenfranchisement* or *self-initiated disenfranchisement* (Kauffman, 2002). In these situations, he may tell himself that he does not deserve to grieve his loss because of his status, the specifics of the relationship, the cause of death, or other factors. For example, a widower self-disenfranchises when he convinces himself that he does not deserve to grieve his partner because he never married her. Another example would be an older widower who believes he should not grieve the death of his wife after 50 years of marriage because he assumes he should feel fortunate to have had such a long time with her.

There is a variety of implications for disenfranchised widowers. These can include an inability to plan or participate in funeral rituals (Doka, 2002a), lack of access to bereavement leave from work, loss of social support, self-imposed shame (Kauffman, 2002), and socially and/or self-imposed limitations on how the widower expresses his grief for fear of being rejected (Doka, 2002b; Harris, 2010). Examples of how psychotherapists can assist widowers who experience various forms of disenfranchisement will be discussed throughout the book.

4

MEDIATORS OF WIDOWERS' GRIEF

Many different factors can mediate the bereaved person's grief experience. While keeping track of the wide variety of mediators and their varying influence on grief can be daunting, it is critical that psychotherapists keep them in mind throughout therapy. In this chapter I will describe the factors or mediators that influence widowers' grief reactions as well as an examination of the course and length of grief. The mediating factors can be grouped into five categories: (1) factors associated with the relationship to the deceased, (2) characteristics of the widower, (3) characteristics of the loss, (4) social factors, and (5) concurrent stressors. My categorization of these factors builds from Worden's (2009) model and is also informed by Parkes (1996) and Rando (1993), but is unique in that it relates them specifically to widowers.

Mediators of Grief

1. **Relationship With the Deceased**
   Nature of the relationship
   Quality of relationship
   Attachment
   Conflicts
   Tasks performed by the deceased
   Family roles
2. **Characteristics of the Widower**
   Gender and gender role
   Age
   Loss history
   Mental health history
   Personality factors and self-esteem
   Religiosity

3. **Characteristics of the Loss**
   Sudden and unexpected death
       Heart attack and stroke
       Vehicle accidents
   Traumatic death
       Homicide or violent death
       Suicide
   Witnessing the death
   Prolonged illnesses
   Preventable deaths
   Multiple losses
   Ambiguous losses
   Stigmatizing deaths
4. **Social Factors**
   Social support
   Social role involvement
5. **Concurrent Stressors**
   Children
   Financial pressures
   Substance abuse

Due to the wide variety of mediators, researchers have focused on a few at a time. While this concentration on a few factors increases the internal validity of the studies, it also creates an impression that the individual factors examined in a particular study are operating without influence from other mediators. Although the individual mediators will be presented separately, I encourage therapists to view them as a broad constellation of mutually influencing factors. Certainly there are times when one aspect of the death (e.g., death as a result of suicide or homicide) will alter the entire context of the widower's reaction, but most losses include a wide variety of interconnected mediators.

The Relationship With the Deceased

Nature of the Relationship

The nature of the relationship is a key factor in determining the extent of bereaved person's grief. The simplest aspect of this relationship is the type of relationship between the deceased and the bereaved. Research suggests that the death of a spouse or romantic partner is one of the most difficult losses (Holmes & Rahe, 1967). Researchers have often focused on married couples because they are common and easy to define. Therapists must be careful not to misconstrue the legal status of the bereaved man's relationship as a direct influence on his grief; men who lose girlfriends, same-sex partners, fiancées, and common-law wives will experience just as much grief just as widowers who were married.

Quality of Relationship

More important than the legal status of the relationship are other factors that influenced how the widower experienced the relationship. These mediators include the quality of the relationship and the roles played by each partner. These factors are more difficult to measure and can only be evaluated fully through prolonged contact with the widower. Worden (2009) suggests that "it is almost axiomatic that the intensity of the grief is determined by the intensity of love" (p. 58) and other researchers have found that emotional closeness to the deceased was a significant predictor of the intensity and duration of grief (Carr et al., 2000; Guarnaccia, Hayslip, & Landy, 1999), but not necessarily higher levels of depression (Wayment & Vierthaler, 2002). However, high-quality marital bonds have been associated with less grief-related anger if both partners had rated their marital happiness similarly (Carr & Boerner, 2009).

Several theorists and researchers have suggested that long-standing relationship discord (e.g., poor marital relationship, ambivalent relationships, or superficial attachments) is associated with inhibited grief or delayed grief in bereaved spouses (Raphael, 1983; Worden, 2009). Bonanno and his colleagues (Bonanno et al., 2002) suggest that this long-standing assumption is false and, instead, suggest that bereaved spouses with strong coping resources would show a resilient response that should not be confused with inhibited grief. These results suggest that widowed persons who had a happy and close relationship may not have intense grief responses assuming they have intrapersonal and interpersonal resources.

Researchers have also examined the influence of conflicting or ambiguous emotions in relationships. Contrary to previous studies (e.g., Gamino, Sewell, & Easterling, 1998), Carr et al. (2000) found that widowed persons with more ambiguous or conflicted relationships actually fared better while those who rated their relationship as being closer reported more yearning. Specifically, yearning was higher in those widowed persons that rated their marriage quality highly and reported low marital conflict. Carr et al. (2000) did not find any differences for older widowers based on their level of dependence on their wife for homemaking tasks.

Attachment

Although criticized as being too narrow of a focus (see Klass, 2006), the type of attachment with the partner is also a significant moderating factor. One definition of attachment, advanced by Bartholomew (1990), includes couples that are securely attached, marked by a positive view of oneself and his partner, or conversely, insecurely attached, in which the widowed person had a negative view of himself, his partner, or both. In a study specifically examining the relationship between this view of attachment and grief-related variables, Waskowic and Chartier (2003) found that those widowed persons with an insecure attachment style "experienced more despair, depersonalization, anger, guilt, death anxiety, social isolation, rumination, and somatic symptoms than securely attached individuals" (p. 88).

Bowlby's (1980) theory and descriptions of attachment are the foundation for most research on attachment; Bowlby divides relationships into three attachment styles: secure, anxious-ambivalent, and avoidant. Bowlby hypothesized that those individuals with a secure attachment style would have an initially strong grief reaction, but would improve gradually. Researchers using Bowlby's definitions have found those with an anxious-ambivalent style to be significantly more likely to experience grief and depression, while those with a secure attachment were less likely to experience depression, and those with an avoidant style were more likely to report somatic complaints (Wayment & Vierthaler, 2002). Taken together we could expect that widowers with a close, but secure relationship would experience high levels of grief, but not high levels of other grief-related concerns such as anger, guilt, depression, rumination, and despair. Conversely, those widowers with a close, yet conflicted and insecure relationship are more likely to experience high levels of grief and grief-related distress.

Conflicts

Related to the closeness and type of attachment is the presence of specific conflicts with the deceased. Conflicts are different than ongoing styles of attachment or emotional closeness in that they related to specific problems, not patterns of associating with one another. These conflicts include ongoing relationship concerns, such as long-term infidelity, or short-term problems including an argument immediately before the partner's death. Either way, conflict during the relationship may result in guilt and anger as part of grief (Rando, 1993; Worden, 2009). In one study, older widowed persons reported lower levels of anger if they had had positive interactions with their partners during their last days (Carr, 2003). Commons examples include having an argument immediately before a partner's unexpected death, or regret associated with not being a better partner throughout one's marriage.

Tasks Performed by the Deceased

A final relationship factor that can influence grief is the variety of roles and tasks performed by the deceased partner. Research suggests that widowed persons who depended on their partner for performing practical household tasks were more anxious post-loss (Carr et al., 2000). A common perception is that widowers are unprepared to manage household tasks including cooking and cleaning. Certainly some widowers, especially older widowers, have little experience cooking and cleaning (Bennett et al., 2003). Some widowers see this as a personal challenge and experience significant personal growth after learning new skills (Carr, 2004b). There may be a wide variety of other tasks and roles that the widower's wife performed including maintaining family and social ties (e.g., organizing family reunions, sending holiday cards, etc.), scheduling medical appointments and check-ups, and maintaining the household's day-to-day finances. Those widowers who depended significantly on their partner to fulfill their psychological needs (e.g., self-esteem, self-worth, etc.) and physical and social needs (e.g., socializing, housekeeping, cooking, etc.) will need to make more significant adjustments after their partner's death (Parkes, 1996; Rando, 1993).

Family Roles

Bowen (1976) has provided one of the most popular theories of family systems and suggests that each family member plays a role within the family system. Therefore, when a person is added or removed from the family, the equilibrium of the family is disrupted. When a family member dies that person cannot perform the roles she or he used to play (although the deceased continue to influence family dynamics). Consequently, the bereaved person often must cope with the death as well as a disrupted family system and new responsibilities that were left by the deceased (Rando, 1984). The variety of roles played by the deceased will influence the widower's and other family member's grief. From a family systems perspective, not all deaths are the same. It is easy to think of examples when a family matriarch has died and left a huge hole in the family. Bowen suggests that these types of death create an 'emotional shock wave' that reverberates throughout the family system. Healthy families may react strongly initially, but adjust to the loss quickly while other families may have a minimal initial reaction, but experience long-term adjustment problems as the ramifications of the loss emerge in the family system.

Characteristics of the Widower

Gender and Gender Role

Characteristics of the bereaved individual are another category of variables that mediate the grief experience. These include the age, sex, loss history, and a variety of psychological factors of the bereaved. Is being a man a risk factor in grief? In Chapter 1, I described the many challenges that widowers experience including poor social support, higher rates of depression, higher mortality, and higher rates of suicide. In Chapter 2, I examined the sources and influences of male gender role identity, male socialization, and other factors that contribute to bereaved men's concerns. As mentioned, if a widower identifies with traditional male gender roles then he will be more likely to express his grief in cognitive or physical ways and less likely to share his concerns with others or seek assistance. Taken as a whole, this information has led many researchers to conclude that widowers, on average, face more challenges than widows (Lee et al., 1998; Lieberman, 1996; Wisocki, & Skowron, 2000).

Bennett, Hughes, and Smith (2003) suggest that being a widower directly challenges three of the four injunctions described by Brannon (1976). Traditional grieving emphasizes the expression of sad and painful feelings (violates No Sissy Stuff). Most men feel a need to withdraw socially as part of their grief experience (violates The Big Wheel). Finally, men fail at being the Sturdy Oak because "men are expected to protect their families, and wives should not die. Indeed, there is an expectation that wives will outlive their husbands, so this failure may seem doubly unbearable" (Bennett et al., 2003, p. 410).

However, I believe it is overly pessimistic to assume that traditional masculinity can only impede a widower's grief. Many of the positive aspects of traditional masculinity (see Kiselica, 2011; Kiselica & Englar-Carlson, 2010) can benefit a widower as he adjusts to the death of his partner. Below are a few examples of these benefits within the context of the Dual Process Model (see Stroebe & Schut, 1999). For example, a widower who practices generative fatherhood can assist his children as they express their grief (loss-oriented coping) while also helping them learn new tasks and fulfill new responsibilities that may have been previously handled by their mother (restoration-oriented coping). Widowers can benefit from distraction and humor (especially when experienced within a group of supportive men; restoration-oriented); a few jokes during a game of golf with trusted friends can help a widower feel supported and can be a welcome respite from focusing on his loss. Conversely, a widower's sense of action-oriented empathy and connection to humanitarian organizations could lead to developing or supporting an organization that assists others; this may be done as a way to remember and honor his deceased partner (loss-oriented coping). These are just a few examples of how the positive aspects of traditional masculinity could be used to benefit the widower.

Age

Most research that examines the differences in grief reactions based on age has found that younger widowed persons suffer more than older bereaved persons (Gamino, Sewell, & Easterling, 1998; Stroebe & Schut, 2001), including more grief severity and poorer physical health (Archer, 1999). It is likely that this is confounded by the characteristics of the loss; specifically, the deaths experienced by younger widowers are more likely to be unexpected and traumatic (Archer, 1999). Lund and Caserta (2001) found that men in their 50s coped best with spousal bereavement. This may be due to men in their 50s being more likely to have both the benefit of social support and a sense of purpose derived from working and avoiding the challenge of being a single parent to young children. Research examining widowers over 50 did not find age to be a significant factor (Lund et al., 1993).

Loss History

Several aspects of the bereaved's loss history can affect his response including the number and types of previous losses, recent losses, and the bereaved's reaction to those losses. One might expect that frequent previous deaths (and other losses) would lead to more problems with later losses. However, the research has been inconclusive (Stroebe & Stroebe, 1987). In some studies, having more previous losses has been found to be related to better bereavement adaptation. One interpretation of these results is that by successfully adjusting to previous losses the bereaved person gains positive self-efficacy for the current loss. In short, the bereaved says, "I have survived significant deaths before, I can do it again."

What is likely more important than the raw number of previous losses is their timing, meaning, and the bereaved person's reaction. Significant losses during childhood, such as the death of a parent, may be related to more difficulty adjusting to later losses (Stroebe & Stroebe, 1987) as well as any previous loss the bereaved coped with poorly (Rando, 1993; Sanders, 1999). Because we learn social rules about grief from our family, one's family history of dealing with losses can also influence later grief reactions (Parkes, 1996). For example, a widower may have learned as a child that grief should be kept to oneself and the deceased person should not be discussed. Previous experiences with death can lay the foundation for more adaptive grieving methods or more restrictive rules about grief.

Mental Health History

Research has found that the bereaved person's prior history of psychological disorders is negatively related to his grief response (Gamino et al., 1998). Psychological and physical stress are linked to recidivism of most psychological disorders; relevant to bereavement, the return of a mood disorder following a loss is a particular concern (Parkes, 1996; Rando, 1993). Widowed persons with a prior history of anxiety disorders have also been found to be more likely to relapse following the loss (Jacobs et al., 1990).

Personality Factors and Self-Esteem

There is a wide range of personality factors or traits that can influence an individual's grief. Certainly individuals with personality disorders are more likely to experience problems during grief (Rando, 1993). Lund, Caserta, and Dimond (1993) found that positive self-esteem and strong sense of personal competency were significantly associated with adaptive bereavement adjustment. They argue that individuals who have a high self-regard are "more likely to be dissatisfied with not coping well, feel that they deserve better, be motivated to take control of the situation, and persist until they have more favorable outcomes" (p. 253).

Religiosity

Reviews of studies examining the link between religiosity and coping with bereavement have found mixed results with some showing positive correlations, some showing negative correlations, and others showing no differences (Stroebe & Schut, 2001). Results from studies on religiosity and bereavement are difficult to integrate given the wide range of definitions and behaviors that are used to measure religiosity. For example, factors related to the external or social aspects of religiosity (e.g., church attendance) have been found to be associated with higher levels of grief, while studies that focus on intrinsic religiosity (i.e., an individual's internalization of their personal spiritual beliefs and a commitment to practice them in daily life) show that these have been associated with lower levels of grief (Easterling, Gamino, Sewell, & Stirman, 2000; Rosik, 1989). When examining the topic in a more global way, researchers report that most bereaved persons feel that their spiritual and religious beliefs have been helpful (Frantz, Trolley, & Johll, 1996).

Characteristics of the Loss

Sudden and Unexpected Death

Traumatic deaths can change the entire experience of grief for the widower. In most cases, sudden deaths are also unexpected deaths. In rare cases the widower may expect that his partner was going to die, but may be surprised by the sudden timing of the actual death. For example, the widower's partner may have frequently discussed suicide. Thus, when the partner commits suicide the death may be sudden, but not entirely unexpected. Most of the previous research regarding the timing and foreknowledge of death assumes that the event was sudden and unexpected for the survivor, as in the case of a car accident or a homicide.

Most studies have found that individuals bereaved by a sudden and unexpected loss have poorer psychological adjustment than those who have some forewarning (e.g., Farberow, Gallagher-Thompson, Gilewski, & Thompson, 1992; Glick, Weiss, & Parkes, 1974; Tolle et al., 1986), although some have found there are no psychological differences for older widowed persons (e.g., Carr, House, Wortman, Nesse, & Kessler, 2001), nor differences in health outcomes (Hansson & Stroebe, 2007). Results from Sanders's (1983) Tampa Study revealed a more complicated situation. When categorized by sudden death, short-term illness (< 6 months), or long-term illness (> 6 months), Sanders found evidence for a stronger grief response from sudden *and* very long-term illnesses while the short-term illness group adjusted the best. Several possible reasons are that those bereaved after a partner's short-term illness avoid the stress of caregiving over a long period of time, maintain the support of friends who may drift away during longer illnesses, and avoid the additional shock that comes with and unexpected loss.

Another reason why sudden and unexpected deaths are particularly challenging is because they tend to be traumatic deaths (e.g., accidents, homicides, suicides, etc.) and the bereaved are unable to say good-bye to the deceased (Frantz et al., 1996; Gamino, Sewell, Easterling, 2000). Another reason that sudden and unexpected deaths can be more difficult to adjust to is these types of death are more likely to challenge our assumptions about the world. For example, Rando (1996) suggests that deaths that result from random circumstances, as unexpected deaths often are, can be even more terrifying than other types of death because the survivor has no way to protect himself or other loved ones from the same fate.

> Therefore, a common tendency on the parts of mourners and those who have been victimized by random events is to assume blame for them. . . . The assumption of blame is the price paid to maintain the

needed perception that the world is not random and unpredictable, but orderly and dependable. (p. 149)

Some of the most common causes of sudden death are heart attacks, strokes, and car accidents.

Heart Attack and Stroke

In 2010, diseases of the heart and cerebrovascular incidents were, respectively, the first and fourth most common causes of death in the US and accounted for almost 30% of all deaths (CDC, 2012). Similar to those bereaved by other types of sudden loss, widowers whose partners die from strokes or heart attacks experience reactions such as shock, disbelief, guilt, and sadness about unsaid sentiments. For example, Ronald Petrie's (2001) wife, Joyce, died suddenly as they walked off the dance floor at a friend's birthday party:

> The music stopped and we were both a little winded. She faced me, and I gave her a kiss and said, "I love you." She said, I "love you, too." . . . As we walked, she looked up at me and smiled, and then just fell to the floor dead! . . . My life changed forever in an instant. (pp. 12–13)

Approximately four months later, Petrie's sister was in the care of hospice and dying from cancer. Petrie described the clear differences between the two losses: "I had an opportunity to lie down in the bed next to her and tell her that I loved her, and she told me that she loved me. We were able to say our goodbyes" (p. 17). Factors that may further complicate the survivor's grief reaction include if the deceased's health condition was unknown by family members and if the deceased partner was not of an age typically associated with heart attacks and strokes. Furthermore, surviving partners may feel guilt about not requiring their partner to seek medical treatment or to reduce their risk factors (Hersh, 1996).

Vehicle Accidents

Auto accidents are one of the most common causes of sudden and unexpected deaths. In 2010, approximately 35,000 Americans died in vehicle accidents, and transportation-related accidents were the most common cause of death for Americans between the ages of 15–44 (CDC, 2012). Lord (1996) suggests that deaths as a result of vehicle accidents are especially unexpected because they result from an activity, driving, that most people do every day. Furthermore, deaths from vehicle accidents typically result in trauma to the deceased's body.

Deciding whether to view the body is yet another added challenge to bereavement as a result of a vehicle accident. Lehman, Wortman, and Williams (1987) compared spousally bereaved individuals whose partners had died in auto accidents with matched controls and found those bereaved by auto accidents had poorer outcomes even four years after the death.

Traumatic Death

Deaths as a result of intentional violence, including homicide and suicide, can be especially traumatic for survivors. There are several reasons why traumatic deaths are more difficult for the bereaved. First, traumatic deaths are inherently sudden and unexpected. Therefore the bereaved must deal with the challenge associated with the loss being unanticipated. Second, traumatic deaths often involve the deceased being in physical pain. This trauma may be heightened in the bereaved if the cause of death creates easily seen physical damage to his partner's body. The bereaved may even be a witness to the accident or the first to find a loved one's body. Third, those bereaved by traumatic deaths often receive less social support due to the stigmatizing nature of the death and the discomfort in creates in others (Parkes, 1993). Finally, the cause of death often forces the bereaved to change their worldview (Worden, 2009). A common example is adjusting from a world that is generally safe to one that includes the reality of violent deaths.

Those individuals bereaved by traumatic losses are at a higher risk of various types of denial, anger, and guilt (Redmond, 1996). The denial can be a reaction to the suddenness and unexpectedness of the death. The bereaved's anger is often justifiably targeted toward those responsible, but may also be misdirected toward those who had no role in the death or the bereaved's caregivers. Furthermore, anger can also be directed at the deceased (often for being in the 'wrong' place or situation) and the bereaved himself (for not stopping the sequence of events leading to the death). While this is sometimes experienced as anger, it may even more likely be felt as guilt. This guilt may be even more intense if the loss occurred while there was a strain on the relationship or if the bereaved individual felt that he had failed to protect his loved one (Parkes, 1993).

Homicide or Violent Death

Complicating factors specific to homicides can include the conduct and sensitivity of law enforcement, medical staff, coroners, and other professionals associated with the death (Lord, 1996). During the initial notification of the death, even relatively small statements and actions can be interpreted as insensitive, degrading, or even threatening. In cases where the culprit is not known it is common practice to view family members, especially the husband, as a potential perpetrator. Between 1980 and 2008, 40.5% of homicides of women were by intimate partners or former partners (Bureau of Justice Statistics, 2011). The outcome of the search for the perpetrator can cause further grief, anger, and disenfranchisement. Possible situations include if the perpetrator is not found (in 2008, only 64% of murders were solved or cleared (Bureau of Justice Statistics, 2011), if there is a lengthy court trial, or if the perpetrator is tried but found not guilty. In some cases, the challenges can be exacerbated by ongoing media coverage that often sensationalizes aspects of the death, deceased, perpetrator, or survivors to increase viewership (Redmond, 1996).

Campbell and Silverman (1987) interviewed a widower, Jan, whose wife was murdered while she walked in nearby woods. Jan had the additional challenge of being the first person to find his wife's body. A little less than a year later, Jan was forced to relive his wife's death when he attended and testified at the perpetrator's trial:

> The trial reopened everything. . . . When I testified (I testified for a morning, I guess), the whole thing became real again. I wasn't testifying, I was reliving the murder in detail, all the events of the day of the murder, and that was terrifically draining. . . . I was reliving the experience of finding my wife's body. It was very, very real. (p. 40)

Given the wide range of extenuating factors, most of which further complicated grief adjustment, professionals should assume that those bereaved as result of homicide will display stronger grief reactions for a longer period of time. Redmond (1989) suggests that these reactions, which may reach levels that qualify for a diagnosis of PTSD and may last up to five years following the loss, should be viewed as normal reactions for this type of loss. Similarly, Parkes (1993) found that those bereaved by homicide frequently found the intensity of their grief remained constant (or increased) during the year following the loss.

Suicide

More Americans died in 2010 from suicide than from homicide or vehicle accidents (CDC, 2012; US Department of Transportation, 2011). Bereaved persons whose loved ones die of suicide (i.e., suicide survivors) go through similar reactions to other bereaved people, including shock, guilt, and anger although they are more likely to experience symptoms of PTSD (Lukas & Seiden, 2007; Zisook, Chentsova-Dutton, & Shuchter, 1998).

Lukas and Seiden (2007) described several reasons why grief will be more challenging for those bereaved by suicide. First, most individuals who die by suicide have made previous attempts. Consequently, the bereaved may have been expecting another attempt and may feel responsible for not preventing it. Whether previous attempts had been made or not, the widower will still have to deal with 'double shock'—the shock of the death and the shock of the cause of death. Furthermore, the survivors have the added burden of disclosing the cause of death to others and receiving less social support (Stillion, 1996) and a greater sense of rejection by others (Barrett & Scott, 1990). The challenges to adjustment may be long-lasting. A longitudinal study of surviving spouses found that those bereaved by suicide rated themselves as having poorer mental health at one year after the loss as compared to those suffering a 'natural death' loss; the differences were still present after two and a half years post-loss (Farberow et al., 1992). Similarly, Reed and Greenwald (1991) found that surviving spouses of suicide had higher rates of guilt, shame, and rejection than those bereaved by sudden accidental deaths.

Anger and guilt are common reactions following a partner's completed suicide. The anger may be directed at one or more of the following individuals: the deceased for taking his or her life, mental and physical health professionals for not being able to save the deceased, and at oneself for not being able to prevent it. Furthermore, family members may blame one another for not doing more to stop the suicide (Lukas & Seiden, 2007). Those bereaved by suicide often feel guilty for not doing enough to be able to save their loved one—even if this guilt is unjustified. Given that protecting one's wife and family is a key aspect of male gender norms, widowers may feel especially guilty following a suicide.

Conversely, suicide survivors may also experience relief. This is most likely in cases where the deceased person frequently threatened or attempted suicide, had a terminal illness, or involved other situational variables that were an ongoing stressor for the survivor. Of course, this relief is often mixed with guilt for feeling some relief that the stress has ended (Lukas & Seiden, 2007).

Witnessing the Death

The influence on bereavement of being present at the time of death is almost entirely dependent upon the circumstances; most widowed persons hope to be present if their partner is dying from a progressive illness (Tolle et al., 1986), while others are haunted by being present at an accident, suicide, or homicide. Carr (2003) found that older bereaved spouses who were present at their partner's death were less likely to have intrusive thoughts about the deceased during the first six months.

As one would expect, witnessing a traumatic death is quite different. Although research is limited, anecdotal evidence suggests that those who witness a traumatic death (suicide, homicide, or accident) are at a much higher risk of some type of complicated grief reaction (e.g., Rynearson, 1994). Even if the death was not directly witnessed, the bereaved can often construct a mental image of what happened based on police reports and other descriptions; some individuals may obsessively replay this constructed sequence of events in their minds (Rynearson, 2012).

Prolonged Illnesses

Due to advances in medical treatments and technology, more and more individuals die after a prolonged struggle with a terminal illness. These struggles frequently stretch over many years and may also allow the ill person to live a long time near the threshold of death. Watching and caring for a dying spouse can influence a widower's grief. For example, one study found that older widowed persons had more intrusive thoughts, yearning, and anxiety if their partners' deaths were seen as painful (Carr, 2003). Furthermore, widowers, especially older widowers, who are highly engaged as the primary caregiver and provide caregiving for a long period of time are at a higher risk of having difficulty postloss (Richardson, 2010). Death after an extended terminal illness is more frequently associated with prolonged grief. This may be caused by the additional stress on the caregiver and guilt from ethical choices related to end-of-life care (Rando, 1993).

Two different models have been used to explain the caregiving bereaved person's reaction following the death of the loved one: the stress-relief model and the chronic strain model (Richardson, 2010). The stress-relief model assumes that caretaker will experience relief after the stress of caregiving has ended. For example, Elison (Elison & McGonigle, 2003) found that in a sample of widowed people whose spouse had died from cancer that over 73% expressed relief as a primary response to their spouses' death. Furthermore, 23% of the sample reported feelings such as 'peace,' 'extreme happiness,' and 'delight.' Conversely, the chronic strain model predicts that caregiving creates stress reactions that can continue even after the loved one dies and the caregiving responsibility has ended (Richardson, 2010). Therefore, the chronic strain model suggests that the chronic stress experienced by a caretaking widower will have negative long-term consequences on his adjustment following his loss. Support for this perspective can be found in Sanders's (1983) study that found poorer bereavement adjustment for those whose loved ones had suffered with an illness for more than six months prior to their death.

A common experience of widowed individuals who face the impending death of a partner is to begin to grieve before the actual death. *Anticipatory grief*, originally described by Lindemann (1944), refers to the experience of non-death losses associated with a loved one after becoming aware of her or his impending death. For a widower this often begins with an initial diagnosis of his wife's life-threatening illness. Thereafter he often suffers many pre-death losses including the loss of an active and mobile partner, the loss of a sexual partner, the loss of a future retirement spent together, and other losses. Because many friends and family members may not recognize that the widower has experienced these cumulative pre-death losses, they assume that the grief should begin at the time of death. They do not realize that the widower started grieving a long time ago.

Individuals wrestling with anticipatory grief may begin to engage in 'role rehearsal'—imagining what it would be like to fulfill new roles after the partner has died. On one hand, this anticipatory rehearsal can improve their ability to actually perform these new roles. Conversely, the bereaved individual may receive criticisms from others who view it as giving up hope, being morbid or pessimistic (Worden, 2009). Some widowers may look back at their role rehearsal in this way and feel guilty about this. It is helpful to reframe this as a necessary, adaptive process.

Preventable Deaths

Losses are viewed as being especially traumatic if the death was viewed as preventable. Examples of losses that could have been avoided include medical mistakes, accidental shootings, and some auto accidents. Research has found that those bereaved by preventable deaths have more negative grief responses (Gamino et al., 1998; Gamino, Sewell, et al., 2000) including anger (Carr, 2003), and rumination (Rando, 1996) as well as longer duration and greater intensity of grief (Guarnaccia et al., 1999). Men who lose a partner (especially a female partner) to a preventable or traumatic death may be even more at risk for ruminating over a preventable death because it violates his traditional gender norm that he should be able to protect his wife from harm (Bennett et al., 2003).

Multiple Losses

A series of deaths in a short period of time can make grief adjustment more difficult (Worden, 2009). Multiple losses may occur independently through happenstance, such as the death of a partner close in time to the death of a parent or sibling, or may be the result of the same event as in the case of a partner and children dying in a car accident or as victims in a homicide. Kastenbaum (1969) referred to one potential reaction to this barrage of losses as *bereavement overload*. This concept originally referred to the cumulative social losses for older adults, but has since been generalized to include the view that the bereaved person is unable to finish grieving a loss before another comes along or is faced with multiple losses simultaneously.

Ambiguous Losses

A less common, but particularly difficult circumstance, is an *ambiguous loss*. Ambiguous losses involve situations when a loss or death leaves the bereaved in a state of uncertainty. Boss (1999, 2006) popularized the term and has written extensively about the topic; Boss separates ambiguous losses into two types: *physically absent* and *psychologically absent*. Examples of ambiguous losses in which the person is physically absent include military personnel that are missing in action, abducted persons, and runaways. In these cases, the lost person is not physically present, but the ambiguous nature of his or her absence leaves the loved one uncertain if he or she has died or not. Given the uncertain status, the bereaved is unable to proceed with the typical rituals associated with death including a funeral or memorial service, viewing the body, and receiving social support.

Ambiguous losses where the loved one is psychologically absent include dementia, coma, severe substance abuse, and severe psychological disorders (e.g., schizophrenia). In these cases the bereaved person can still interact with the psychologically 'lost' individual, but feels she or he is not the same person she or he used to be. Given that the loved one is still alive and physically present, it can be difficult to recognize the extent of the loss and receive social support. Furthermore, even if the loss is not the fault of the afflicted partner, the bereaved spouse may feel depressed, guilty, anger, and confused as well as abandoned for not receiving the expected companionship (Doka & Aber, 2002).

Difficulty adjusting to the loss of a loved one is often referred to as being 'stuck' in one's grief. In ambiguous losses, the bereaved begins with a sense of being stuck even before a loved one's death is confirmed or has happened. Obviously beginning with this unsettled status makes adapting to one's grief more difficult (Worden, 2009).

Stigmatizing Deaths

Stigmatizing losses involve situations where the cause of death creates anxiety in the bereaved and others (Doka, 2002c). Doka provides several examples of causes of death that are likely to be stigmatized, including suicide, AIDS, homicide, capital punishment, developmentally unexpected deaths (e.g., the death of a 4-year-old for no obvious reason), death from autoerotic asphyxiation, and assisted suicide.

All stigmatized deaths are potentially disenfranchised losses. To review, a disenfranchised death is one that is not fully acknowledged because one or more of the following aspects of the loss are not recognized or accepted: the relationship to the deceased, the loss itself, the bereaved, the circumstances of the loss, or the ways of expressing grief. The disenfranchising characteristics of the loss that mediate grief are most frequently related to a specific cause of death that is stigmatized (e.g., suicide, homicide, etc.) and/or the cause of death challenges our worldview and creates anxiety. For example, widowers bereaved by a suicide may have to deal with the stigma from others, including religious leaders (Echelbarger, 1993). Further complicating the situation is the cause of death (as in a suicide) is often selectively shared. This forces the bereaved to self-censor what he shares with others based on how much each person knows about the reality of the cause of death (Worden, 2009). If a widower experiences shame or expects others to react negatively to learning about the cause of death, he will avoid sharing his grief and, consequently, be less likely to receive social support.

Any cause of death that violates our assumptions about the world and creates anxiety may evoke a strong response from others. For example, Redmond (1996) states that "we have held the belief that those who are murdered have in some way led to their own death" (p. 62). This self-protective perspective for the non-bereaved allows them to maintain a view that the world is safe and their loved ones are protected. For many non-bereaved supporters it can be easier to not interact with the bereaved than to jeopardize this treasured perspective of the world as safe and just. This leads to the bereaved receiving less social support at a time when they need it most.

Social Factors

Social Support

A variety of social and external factors also mediate widowers' grief reactions. These factors include the widower's desire for social support, his access to confidantes, and the number of social roles in which he is involved. The role of social support in grief adjustment is a complicated relationship. Widowed men are less likely to ask for and receive less social support than widows (Lee et al., 1998; Stroebe & Schut, 2001). Widowers may receive less support because they are perceived to not need it or because they are hesitant to ask for it because it goes against male gender norms (Bennett et al., 2003).

Some research on social support for the bereaved has focused primarily on the numbers of supporters (e.g., Davidson, 2004; Lee et al., 1998). It is likely to be at least as important to have at least one or a few confidantes. Balaswamy et al. (2004) found that widowed men's confidantes are almost equally split between men and women, yet when they were depressed they were more likely to turn to a woman (most commonly a daughter or sister).

Conventional wisdom and a few qualitative studies (e.g., Campbell & Silverman, 1987; Troyer, in press) suggest that some widowers are more comfortable being alone immediately following their loss. While less social support is generally linked to poorer grief adjustment, there is nothing inherently harmful about allowing a widower to focus on his grief alone. Of course, isolating oneself can be harmful if the widower believes that he maintain a façade of No Sissy Stuff and can be dangerous if he is considering self-harm. Furthermore, if the widower rejects support early in his grief when it is most likely to be offered (Stelle & Uchida, 2004), it may be more difficult to regain later when he is ready for more social contact.

Widowers may seek solitude following their losses to communicate to others that they have not been significantly hurt by the loss and therefore do not need assistance. This isolation would match the injunction to be a Sturdy Oak (Brannon, 1976). However, the limited research on this topic suggests that most widowers do not isolate themselves as a way to deny their pain to themselves or others, but instead to use their own methods to deal with grief-related psychological pain alone (Brabant et al., 1992).

Social Role Involvement

Bereaved individuals who are involved in a variety of social roles adjust better to loss (Hershberger & Walsh, 1990) although most of this research has focused on women (e.g., Moen, Robison, & Dempster-McClain, 1995). This reflects the assumptions of Role Enhancement Theory (Sieber, 1974), which suggests that multiple roles are beneficial because individuals can draw support from a wide range of support networks associated with each role and can derive satisfaction from performing a variety of tasks. For example, a widower who is employed, belongs to the local Rotary club, regularly attends religious services, and maintains close contact with his extended family will have multiple sources of support compared to the self-employed widower who isolates himself from his family and does not belong to local service or religious groups. Furthermore, the socially connected and active widower may be receive personal satisfaction through continuing to be active in each of his vocational, service, religious, and family groups. The significance of being active in these groups may be particularly important for men who tend to be more likely to view their self-worth as being closely tied to their ability to contribute tangible services to their workplace, fraternal organizations, and family.

Concurrent Stressors

Some of the competing stressors, including those associated with various secondary losses, financial losses, and relationships with extended family members, can also be important mediators of the widower's grief response.

Children

One concurrent stress common with widowers is becoming a single parent for their children. This is especially true for widowers who have young children living at home. However, even if the children are no longer living with the widower the death of a co-parent/mother can create new stressors for the widower. Children may expect the widower to perform all of the previous roles fulfilled by their deceased parent in addition to his previous roles. They may also be hurt and angry if the widower is not grieving in a way that matches their expectations. Finally, widowers who choose to date and eventually remarry may have to deal with children who view this as a betrayal of their deceased parent. These problems may arise even in adult children who no longer live with the widower and may also be concerns raised by the widower's partner's family.

Research is limited comparing the grief of widowed men with children versus those without. In the Harvard Children's Bereavement Study, Worden (1996a) found that widowed fathers were more likely than widowed mothers to say that they were not prepared for being a single parent and had difficulty negotiating time between work and parenting. Given that family members, and especially children, are cited by widowers as their most common confidantes and supporters (Balaswamy et al., 2004), conflict with children can remove one of the most important sources of support. Furthermore, the widower may view his children as one of the few groups of co-grievers who truly understand his loss.

Financial Pressures

There are two primary ways in which financial variables can influence grief. One is the overall financial resources controlled by the widowed spouse which determines their general standard of living. The other factor is the familiarity and proficiency with which the surviving spouse handles ongoing financial transactions.

Historically, one of few areas where research has shown a benefit to being a widower instead of a widow is regarding overall financial resources. Widowers typically have more financial resources than widows (Utz, 2006). Given the increase in the percentage of families where both adults work and the increasing number of wives who outearn their husband (Utz, 2006), it is likely that this advantage will erode over time. The biggest concern is for those widowers whose financial lives will be significantly altered following the loss of their partners.

While a widower's overall economic status is the most important financial factor, one should not underestimate the stress associated with learning how to manage all of the finances. A prevailing assumption is that men are typically adept at handling financial matters. However, Lindamood and Hanna (2005) found that wives were just as likely to be the partner who knew the most about a couple's finances. Widowers who had completely turned the financial matters over to their wives may find that learning and maintaining all aspects of their personal finances may be a significant stressor. Furthermore, widowers will often feel immediate stress from dealing with the numerous financial and legal changes and notifications required after the death of a marriage partner.

Substance Abuse

Given the stress that results from bereavement and the tendency for widowed men to increase their binge drinking (Barusch & Peak, 1997; Byrne et al., 1999), one can reasonably assume that the loss of a partner may cause the widower who had a prior substance addiction to relapse. Furthermore, widowers with no prior history of substance abuse may use substances inappropriately in an effort to cope. Alcohol is the most likely substance to be abused. Widowers may use alcohol in a variety of ways including to help fall asleep (Tolle et al., 1986) and/ or to dull their emotional pain. While some widowers may simply misuse alcohol, others (especially those with a prior history of alcohol dependence) may find that it completely overtakes their life (Hughes & Fleming, 1991). Widowers may abuse prescription medications including medication that had been prescribed for their partners. Widowers may also use illicit drugs to cope. Phillip, a middle-aged widower I interviewed, explained how he believed that smoking marijuana had helped him—at least early in the process:

> I started smoking a lot of pot a couple days after she passed and basically that was my crutch from then all the way up until I felt like I was ready to start dating. I'd been a recreational user in the past and I liked it better than alcohol. I think that it did allow me not to be wallowing in self

pity to some degree and kind of deadened everything, but I don't think it was especially healthy after the first little bit and—maybe a month or two and done would've probably been a much better approach.

Most researchers and therapists assume that substance abuse can dull the bereaved's reaction to the loss and impair his ability to fully experience the pain of the loss. Many grief models (i.e., Worden's Tasks, etc.) presume that fully acknowledging the pain of the loss is a key step in coping with grief. Therefore anything that impairs the experience of loss, including substances, can impair the widower's adaptation.

Mediators and Grief Counseling

Examining the mediators of a widower's loss can be a useful tool in developing a comprehensive view of his grief situation. Furthermore, it can provide a framework for conceptualizing clients with especially difficult concerns. However, psychotherapists should be careful to not become too focused on specific variables and overemphasize their importance especially if the circumstances are atypical or especially morbid. Furthermore, this list is not meant to be an exhaustive summary of every factor that can influence a widower's grief. Numerous other factors (e.g., his physical health, employment status, new romantic relationships, etc.) can significantly affect his grief reaction. This chapter summarizes most of the factors that have been studied empirically.

Course of Grief

The popular view of the 'normal' course of grief is that bereaved individuals suffer the most immediately after the loss and slowly improve. While there is some evidence that grief reactions generally lessen over the course of years (Zisook & Shuchter, 1985), research examining a shorter time period provides a more complicated picture. When the overall functioning of 1,200 adult grievers was examined over the first two years, the bereaved individuals experienced the poorest functioning at five to six months post-loss (Davidson (1979) as cited in Neimeyer (2006)). This reaction may be due to the insulating effects of shock and the high level of social support immediately following the loss, and conversely, the relative lack of support and increased awareness of secondary losses beginning within several weeks of the loss (Neimeyer, 2006). Davidson's study provides empirical support to a common belief among grief therapists—the grief reaction of some bereaved individuals will get more intense before it gets better. This is one reason why bereaved individuals seek out grief therapists several months after their loss with the presenting concern of feeling worse than before. For some, it may be a sign of a form of complicated grief, yet for others it is a normal grief reaction.

There is a wide variety of other reasons for why grief reactions may not follow a gradually improving course. Significant dates can serve as important factors in a widower's grief response. Wedding anniversaries, partners' birthdays, and other important dates can trigger strong grief reactions for widowed individuals.

Length of Grief

There is no consensus for a typical duration of grief. However, most thanatologists agree that grief lasts longer than early theorists stated (Shuchter & Zisook, 1993). Much of the disparity in answers given by early theorists is likely due to the range of definitions of *grief* and *resolution*. For example, Lindemann (1944) suggested that 8 to 10 sessions with a psychiatrist and approximately "four to six weeks duration, it was ordinarily possible to settle an uncomplicated and undistorted grief reaction" (p. 192). Based on his emphasis on behavioral reactions, it is likely that Lindemann was referring to clearly observable responses as opposed to a cognitive, emotional, or spiritual sense of loss. Conversely, Rando (1993) suggests that Freud believed the normal period of mourning was one to two years.

While most theorists are hesitant to give a specific time frame for grief, modern authors are more likely to agree with Freud than with Lindemann. Popular grief researchers and practitioners generally talk about grief related to the death of a spouse or partner lasting one to two years (e.g., Worden, 2009; Wortman & Boerner, 2011), while some argue for a longer period of time (Glick et al., 1974; Sanders, 1999) and others suggest less (Tatelbaum, 1984). To be clear, no modern researcher or practitioner places a clear boundary on the length of time necessary for healthy grieving; all recognize that significant individual differences among the bereaved and the circumstances of the loss will influence the time necessary.

Perhaps more important than an estimate on how long grief 'should' take is the fact that it is likely to be longer than the average person expects. A common concern of bereaved persons is that they are not progressing quickly enough. Given the emphasis on grief being hidden from others, the lack of external symbols of grief, and an emphasis on 'getting back to normal' (Cable, 1998), it is easy to see why many bereaved persons erroneously believe that they should not experience grief after a few weeks or months. Worden (2009) argues that dispelling this misconception is a key aspect of grief counseling:

> One of the basic things that education through grief counseling can do is to alert people to the fact that mourning is a long-term process and that the culmination will not be a pre-grief state. The counselor can also let mourners know that even though mourning progresses, grieving does not proceed in a linear fashion; it may reappear to be reworked. (p. 77)

Worden mentions an important concept. Although the question of how long grief should last is more commonly asked by clients, a more important question that is rarely discussed is: "Is grief resolution possible?" Moreover, should terms like *resolution* or *recovery* be used in relation to grief? I address this topic in Chapter 7.

5

MEN'S GRIEF

Theories on men's grief have changed considerably in the last two decades. In this chapter I will examine the major developments in men's grief and review the most current perspectives. To put these changes in context, it can be helpful to briefly glance back and review the previous perspectives on gender differences in grieving. As described in Chapter 3, grief theorists have shifted their views on several key aspects of grief. One of these shifts is from a 'cutting ties' perspective to a more empathic view of continued relationships with the deceased. Another significant shift is the critique of the long-held assumption that the bereaved must engage in 'grief work' before grief can be resolved. These requirements for successful grieving, that ties *must* be cut and that grief work *must* happen, have been applied equally to women and men. Under these assumptions, it was generally expected that women were better grievers than men—certainly in terms of engaging in grief work (Rando, 1993). Remember, grief work is about "confronting a loss, of going over the events before and at the time of the death, of focusing on memories . . ." (Stroebe, 1992, pp. 19–20). Furthermore, grief work "requires that the bereaved confront and express their feelings and reactions to the death of a loved one, and that failure to do so is maladaptive" (Stroebe, Schut, & Stroebe, 2005, p. 396).

Historical Perspectives on Men's Grief

Given the pervasiveness of these grief concepts, it is useful to examine how more recent perspectives on men and grief have evolved from the grief work assumption and the expectation to cut ties over the last 20 years. I have chosen two authors, Carol Staudacher (1991) and Elizabeth Levang (1998), to show how these perspectives have been previously applied to male grievers and how the field has evolved.

In 1991 Staudacher wrote *Men and Grief*. It is not surprising that she affirmed the grief work hypothesis which was still prevalent at the time:

> Simply put, *there is really only one way to grieve*. That way is to go through the core of grief. Only by experiencing the necessary emotional effects of your loved one's death is it possible for you to eventually resolve the loss. If you try to walk around the perimeter of loss, that loss will remain unresolved, and you will be more likely to endure painful emotional, psychological, or physical consequences. The death of a loved one is a wrenching, painful, and sometimes almost unendurable experience. Both men and women may respond to a loss in ways that block, delay, or distort the grieving process. A successful grief experience allows you to resolve the loss, to integrate the loss into your life, and to go on living, free of grief-related disturbances. (pp. 3–4)

This quote highlights several specific aspects of the 'grief work' perspective: (1) expressing feelings is the only way to deal with grief; (2) grief can be completely 'resolved'; (3) to not express feelings is to set yourself up for a delayed grief reaction; and (4) the loss of a loved one *must* be an overwhelming emotional event that significantly disrupts your life. A few pages later she partially endorsed the necessity of cutting ties: "You must endure the traumatic experience of detaching from your loved one; but the emotions that are produced as a result of the death must not be similarly detached. If they are, they become suppressed or repressed" (Staudacher, 1991, p. 6).

I am using Staudacher's work as just one example of using the assumption at the time with men. In her defense, she urges therapists and women to be more empathetic toward grieving men because they are not used to embracing and expressing their emotions. Furthermore, I am sure that some widowers, especially those who are comfortable with emotional expressions of grief, could benefit from a book that helps normalize their expression of grief feelings. Despite this, her assumption, like many others at the time and some still today, was that the *only* way through grief was through the confrontation and expression of emotions. I am not the only one who takes issue with Staudacher's stance. Doka and Martin (2010) have discussed their concerns with Staudacher's perspective, and Robert Howell (2013), a widower, wrote about his reaction to reading Staudacher's book:

> At the beginning of the 1990s, there was a dearth of literature for grieving men. . . . Several years after Diane's death, I did run across

a book, *Men and Grief* by Carol Staudacher. However, Staudacher's approach to grief only increased my own sense of distance from how I was *supposed* to be responding to loss and grief. (p. 9)

Although most mental health therapists at the time recognized that the socialized and internal pressure of men's gender roles would cause them to react differently to grief, this did not result in acknowledging any differences in the grief process. Essentially, 'normal' grief was viewed as what tends to work for most women (Doka & Martin, 2001; Martin & Doka, 1996; Zinner, 2000), and men and women were still expected to grieve the same way. Wolfelt (1990) recognized that, based on these assumptions, men were stuck:

> Observers might assume a blaming attitude toward the male thinking that he consciously chooses to repress his grief. However, to openly mourn is not something he won't do; it is something he often can't do. A prisoner within himself, he often experiences total frustration of even where to begin in the healing process. To simply urge the bereaved male to openly mourn is unhelpful and inadequate. To urge the male to mourn is like asking a carpenter to build without his tools. (p. 24)

In my opinion, this was a clear step in the right direction. Wolfelt recognized that we cannot assume that men and women can or want to grieve the same way.

Elizabeth Levang's (1998) book, *When Men Grieve: Why Men Grieve Differently and How You Can Help*, represents a transition away from traditional assumptions and toward a new way of understanding men's grief. In it, Levang recognized the importance of cognitions in men's grief: "Men grieve on the inside, and their grief work tends to be more cognitive than emotional" (p. 44). Though she also warns that this can simply be a way for him to rationalize and avoid his grief. Levang also warns that physical and practical tasks related to the loss have only one goal which is "to keep the negative and painful from penetrating their soul" and to provide "another way to escape reality" (p. 44, 45). She acknowledged that grieving men may be drawn to dealing with solvable problems (such as planning the funeral or dealing with legal details), but assumes the primary reason for this is so that men can show everyone that they have not 'lost' to grief. She does not consider the view that grief (as well as love for other survivors) can be expressed through the completion of these tasks.

Therefore Levang's (1998) perspective represents one step away from the 'grief work' perspective and its exclusive focus on the goal of affective expression. Levang recognized that men view and experience grief differently. For example, she understands that men will be more likely to process grief in a primarily cognitive and behavioral way, but she still expects the goal of thinking and action to be a return to expressing emotions.

Although the books by Staudacher and Levang represent common assumptions about men and grief over the last few decades (and assumptions that continue to today), there were others who began to acknowledge that men and women may grieve differently. Therese Rando (1993) was one of the first to outline a new perspective when she argued that men and women may experience loss quite differently. She admonished therapists to avoid the pitfall of assuming uniformity in grief response:

> Many caregivers strive to have male mourners respond to mourning as do their female counterparts. This is an unwise, to say nothing of almost always fruitless, goal. The caregiver would do better to direct energy toward translating what is required in grief and mourning into terms acceptable to the male mourner (e.g., discover methods by which the male mourner can release sorrow that do not violate his upbringing as much as sitting in a support group and crying). (p. 352)

Furthermore, she recognized that therapists who try to force men to experience grief in only affective ways would likely create a power struggle. She was one of the earliest theorist-clinicians to reject the perception that expressed emotion was the only way to grieve successfully:

> Some caregivers are determined to wring tears from male mourners, and doing so becomes the primary focus of the treatment. . . . A prevalent misconception held by caregivers, mourners, and the general public is that one's extent of and/or success in mourning is measureable by the amount of tears released. (p. 353)

Grieving Styles

The most significant shift in theories on gender and grief has been a result of the work of Ken Doka and Terry Martin (Doka & Martin, 2001, 2010; Martin & Doka, 1996, 2000). Doka and Martin provide two critical insights into the relationship between gender and grief. The first is the recognition that how people respond to loss is *related* to gender, but is not *determined* by it. The other is that grief expressed through cognitive, physical, and behavioral methods can be just as healthy as grief expressed through affective means.

Instrumental, Intuitive, and Blended Grieving Styles

Doka and Martin (2010) provide a foundation for a theory of *grieving styles*. They suggest that an individual's grief reactions, experiences, and conceptualizations can be plotted along a continuum. At one end of the continuum is an emotionally based style in which the grief is expressed affectively. Their term for this pattern is called the *intuitive* style. The intuitive grieving style is similar to what most people think of as traditional or typical grief. Grief is expressed through emotions, particularly crying; the individual not only feels comfortable sharing his or her grief with others, but gains comfort from it. On the opposite end of the continuum is the *instrumental* style. This style is characterized by responding to grief in a cognitive, problem-solving, and intellectual manner. Furthermore, instrumental grievers avoid intense emotions and tend to be uncomfortable sharing their grief with others. It is important to note that neither intuitive nor instrumental grievers will exhibit all of the characteristics. The differences between intuitive and instrumental styles are delineated in Table 5.1.

In their earliest writing, Martin and Doka (1996) used the terms *feminine* and *masculine* instead of *intuitive* and *instrumental*. Later they (Doka & Martin, 2010; Martin & Doka, 2000) changed the terms in recognition that some men utilized an intuitive style (as well as some women employed an instrumental style). While this change was important to signify that grieving style was not dictated by biological sex, Doka and Martin (2010) acknowledge that "there is a clear relation between gender and grieving style" (p. 4). Therefore, men and women can either use an instrumental or intuitive grieving style, although

Table 5.1 Characteristics of Intuitive Versus Instrumental Grief/Grievers

Characteristics of Intuitive Grief/Grievers	*Characteristics of Instrumental Grief/Grievers*
Grief experienced primarily as deep and intense feelings	Grief experienced primarily cognitively/intellectually
Feelings come in overwhelming waves	Feelings are dosed in manageable amounts
Frequent and prolonged crying	Rarely or never cry
Sharing emotional pain is comforting	Solving problems is comforting
Experience a need to share emotions	Experience a need to control behaviors
Expend most energy through emotional expression	Expend most energy through problem-solving and task management
Easily experience the pain expressed by others	Uncomfortable with intense emotions of others
Generally comfortable sharing grief with others	Generally uncomfortable sharing grief with others

Source: Adapted from Doka and Martin (2010).

men (and therefore widowers) are more likely to be instrumental grievers. It is important to note that while gender and gender role socialization play the largest roles in influencing people's grieving styles, their personalities and culture also important factors.

Doka and Martin (2010) are quick to point out that few grievers, if any, are purely instrumental or intuitive in their style; most incorporate some aspects of each. Therefore when I discuss instrumental or intuitive grievers, I mean those whose style falls largely to that side of the continuum. The term *blended style* is used for individuals whose style is a relatively even mix (the middle of the continuum) of intuitive and instrumental traits. (However, Doka and Martin hypothesize that most grievers prefer one style or the other.) For example, Robert Howell (2013), a widower, reflected on his reaction to his wife's death 20 years previously. He described his own grieving style as instrumental, but that did not mean that he was unemotional regarding the death of his wife:

> While my responses to Diane's death and my experiences of grief fluctuated along the Intuitive-Instrumental continuum, the predominant pattern was more closely aligned with the Instrumental. While I experienced more intense feelings than I ever before had encountered and I was a frequent visitor to what I came to call "the abyss" of despair; my preeminent and most powerful need was to understand what had happened to me; what I was experiencing and how I might construct a life after Diane. (p. 10)

Consequently, it is important to not judge an individual's grieving style based on limited contact. Instrumental grievers will cry and intuitive grievers will engage in problem-solving. It is more important to consider their overall approach to grief and their level of comfort with different behaviors and attitudes related to grieving.

A significant shift from previous perspectives is that no one grieving pattern, instrumental, intuitive, or blended, is viewed as superior to any other, nor should the goal of grief counseling be to encourage a certain pattern (Doka & Martin, 2010). This is different from the assumption that the only healthy responses to loss are those that conform to the grief work hypothesis. Or put another way, Doka and Martin propose that the intuitive grieving style (which matches more closely with the grief work hypothesis) is not the only adaptive way to grieve—instrumental methods can also be healthy and adaptive. This is not to suggest that any particular grieving style is inherently beneficial for the bereaved individual; individuals using any grieving style can employ effective or ineffective strategies. For example, intuitive grievers may express their grief in ways that match the grief work hypothesis (e.g., crying, sharing their grief, frequently reflecting on their loss, 'going through the core of their grief,' etc.) yet find over long periods of time that they remain stuck.

Central to accurately understanding Doka and Martin's theory of grieving styles is their view of emotions and feelings. Doka and Martin (2010) define *emotion* as "biologically based, adaptive reactions involving changes in the physical, affective, cognitive, spiritual, and behavioral systems in response to perceived environmental events of significance to the individual" (p. 38). This definition uses the term *emotion* more broadly than is typical and makes it distinct from the common use of the term *feelings*. Based on their definition of emotion, grief is viewed as "an instinctual attempt to make internal and external adjustments to an unwanted change in one's world—the death of someone significant to the griever. Grief involves both inner experience and outward expression" (p. 38). As such, both instrumental and intuitive grievers will experience emotions related to their loss, yet their expression of emotions may differ significantly. Other authors (e.g., Winokuer & Harris, 2012) use the term *emotions* synonymously with *feelings*, so it is important to understand each theorist's definition.

Adaptive Strategies

Another critical concept of the grieving styles perspective is the bereaved individual's use of *primary* and *secondary adaptive strategies*. Primary adaptive strategies are defined as "the principal ways grievers express their grief and assimilate and adapt to their losses over long periods" (Doka & Martin, 2010, p. 53). Grievers can also use secondary adaptive strategies; these strategies are used to express the aspects of their grief that do not come as naturally. For example, instrumental grievers are more likely to focus on solving problems and other goal-directed activities (primary strategies). Conversely, because expressing their feelings is not a natural response to grief they may be more likely to plan time to accomplish this. Intuitive grievers would typically feel comfortable expressing intense emotions (primary strategy), while expressing their cognitive and physical aspects of grief as disorganization, confusion, exhaustion, and/or anxiety (secondary strategies). For a widower who grieves in an instrumental style he may channel his grief into problem-solving (primary strategy; e.g., planning the funeral, setting up child care for dependent children, settling legal matters, etc.) while occasionally planning time (usually alone) to express his feelings (secondary strategy; e.g., looking at pictures of his wife, taking a drive, etc.). Table 5.2 provides a comparison of the adaptive strategies of grievers with instrumental or intuitive grieving styles.

Table 5.2 Adaptive Strategies of Instrumental Versus Intuitive Style of Grieving

Intuitive Style Openly Expressing Feelings by:	Instrumental Style Actively Controlling Feelings by:
Allowing time for full experience of pain	Shelving thoughts and feelings to meet obligations
Outward expression of grief matches internal experience	Using humor and other indirect ways to express feelings
Identifying others in environment as receivers of feeling expressions	Choosing active means of expressing grief externally
Choosing support groups	Seeking companionship through activities but not for direct emotional support
Seeking trusted others with whom to share grief	Employing solitude as set aside time for reflection, adaptation
Grief expressed directly	Dosing feelings in controlled settings

Sources: Expanded and adapted from Doka and Martin (2010); Martin and Doka (1998); and Zinner (2000).

It is easy to overlook the importance of the secondary strategies for bereaved individuals. Furthermore it can be easy to confuse an instrumental or intuitive griever who has well-developed secondary strategies with a bereaved individual with a blended style. Secondary adaptive strategies are methods of expressing the aspects of grief that feel unnatural. Instrumental widowers who can find ways to express their feelings, despite the discomfort, will benefit. Doka and Martin (2010) describe the importance of well-developed secondary strategies:

> It is important to stress the significance of intuitive grievers discovering outlets for cognitive-driven action, while instrumental grievers must find ways of discharging affective energy . . . instrumental grievers who have choices among various vehicles for expressing feelings will adapt sooner and better than those whose tools for expressing feelings are confined to one or none. (p. 117)

Psychotherapists should not be too quick to judge a widower's grieving style because most grievers go through an initial period of shock or disorientation. Therefore a widower's early response may not be representative of his true grieving style (Doka & Martin, 2010). For example, a widower with an intuitive grieving style may be misconstrued as an instrumental griever because his initial efforts are focused on taking care of the necessary funeral arrangements and other tasks. In essence, his gender role needs of providing and protecting temporarily supersede his grieving needs. Only later will his natural grieving style have an opportunity to surface.

Instrumental Style: A Closer Look

Psychotherapists and laypeople are likely to have an understanding of intuitive grief because it matches many popular assumptions about grief—specifically that feelings must be expressed, concerns shared, and that avoiding these things will necessarily lead to maladaptive grief. Conversely, the instrumental grief style is the newer and more controversial concept. It is not a huge leap for most people to accept that there may be differences between how most men and women grieve. The challenge for some is to accept that it is possible to grieve adaptively by expressing grief in cognitive and problem-solving ways and in a more solitary manner. Personally I agree with Doka and Martin (2010) and believe that instrumental grief can be an equally healthy expression of grief. But, I can understand why some may not be convinced. Given that it is a newer concept and most widowers are instrumental grievers, it is important to examine it in more detail.

Instrumental grievers channel their mental energy into planning, thinking, and focusing on their internal experience. Although commonly viewed as a method for controlling their feelings, their goal is actually larger: to master their environment and their inner experiences. While instrumental grievers may be hesitant to share their feelings with others, this does not mean that they are unwilling to talk about grief-related concerns. They are often willing to talk about problems when it does not require disclosure of their feelings. Doka and Martin (2010) attribute the lack of attendance by men at support groups to the topics usually discussed: "This aversion to seeking help from support groups is often misinterpreted as isolation, when, in fact, it is not the company of those present that the instrumental griever is avoiding; it is the nature of the discussions" (p. 72). For example, Bob, a younger widower that I interviewed, reported that he did not return to a grief group after his first meeting despite having a graduate degree in psychology and being open to the experience. Bob did not return because the group experience was based entirely on venting feelings, reflecting on the loss, and sharing emotional support. For an intuitive griever, this group format might be ideal. However, for instrumental grievers, this group design offers little benefit. (In Chapter 8, I discuss this mismatch between instrumental widowers and the traditional format of grief groups in more detail.)

Widowers who exhibit an instrumental style of grieving often share several patterns in responding to their losses. These patterns include using intellectualization as a strategy to understand their loss, using planned action to accomplish various goals, and being strategic about dosing their expression of emotion.

Intellectualization

Instrumental grievers also tend to use intellectualization as part of their grief reaction. While typically viewed as a harmful defense mechanism, Doka and Martin (2010) suggest that using intellectual inquiry as a way to respond to a loss can be beneficial: "Far from being seen as pathological, using one's intellect to solve life's problems is as important as being aware of one's sensory experiences" (pp. 80–81). Furthermore, this does not mean that widowers using an instrumental style will not have emotions, but they will be more likely to understand their losses through their thoughts.

Planned Action

As mentioned, instrumental grievers' primary adaptive strategies tend to revolve around planned action. Doka and Martin (2010) describe four goals that may be the focus of this planned action: (1) a channel for emotion; (2) a method of memorialization; (3) problem-solving; and (4) return to normal.

ACTION AS CHANNEL FOR EMOTION

While instrumental grievers focus their mental energy primarily on cognitive-related tasks, they still experience affective energy. Sometimes they will use physical activity to "channel excess psychic energy"; examples include "running, weightlifting, martial arts, and 'mindless' work like mowing grass or stacking wood. Less intense ways of displacing energy include needlepoint, knitting, sewing, gardening, painting, walking, and low-impact sports like golf or horseshoes" (Doka & Martin, 2010, p. 76). Widowers may use these types of activities as a way of dealing with feeling restless and confined. I believe C. S. Lewis (1961) was referring to this when he said, "I do all the walking I can, for I'd be a fool to go to bed not tired" (Lewis, 1961, p. 60).

ACTION AS A METHOD OF MEMORIALIZING

Another action that can be used as an adaptive strategy is to create or build something with the specific intention of memorializing the deceased. This can take the form of performing an action with the intent of remembering (listening to specific songs, watching videos on an anniversary, etc.), creating an artistic item (e.g., a sculpture, a painting, a scrapbook, etc.), cultivating a 'natural' item (e.g., maintaining her flower garden, planting a tree, etc.), or a performing a service (volunteering for an organization in her memory, creating a scholarship/

fund, etc.), among others. I have found that widowers use an average of eight different rituals related to the loss of a partner. In fact, I have never found a single widower who did not use any rituals and some have used more than 15 different types (Troyer, 2011).

ACTION AS PROBLEM SOLVING

The instrumental griever may focus on solving a specific problem connected to the loss such as joining an organization that works to promote a cause related to the death (e.g., walking in Susan G. Komen events after losing wife to breast cancer, etc.), finishing or continuing a project that the wife started (i.e., finishing a book that his wife had started, maintaining a website that she had created, etc.), or "making restitution for damage or injury in the wake of the death" (Doka & Martin, 2010, p. 78). Levang (1998) described other examples of how men may focus on problem-solving connected to their losses:

> To create meaning from their loss, many men devote great amounts of time and energy to issues or concerns related to their personal tragedy. They may, for example, mobilize groups to fight teen suicide, educate the public about the effects of depression, lobby government entities against the tobacco industry, volunteer in hospice programs, organize AIDS marathons, develop programs for bereaved families, or lead cancer support groups. (p. 89)

ACTION AS A RETURN TO NORMAL

This method of action is commonly viewed as returning to typical activities as a way of restoring a sense of security and routine. The most common examples are returning to activities that are a significant part of the widower's life including returning to work or a long-term project (Doka & Martin, 2010). Note how this type of activity is viewed quite differently when examined from a grieving styles perspective. Instead of focusing on accomplishing traditional 'grief work,' the widower believes his most productive course of action is to try to return to normal. While some may view this as avoidance, the widower may see this as the best way to honor the deceased and also deal with his grief.

The widower may satisfy several of these goals for planned action through a single activity or project. For example, a widower whose partner died from cancer could create a scholarship for undergraduate students who plan to pursue medical school and become an oncologist (solve problems). To create this scholarship he meets with a college's representatives to learn about how to establish the scholarship (channel emotion) and also pays tribute to his wife by naming the scholarship after her (memorializing). Based on a single project the widower has used planful action to accomplish three of the four goals described by Doka and Martin (2010).

Dosing

A common concern of instrumental grievers is that their feelings may overwhelm them. Therefore, widowers employing an instrumental grieving style may use planned activities to release their feelings. Since expressing feelings is not their 'natural' style (hence, this is a secondary adaptive strategy), the use of controlled environments and deliberate timing helps them feel more in control. This process of regulating the expression of feelings so as to "allow the survivor to face reality while simultaneously protecting against too great an onslaught of affect" is referred to as *dosing* (Shuchter & Zisook, 1993, p. 30). Golden (2000) refers to a similar construct using the term *sampling*. Doka and Martin (2010) provide an excellent example of a griever using a controlled environment to dose his feelings. Willie, a widower, typically focused on the practical problems related to raising his two daughters. Willie had figured out his own way to occasionally spend time alone and focus on his feelings: "Alone in his car he would put on a tape with 'Earth Angel,' their song, and he would weep. But most of the time, he was focused on holding his job and raising his children" (p. 74).

Psychotherapists may mistakenly assume that a widower never expresses his feelings if he is unwilling to do so in a group or in psychotherapy. For intuitive grievers, this is the ideal setting in which to express feelings—in a situation where supportive companions are present. They may ask an instrumental griever, "Why would you want to cry alone when you can share the burden?" Most instrumental grievers do not see it this way. They may presume that the situation is too uncontrolled, they may not be able to stop their emotions once begun, or they will be viewed as unmasculine. Unfortunately, others (including therapists, family, friends, co-workers, etc.) may assume that if the widower does not share his feelings with them, then he must never express them. This is not necessarily true—he may be carefully choosing the time and setting where he is most comfortable.

Given that instrumental grievers are more comfortable grieving in active and planned ways, I believe rituals are especially helpful for them. Without a doubt, instrumental, intuitive, or blended grievers can benefit from rituals. In particular, rituals allow instrumental grievers to use their strengths (i.e., cognitive approach, activity-based orientation, and thorough planning) to help create meaningful experiences and express emotions in a carefully dosed manner.

Blended Style

Although most individuals are viewed as either intuitive or instrumental in their grieving style, some bereaved individuals are most accurately described as a having a blended style. The blended style is not superior to other grieving styles. On one hand, blended grievers may feel more comfortable with a broader range of strategies to deal with their grief. However, just because a wider variety of strategies are available to the 'blended' griever, that does not mean that he will have access to, nor the ability to employ them (Doka & Martin, 2010).

This goes against the common perception that grievers should focus on developing their 'weak side.' For example, a psychotherapist who pushes an instrumental widower to focus exclusively on expressing his feelings and sharing them with others despite his discomfort is not respecting the widower's natural process.

> To urge oneself or another to express feelings that are, in fact, not really a significant part of the grief experience is counterproductive... such calls ignore both the basic principle of self-help and counseling—lead with strengths. Crises are poor opportunities to attempt to comply with uncomfortable or unfamiliar approaches. One is better served by effectively employing the adaptive strategies that seem most natural. (Doka & Martin, 2010, p. 185)

This perspective blends nicely with the positive psychology/positive masculinity (PPPM) perspective described in Chapter 2 (see Kiselica & Englar-Carlson, 2010) in that both perspectives seek to begin working with male clients' natural strengths.

Dissonant Response

Dissonant responses occur when the individual's grieving style and primary adaptation strategies do not match. For example, a widower with an intuitive grieving style may initially suppress his feelings because of a choice (cognition) to be useful in planning services, to demonstrate emotional 'strength' to his children by not expressing his feelings of loss, or due to adopting cultural proscriptions against grieving openly. If this naturally intuitive griever continues to adhere to one of these reasons for not opening up and expressing his emotions (his natural grieving style), then he may remain stuck in a dissonant style. This suppression requires a large amount of emotional energy—energy that cannot be used to deal with other planned and unplanned events (Doka & Martin, 2010).

A widower's grieving style may take awhile to surface given that the initial shock of his loss, arrangements for funerals and other death rituals, and dealing with other grieving family members and friends can create a situation where he feels he must focus on taking care of the needs of others. Doka and Martin (2010) suggest that a common pattern is for men who are naturally intuitive grievers to initially appear to be instrumental because they are actively taking care of others. Only later can he feel more comfortable expressing his innate grieving style. However, some men in these circumstances never feel comfortable using their natural style and remain locked in a gender-norm straitjacket.

Intuitive male grievers are more likely to have a dissonant grief response because the intuitive style goes against traditional male gender norms. "For these grievers, their need to express their feelings and share them with others is overshadowed by a rigid definition of manliness. In disenfranchising their own grief, these unfortunates may contribute to the stereotype of the poker-faced male griever" (Doka & Martin, 2010, p. 91). This can make a psychotherapist's job especially tricky. On one hand, no one grieving style (instrumental, intuitive, or blended) is viewed as being superior, therefore, psychotherapists should not try to force a widower to adopt an unnatural style. However, a widower may resist his style based on gender norms and cultural factors—as when a widower who is naturally intuitive restricts his grieving style because it is a poor match with his views of masculinity. And don't forget that his initial appearance and behavior may not match his natural grieving style because of the unique pressures that come with the initial demands after the loss (as when an intuitive widower may appear instrumental because he feels responsible for keeping up appearances for his children and completing specific tasks). Psychotherapists need to have a trusting relationship with the widower in order to have accurate information about how the widower is responding to his loss and if his grief reaction has been altered or curtailed for any reason. Contrary to previous models that focused almost exclusively on the expression of feelings, a therapist's goal should not be to get a widower to cry. But the therapist should be open and ready to support a widower if the therapist's office is the only place he feels comfortable expressing his feelings (see Wolfelt, 2006).

Disenfranchised Grief and Grieving Styles

In Chapter 3, I discussed the importance of understanding how a widower's grief could be disenfranchised (see Doka, 1989a, 2002a). Disenfranchised grief is when the relationship, loss, griever, circumstances, or method/style of grieving is not fully acknowledged or recognized by others. Widowers with an instrumental grieving style tend to violate the expectation that dealing with a significant loss should be visible to others. As Zinner (2000) states:

> To the extent that men are not culturally sanctioned to outwardly demonstrate their grief or to share their emotional experience of grief, their style of bereavement will be open to misinterpretation and will elicit limited outside support. Thus, when men do not demonstrate their bereavement and are not seen as being bereaved, they will find themselves to be marginalized as grievers, left outside of the ranks of those who grief is responded to and validated. (p. 181)

Therefore, grieving styles can have a profound influence on the widower if the widower is viewed sympathetically by others and on the level of support he receives. Undeniably, individuals who use any grieving style, instrumental, intuitive, or blended, may be disenfranchised for various reasons. I am focusing on how widowers using an instrumental style can be disenfranchised because that is the most common grieving style they use and it goes against common assumptions about the 'best' way to grieve.

In some cases widowers who use an instrumental grieving style may suffer from 'double disenfranchisement' (Martin & Doka, 2000). In these cases men may not be supported because of their grieving style in addition to one of the other types of disenfranchisement. For example, a widower grieving the death of his wife after she committed suicide may need to contend with the disenfranchisement from his instrumental grieving style and from the additional stigma associated with deaths by suicide.

Grieving Styles and Grief Counseling

Based on the grieving styles perspective, psychotherapists can be more welcoming and empathic toward instrumental widowers by adjusting their therapeutic process in the following ways:

- Begin with and focus on the widower's presenting problem
- Reinforce positive aspects of traditional masculinity
- Encourage problem-solving and action-based strategies
- Consider gender role, grieving style, and other mediators

Begin With Presenting Concerns

The widower's presenting concerns may be related to problems that are caused by the loss, but do not involve the grief expression. It is important for the therapist to not supplant the widower's opinion about what his own most pressing concerns are. A widower may be seeking information related to parenting, managing household tasks, and other practical matters. Certainly it is necessary for the therapist to have the 'big picture' of the widower's life, but taking control of the focus of therapy is a sure way to chase off a client. Earlier in the chapter I used Doka and Martin's (2010) example of Willie who felt most comfortable expressing his feelings by listening to music in his car. Willie

> attended a [hospice-sponsored] group once, hoping to discuss the practical concerns he had in raising his 9- and 10-year-old daughters. But every time Willie tried to talk about his children, the group leader would interrupt and ask, "What about your feelings?" Willie, quite frankly, was uncomfortable with the question. (pp. 73–74)

Psychotherapists should keep in mind that many men question the utility of counseling and are, therefore, hesitant to seek out professional psychological help. Ignoring a widower's presenting concerns is a sure way to reinforce these assumptions and drive men away from psychotherapy.

Reinforce Positive Aspects of Traditional Masculinity

As described in Chapter 2, there are many positive aspects of traditional masculinity, including self-sacrifice, loyalty, self-reliance, and the ability to remain calm in the face of danger, among others. Often the widower's presenting concerns will coincide with one or more (positive or negative) aspects of traditional masculinity. For example, Willie was seeking guidance from a support group in regard to being a better parent. The group leader could have built a relationship with Willie by affirming his desire to be an active and caring father and the obvious self-sacrifices that come with being a single parent.

Encourage Problem-Solving and Action-Based Strategies

Psychotherapists should encourage widowers with an instrumental style (as well as intuitive or blended grievers who endorse traditional gender norms) to act and problem-solve as part of their grieving strategy, especially given that these are characteristics of traditional masculinity and instrumental grief (Doka & Martin, 2001, 2010; Kiselica & Englar-Carlson, 2010; Levant, 1995). Men often genuinely want to 'fix' things, be part of a solution to a problem, or simply want to be doing something physically active. Golden (2000) argues that the trend toward deritualization leaves little opportunity for men to express their grief in culturally sanctioned, active ways:

> Given this void of ritual, men and women are put into a precarious state. Often, women are able to overcome this void by using their skills of relating and their natural tendency towards verbally sharing their grief with others, but men, usually with strengths of a different nature, are at more of a disadvantage. Without culturally-endorsed rituals men are left with nothing to *do* following a death. (p. 112)

While there is no way to repair a loss, he can choose to solve problems caused by his loss and also help others.

A common reaction is for widowers to return to their workplace. There are many examples of men who returned to work quickly and reported that it is what 'saved them.' While it is possible to avoid grief by overworking, many bereaved men report that it provides a balance to their lives. Viewing this through the Dual Process Model (Stroebe & Schut, 1999), these widowers are using work as a restoration-oriented coping strategy. They believe that being at home, where they would likely spend most of their time grieving, is not useful or productive. Instead, work provides an opportunity for them to dose their grief.

Consider Gender Roles, Grieving Style, and Other Mediators

In Chapter 2 I discussed the importance of the psychotherapist understanding the influence of gender role socialization and adherence to traditional gender norms on a widower. While this information is important and is related to an individual's grieving style, it is important to recognize that grieving style must be examined as a separate variable. For instance, an older widower may view himself as traditionally masculine, yet his grieving style may be intuitive or dissonant. Simply knowing that his attitudes and behaviors, in general, follow traditional gender norms does not mean that his grieving style will necessarily follow. Assessing the widower's gender norms and his grieving style will provide the psychotherapist a more complete picture.

There is a wide variety of other factors that will influence a widower and his reaction to his loss including culture, acculturation, prior personal experience with death and grief, and specific factors related to the death. Culture not only influences how death is viewed and grief is expressed, but also defines relationships and their importance (Doka & Martin, 2010). A widower who identifies with a culture other than the dominant culture may be influenced by his level of acculturation. It is important to look at many factors that are interconnected and avoid viewing constructs like gender roles or grieving styles in isolation.

Limitations of Grieving Styles Perspective

The primary limitation of the grieving styles perspective is that it lacks extensive empirical support. Given the limited time that the theory has been around (their first book was published in 2000) and the limited time since an initial scale for assessing grieving patterns (Doka & Martin, 2010), this is not surprising. Offsetting these limitations is the positive reactions from clinicians and clients (men and women) that find the theory to have tremendous face validity and usefulness. The basic assumptions are easily understood by clients and therapists and help them view their attitudes and behaviors regarding grief in new ways. A significant advantage of the grieving styles perspective is that it works with and expands other models that focus on gender roles and masculinity such as positive psychology/positive masculinity (PPPM) (Kiselica & Englar-Carlson, 2010) and the New Psychology of Men (Levant & Pollack, 1995).

In this chapter I have focused primarily on widowers who are instrumental grievers. This has been intentional for several reasons. First, most men exhibit an instrumental style (Doka & Martin, 2010). Furthermore, widowers who are intuitive grievers are likely well served by current practices in individual and group grief counseling (assuming the widower is open to seeking professional assistance). It is likely that men with an intuitive grieving style are comfortable with these practices given that many therapists endorse the grief work perspective which matches well with the focus on expression of feelings. I have yet to hear a therapist say that a widower is too skillful at expressing his feelings. What I have heard again and again is therapists complain about men who are 'avoiding' their feelings and focusing on 'surface' problems or concerns. I have also heard therapists worry about men that prematurely leave therapy or a support group and wonder why they never return. In many of these situations therapists can benefit from a deeper understanding of the grieving style perspective.

6

COMMON AND COMPLICATED GRIEF RESPONSES

In Chapter 4, I described the wide variety of factors that can mediate a widower's response to loss including the relationship with the deceased, characteristics of the widower, characteristics of the loss, social factors, and concurrent stressors. Although there are many factors included in these five groups, there are only a handful of different responses to a partner's death. Of course, these responses are widely varied in their specific expression (e.g., a 90-year-old, Caucasian, heterosexual widower from Iowa may respond quite differently than a 24-year-old homosexual, first-generation Latino widower from California) and often change over time. While it is necessary to keep in mind the specific nuances of a widower's situation, it is at least as important to understand his core reactions. Most widowers (and, for that matter, most bereaved individuals) will experience one or more of the following reactions to his loss: denial, shock and numbness, guilt, anger, shame, fear, helplessness, meaninglessness, loneliness, relief, or deification.

In this chapter, I will briefly examine each of these reactions and possible precipitating factors. I will also briefly describe counseling techniques associated with each reaction. Which grief reactions are normal and which are abnormal? There is an ongoing debate among grief researchers and psychotherapists about whether or not an individual's response to loss can be pathological. For example, Worden (2009) argues that:

> It is not the grief that people experience that is abnormal. Their experience of grief *is* their experience of grief. . . . The difficulty lies in the mourning process. There is something that is impeding the mourning process and not allowing it to move forward toward a good adaptation to the loss. (pp. 137–138)

I believe that an individual's grief reaction, if persistent and severe enough, can be an abnormal or complicated reaction; however, this is not typical. (An example of a complication is when the grief reaction is intertwined with severe pathologies, as in the case of a severe delusion.) I prefer the terms *atypical grief* and *complicated grief* to *abnormal grief* or *pathological grief* and never use the latter terms with clients. Later in the chapter I will outline several different forms of complicated grief.

While many of these reactions could be described as feelings, I purposely use the terms *reactions* and *responses*. This is done intentionally because each of these responses is much more than a feeling, and it is important to address the cognitions, behaviors, and spiritual implications of each reaction. For example, anger certainly has an affective element to it, but also involves thoughts and behaviors. Anger can be accessed through shedding tears, discussing its roots, and punching a pillow. Therefore, psychotherapists can access any of these reactions through a variety of methods.

Common Grief Responses

Denial

There is a good reason why many grief models—including Worden's (2009) Tasks of Mourning and Kübler-Ross's Stages of Grief (Kübler-Ross & Kessler, 2005)—begin with denial or overcoming denial. The initial shock of the loss is a very common experience. Many people, mental and physical health professionals included, often misunderstand the potential range of denial reactions. Unfortunately the most dramatic cases of denial (especially cases where the deceased is kept within the home for weeks or months) receive the greatest attention and create the perception that denial is always a terrible thing. This form of extreme form of denial is associated with more severe psychological disorders (Worden, 2009).

In reality, denial reactions are almost always more subtle, and they are a normal part of the early grief process. For example, widowed persons frequently report reaching for the phone to call their partners, walking to another room to find them, or waking up and expecting to find their partner in bed next to them. Rando (1993) suggests that each of these experiences is a normal reminder for the bereaved person that his partner has died and is a critical part of the process:

> Each time the mourner is frustrated in his desire to be with the deceased, he "learns" again that the loved one is dead. Each pang of grief, each stab of pain whenever the mourner's expectation, desire, or need for the loved one is unfulfilled "teaches" the mourner that the loved one is no longer there. . . . It will take a long time and hundreds, perhaps thousands, of these painful experiences of unfulfilled longing

for the deceased before the mourner will be able to transfer to his gut what he knows in his head—that the loved one is really, truly, irrevocably gone. (p. 34)

This form of denial can allow the widower to 'take a break' from thinking about and feeling his loss; this is often necessary to allow the bereaved to complete other necessary tasks related to death rituals (e.g., funerals, etc.), dealing with the ramifications of secondary losses, assisting others (including bereaved children), and resuming daily tasks. As such, denial can be quite beneficial assuming that it is not pervasive or unrelenting (Stroebe & Schut, 1999).

In the vast majority of cases, widowed persons will naturally acknowledge the physical reality of the loss. Simply acknowledging the experiences and any distress that accompanies it is often enough for the widower to begin to integrate the reality of the loss. As Rando (1993) says, it may take many repetitions, but the widower will eventually accept the reality and permanency of his partner's death. Well-intentioned therapists that endorse stage models of grief may take it upon themselves to expedite the process of moving the widower to the next 'stage.' With this goal the therapist may encourage or even harangue the client into using the past tense when talking about the deceased, insist on using unambiguous terms such as *dead* and *deceased* instead of *gone* or *lost*, and attempt to provoke a strong emotional reaction as proof that the denial has been broken. I believe (and widowers have reported to me) that bereaved persons generally find this badgering to be unhelpful, and it may be ultimately harmful to the counseling relationship. While there are a minority of widowers with whom reinforcement of the permanence of the loss is essential, it is unnecessary and unhelpful for the majority of widowers.

More severe denial reactions are often associated with sudden and traumatic losses; this may be a result of attempting to reconcile the loss with our expectations (Redmond, 1996). An example of this is when a widower maintains an ongoing hope that a mistake has been made and his partner will walk through the door. Denial may be particularly difficult in ambiguous loss situations. The absence of the partner's body or other evidence of the death can allow the surviving partner to maintain his denial about the reality of the loss (Boss, 1999, 2006).

As mentioned in Chapter 3, widowers may be especially prone to a specific type of denial—the denial of the meaning of the loss. Widowers who are more likely to deny the importance of their loss are those who endorse Brannon's (1976) Sturdy Oak and No Sissy Stuff injunctions. In other words, if a widower believes that being a 'real man' involves being self-sufficient, then one way to prove this to others is to appear as though he is generally unaffected by the death of his partner. To express a strong sense of loss would be to admit that he was not as self-reliant as he believed himself to be. We do not know what percent of widowers endorse these views and to what extent; but, if your client is trying to live up to these ideals, then he may attempt to move quickly past any self-reflection of what has been lost. Widowers using this form of denial—ignoring the meaning of the loss—can be especially difficult to work with because they fail to recognize the connections between their losses and any post-loss concerns.

Shock and Numbness

Shock is a common initial reaction for bereaved individuals; Sanders (1999) included it as her first phase in her Integrative Theory of Bereavement. Shock can linger beyond a widower's initial reaction and is often a response to unexpected losses including traumatic deaths. One form of shock is *bereavement overload*—the cumulative negative effect of multiple losses on one's grief reaction (Kastenbaum, 1969; Rando, 1996). This can occur when a widower suffers multiple individual losses close in time or when multiple deaths occur simultaneously (e.g., his wife and children are killed in a car accident). The widower does not have to lose his entire family to experience shock. He may experience shock because the death goes against his expectations at a specific age. Mark was 29 when his wife died:

> At first, I was in shock. I was numb. I would find myself saying to myself, "Why did this happen to me?" But there was also an element of fascination with adventure—I mean, to be a widower at the age of 29? . . . There was this unbelievability to it. (Campbell & Silverman, 1987, p. 65)

A widower may refer himself or be referred to counseling because of his shock. He (or concerned others) may believe that he is not grieving correctly because he is not feeling more—this may be especially true if he believes he should be going through some pre-determined stages of grief. It is important not to pathologize shock as it is often a normal initial reaction. Furthermore, Clark (1982), a Gestalt therapist, reminds us that it can be important to respect the function or purpose of shock and not see it as something that must be immediately conquered.

> There is wisdom in knowing that massive change is better realized slowly because a slow pace allows for gradual assimilation, and prevents us from becoming overwhelmed. Overwhelming change can be

so shocking and disruptive that our resources are swept away, leaving us too vulnerable and too defenseless for personal survival. At this point, with unawareness of process, to insist that someone face reality is gravely inappropriate. The wisdom of self-regulation is that "I know as I am able to know." (p. 53)

Given that men may prefer to dose their emotions as a way to feel more in control of them, it would be easy to misinterpret the grief response of a widower who is more instrumental in his grief style.

Guilt

Guilt is frequently viewed as anger turned inward (Kübler-Ross & Kessler, 2005) and can be a reaction to a wide variety of different causes of death. Like anger, guilt is common in situations where death was potentially preventable (including homicide and suicide) as well as in cases where the death is viewed as liberating (Elison & McGonigle, 2003). A man may be more likely to respond with guilt at not being able to protect his partner (Martin & Doka, 2000; Levang, 1998)—even if this is a completely unreasonable standard. This guilt may be even more intense if the loss occurred while there was a strain on the relationship (Redmond, 1996).

Shuchter and Zisook (1993) discuss three types of guilt associated with grief: (1) survivor guilt, (2) guilt related to a sense of responsibility, and (3) guilt associated with betrayal. Survivor guilt often includes themes related to why 'she had to die and not me,' and guilt associated with being able to enjoy things that his partner cannot (Elison & McGonigle, 2003; Sanders, 1999). This can lead a widower to intentionally denying himself pleasure or assistance. Martin and Doka (1996) recounted a widower who had spent most of his time either working as a postal employee or volunteering as a firefighter despite his wife's requests to travel together. Tragically, his wife died three weeks after he retired. "I should have stopped working sooner so we could have taken some of those trips" (p. 163). His guilt was a key factor in initially denying any support: "I don't deserve help. My wife can't enjoy our friend's company, so why should I?" (p. 163).

A widower may blame himself, with varying amount of justification, for being responsible for his wife's death. Sanders (1999) describes a 72-year-old widower's sense of guilt after his wife died in a car crash in which he was unscathed:

> To this day, I am haunted by the lingering sense of shock, loss, and memory of her poor little limp body, broken and bleeding, lying in that

> wreck.... Daily, I go over a litany of a thousand "ifs," any one of which would have saved her life—a deadening treadmill. I was driving—thus a sense of guilt.... Daily, I go calculate the value of survival and wonder if it is worth the effort. (p. 211)

Often the guilt is based on an unreasonable expectation of the capabilities of the widower. The widower may express regret at a variety of things that are beyond his control: how he shouldn't have let his wife drive that day, how he should have encouraged her to improve her diet and see her physician, how he should have been able to protect her. In situations where long-term care was needed, a widower may also express guilt over the perceived inadequacy of the care he provided (Elison & McGonigle, 2003). Careful examination of what was actually possible is necessary, but recognizing that he has a limited ability to protect his loved ones can be a difficult and painful realization.

The third form of guilt results from a view that he is betraying his deceased partner. This type of guilt is frequently associated with three situations: after his acute grief is beginning to lift, after lengthy caregiving, and/or as he begins to consider dating. A widower may begin feeling better after going through a long bereavement process, but may hold back if he assumes that his happiness somehow diminishes his partner or her memory. He may also, quite understandably, feel relief after a lengthy period of caregiving for his wife. This feeling, what Elison and McGonigle (2003) refer to as 'dual relief,' is often a combination of relief that his partner is no longer in any physical pain and relief that the stress of caregiving has been lifted. Frequently the three types of guilt described by Shuchter and Zisook (1993) overlap with one another.

An additional source of guilt not described by Shuchter and Zisook is guilt associated with *unfinished business*. One form of unfinished business is when a widower makes a promise to his deceased partner. The promise may have been made explicitly while his partner was still alive, or internally before or after the partner has died. One common promise is to not repartner or remarry. Sometimes this is promise is made to ensure the griever will never again have to deal with a loss like this—in this way it is a protective promise for the widower. For other widowers it may be a sign of respect and faithfulness to his partner.

A widower may make other promises depending on the circumstances of his life and his loss. For example, he may vow to raise their children a specific way, he may pledge to never forget his partner, or he may promise never to trust doctors or never to go to a certain hospital. I am not suggesting that these promises are always a bad thing. Promises to get sober or to become a more attentive father, for example, can lead to long-term positive changes for the widower (and by extension, his loved ones). The widower may find that this is a positive way to maintain a connection to his partner; keeping his promise honors his partner.

What is more likely to be seen in counseling is when promises create unnecessary obstacles in his grief. For example, a promise to never remarry can feel quite different to a man who was widowed ten years ago. The widower may feel extreme guilt over breaking a promise. A psychotherapist may need to help the widower examine his original intention and how he can remain true to the intent of the promise without impeding his grief process. Keeping the promise hardly seems worth it if it eventually causes the widower to resent his deceased partner. A variety of techniques discussed in Chapter 7, including letter writing, empty chair, and other role-playing techniques can help in this process.

Regardless of the cause, psychotherapists can assist widowers with their guilt with a realistic examination of the guilt. As with anger, knowledge about the illogicality of feeling guilty is not likely enough to change it, but it is still the best place to begin. In some cases, the guilt may be somewhat justified; in these cases the therapist can help the widower with ways to express his sorrow and pain. Specific techniques can also help the widower 'take a break' from his guilt. Jennifer Elison, a practicing grief therapist, recommends that her clients take a 'guilt-free day.' On these days, the client is encouraged to live as if he were guilt-free. This is intended to help the client determine if the self-created guilt has become simply a habit or if it is a true emotion. At the end of the day, the client is encouraged to think carefully about how he felt that day without the guilt. Is the guilt holding him back emotionally, physically, socially, and psychologically? Gaining some distance from the guilt may also help the client recognize the source of the guilt. Furthermore, simply the process of reducing his guilt for a day signifies to the widower that he may have more control over it than he first suspected (Elison & McGonigle, 2003).

Anger

A widower may experience anger for a wide variety of reasons. His anger may be primarily directed toward others or toward himself. Anger toward others may occur following a homicide or losses that were viewed as preventable. Who couldn't understand a widower's rage toward a murderer or a negligent physician who botched an easy operation? The anger may take the form of fantasies about harming or killing the perpetrator(s). It is not uncommon for this anger to reduce the support that the bereaved receives either because he actively pushes away supporters that try to quell his anger or because he alienates potential supporters through his anger—they simply aren't comfortable in the face of such raw anger. At times, the anger can be misdirected at those who did not have a role in the death and even toward those who are attempting to help the griever (Redmond, 1996).

Anger toward a deceased partner is common although not always commonly expressed. In situations where the partner committed suicide, the widower may be angry with his partner for being selfish. Blaine is a 35-year-old widower whose partner committed suicide with a gun after his partner's family discovered he was gay and in a relationship. The day of the suicide was Blaine's birthday. Blaine recognized immediately that he was angry with his partner:

> It hurt but I had no one to turn to. He left me—I was angry. He didn't realize who all was going to get hurt by his actions. . . . I was angry. I was mad. I was sad, I was angry, I was mad. All these emotions built up inside of you. It's so much emotion that some people would explode— I dealt with them every second of every day.

A widower may also be angry at his partner if the death could have been prevented by the partner. For example, the partner may not have sought or followed up with medical treatment or engaged in risk-taking behavior. The widower may express anger even if his partner was a victim. For example, he may be angry that his partner was willingly spending time with dangerous people and environments.

Simply having a safe person with whom to share their anger and an open invitation is often all that most widowers need to express anger. A man may be especially concerned about losing control if he begins to express even a little anger. This makes the support and physical presence of a psychotherapist so important—as a support to ensure that the bereaved will be able to regain control after expressing his anger (Clark, 1982). An angry griever may feel caught between his anger and his view of himself as a loving, kind, compassionate person (Redmond, 1996). For these widowers to feel comfortable expressing and discussing their anger it may take a strong relationship and reassurance that being angry at the deceased does not negate their love for their partners. Worden (2009) provides a less confrontive way to ask the client about his anger:

> I sometimes ask a survivor, "What do you miss about him?" and the person will respond with a list that often brings on sadness and tears. After a short while, I will ask, "What don't you miss about him?". . . . Another useful word is the word "disappointment." I ask, "How did she disappoint you?" It is rare that any close relationship does not have its share of disappointments. The word "unfair" can also be useful here. (pp. 92–93)

The goal is not to vilify the deceased but to give voice to the anger and help the bereaved find a balance between the positive and negative memories of the deceased.

Men who endorse traditional male gender norms and buy into the view that men do not engage in 'sissy stuff' (Brannon, 1976) may view anger, and even rage, as one of the few emotional expressions that do not violate their gender norms (Levant, 1990). Furthermore, men with an instrumental grieving style may be particularly likely to express anger in place of other feelings (Doka & Martin, 2010). Consequently, men may be more likely than women to use anger to cloak other reactions (Golden, 2000). Psychotherapists working with widowers should be prepared to be fully present with their clients as they share their anger, but should also be on the lookout for other reactions masked within the widower's anger.

Shame

Shame is frequently experienced alongside guilt and anger. This is not surprising given that shame often arises from the same types of losses associated with guilt and anger, but is particularly associated with stigmatizing losses. The most common stigmatizing loss is suicide; those bereaved by suicide experience higher levels of shame (Lukas & Seiden, 2007; Reed & Greenwald, 1991). This shame is often heightened because those bereaved by suicide often experience social isolation (Stillion, 1996).

Shame can also come from other sources. A widower may experience shame simply because he is a man asking for help (Brooks, 1996). He may also experience shame in not fulfilling his protector role if he views his wife's death as a failure to protect her (Bennett et al., 2003). Levang (1998) described how this could lead to shame and anger:

> Society has bestowed on men the righteous honor of being protectors and defenders. The reality of grief leads many men to believe that they have somehow failed in what they sense as their most important life role. These feelings of degradation and self-loathing torture their soul, defying their sense of goodness and honor. Anger is a way to protest these emotions without slipping into an even deeper abyss of self-hatred. (p. 73)

Another cause of shame may come from a widower's own views of his grief response. Although not common, some widowers berate themselves for not experiencing more intense grief (often discussed as not crying enough). More common, especially among older widowers in my experience, is a tendency to feel shame because he has not 'gotten over' the loss more quickly. Often this latter version of shame is associated with a widower who assumes that grief should be concluded in an unreasonably short time (e.g., a few weeks or months). The widower may also experience shame following a wide variety of specific responses (e.g., feeling relief after the death) or specific thoughts (e.g., having sexual desires, thinking about dating, etc.).

Psychotherapists can greatly aid widowers with their shame by helping them identify the source of the shame (e.g., internal vs. external, related to the cause of death or widower's grief reaction, etc.) and providing a safe environment in which they can share their shameful thoughts and reactions. Similar to Worden's (2009) indirect method of accessing anger, a therapist may ask, "Are there thoughts that you've been trying to push out of your mind?" Or a more direct approach: "Is there anything that you've been thinking about that you don't feel you can tell anyone?" A reminder to the client to take full advantage of psychotherapy and to 'get a good return on his investment' or his 'money's worth' (see Yalom, 1989) may help nudge him to disclose his shameful reactions.

Fear

A widower can experience a strong sense of fear following his partner's death. The death of a close loved one invariably makes the surviving spouse more aware of his own mortality. This may be especially difficult for younger widowers for whom this realization is incongruous with their avoidance of their own mortality. (Although some older men can vigorously maintain their denial of mortality too.) Grief related to their deeper understanding that they too are mortal can be deeply embedded in their grief for their lost partner. Therapists can easily fall into the trap of focusing exclusively on the widower's grief for his wife and forget that he is also grieving the recognition of his own mortality. Moreover, men may be reluctant to report being afraid in counseling and may be afraid that the psychotherapist will try to trick them into feeling weak (Mahalik et al., 2003).

A widower's fear can also come from specific types of loss especially sudden, unexpected, and violent deaths. Some bereaved individuals find that they struggle with more vague fears about the world as a result of the new perception of the world being unsafe; this fear may focus on their own safety and may also extend to other loved ones including children (Redmond, 1996). A widower may also worry about very specific fears, typically related to his partner's cause of death. Therefore a widower may be desperately concerned about his children's likelihood of also being killed in a car accident or his own chances of developing cancer.

It is critical for the therapist to evaluate the widower's anxiety and carefully consider whether he is experiencing a trauma reaction—especially if the death was witnessed. Surviving spouses whose partners have died as a result from suicide, homicide, or an accident are significantly more likely to meet criteria for PTSD, although a small percent of widowed individuals whose partners die after an extended illness can also met the criteria (Zisook et al., 1998).

Psychotherapists working with widowers with a strong sense of fear can help them by first empathizing with their fear and why it is perfectly reasonable for these concerns to surface. Even though their reaction may be extreme and their self-protection (or protection of loved ones) may be excessive, the response is understandable. It can be quite useful to look at the trade-offs that the fear has created. For example, is it preferable to never ride in a car again because of the fears of another crash compared to what must be given up? However, I believe that expressing empathy and validating the widower's normal reaction to a tragic death is critical before critically examining his fears.

Helplessness

Helplessness is a common cousin of fear. Similar to fear, it often accompanies sudden, traumatic, and/or unexpected losses. However, unlike post-loss fear, helplessness can also be a remnant from long-term losses where the widower often felt there was little he could do to assist his partner. Furthermore, the widower may experience a feeling of helplessness as he begins to more fully realize the extent of his secondary losses. As the widower recognizes the long list of roles that his partner filled and tasks his partner completed, he may begin to feel overwhelmed and helpless to know where to begin. For widowers with children in the home, this list of responsibilities may grow especially long.

There are several ways to assist a widower with his sense of helplessness. First, it can be helpful to genuinely acknowledge his feeling of hopelessness and avoid beginning with a list of reasons or steps to taking charge of the situation. This is a key time to avoid clichés about 'everything working out for the best' and other platitudes. At the appropriate time, introducing grief models (e.g., Tasks of Mourning, DPM model, etc.) to the widower can help put the widower's grief response within a larger context that makes it feel more manageable (Worden, 2009). When he's ready, these models can give the widower some type of starting point and a general map of the terrain to come. Of course, it is important to emphasize the client's unique circumstances and that deviating from a model is not necessary pathological or harmful.

As described more fully in Chapter 7, rituals can provide the bereaved a chance to 'do something' at a time when he is feeling helpless (Golden, 2000; Weeks, 1996).

Meaninglessness

Men are likely to view their primary purpose in life as provider and protector for their families and especially their wives (Doka & Martin, 2001; Golden, 2000). While this sense of providing and protecting invariably changes throughout the lifespan, it should not be underestimated. Following the death of his wife a widower may feel that his purpose or meaning is gone. The shift from focusing on providing for another to focusing on himself can be difficult. This is especially true if the widower believes that he has been at fault for failing to protect his wife in some way. This sense of failure may be illogical—after all, he cannot heal a wife with cancer or save her from an accident at which he was not present—but a sense of failing to live up to his responsibilities may still be present/influential/relevant.

Psychotherapists can assist a widower with a strong sense of meaninglessness through aiding him with reconstructing meaning in his life (see Neimeyer, 2001). This does not mean that he must shift his focus from his partner to someone or something else. After all, he can still maintain an ongoing connection to his deceased partner and use her as inspiration for various actions. For example, a widower can continue gaining a sense of helping his partner when he raises money or volunteers for causes in which she believed.

Loneliness

Loneliness has been described as the most difficult long-term aspect of spousal bereavement (Davidson, 2002; Lund et al., 1993) and widowed men may feel it even more acutely than widows (Peters & Liefbroer, 1997). One widower described his realization of how connected he was to his wife until after she died: "I thought I was a real individual before she died, but afterwards I realized she was a big part of me. That surprised me" (Brabant et al., 1992, p. 43). In most situations, the widower's partner is an integral part of most of his daily life and routines—older widowers can be married 70 years or more. This is especially true for widowers who are retired and spend a significant amount of time at home.

Loneliness can affect older and younger widowers differently. Older widowers must deal with changes to long-standing patterns and, especially if retired, may be used to spending most of their time with their partners. Younger widowers are unlikely to know any other younger widowers and face the challenge of feeling like an oddity.

In addition to their partners' physical presence, widowers also feel emotionally isolated. As mentioned previously, men frequently rely on their partners as their sole emotional confidante, whereas women are more likely to have a broader emotional support network (McGill, 1985). Widowers tend to have smaller social networks and receive less support from their friends after their partners' deaths (Lee et al., 1998; Stroebe & Schut, 2001). Widowed men may have a group of friends to share physical activities (e.g., fishing, golfing, etc.), but would rarely experience intimate physical contact (e.g., hugs) in these contexts. This is one reason why group interventions can be particularly helpful for widowers; grief groups can assist the widower with his reaction to his loss and simultaneously provide ongoing social interactions.

Relief

A widower's primary response to his partner's death may be relief. It is easy to assume that after his partner's death a widower will feel something negative (e.g., anger, shame, guilt, helplessness), but there are two situations where a sense of liberation is a common reaction: when the widower was a primary caregiver and when the relationship was conflicted. Although each situation results in the same emotion, these two situations will typically be vastly different.

Caregiving for an ailing partner is often very taxing for the widower. Widowers who have been caregiving for months or years and have seen their partners withstand various treatments, pain, and setbacks will eventually be relieved when their partners will no longer have to endure these hardships. While sadness and grief are still present (and likely have been for some time), relief is the new reaction.

This reaction can be the focus of psychotherapy when the widower experiences relief, but does so with guilt. This may be in response to other family members who expect the widower to feel only sadness and grief after the loss, or it may be the widower himself who believes he should not feel anything resembling pleasure or liberation. Psychotherapy can help remind the widower that he has likely been grieving throughout his partner's illness and caretaking. Furthermore, psychotherapy can be a safe place for him to discuss the challenges of caretaking and any guilt regarding his feelings or attitudes toward his partner.

The second situation where a widower may feel relief after the death of his partner is when the relationship was filled with conflict and discontent. In these 'liberating losses' (Elison & McGonigle, 2003), the widower may have had to deal with a partner who suffered from substance dependence, psychological disorders, infidelity, or other concerns. Furthermore, the widower himself may have been subjected to physical, emotional, and/or sexual abuse by his partner.

Despite the description of being 'liberating,' widowers may still find these losses to be conflicting. Elison and McGonigle (2003) suggest that "there is often a great deal of unfinished business in the wake of a relief death [liberating loss], especially if it was sudden" (p. 150). A survivor may find himself wanting to know why his partner was so cruel, mean, dismissive, absent, addicted, and so on. Furthermore, any hopes and fantasies he had about his partner being reformed or changing died with the partner. These situations can be further complicated if the deceased partner was viewed positively by others. When the survivor has a radically different perspective on the deceased than the rest of the community, the discrepancy can be difficult. Jennifer Elison described her conflicting feelings after her emotionally abusive husband (a well-liked, small-town physician) died in a car accident the day after she asked for a divorce:

> Irrationally, even though I was planning to leave him, I was angry at Paul for leaving me, and I vacillated between fury, overwhelming sadness at the death of a man I had once loved, and relief that my marriage was over. . . . People arrived at the house in droves. The situation was more than a little bizarre for me. These kind people needed consolation, and they looked to me to share their sorrow, but I was the last person who should have been asked to do this. Comforting them meant acting out a lie. (Elison & McGonigle, 2003, pp. 118–119)

Widowed individuals can experience a form of disenfranchised grief when their primary reaction to the death is relief while everyone else expects them to be sad (Elison & McGonigle, 2003).

In some cases, the widower will feel relief at the end of caregiving *and* at the end of a difficult relationship. Patch, a 66-year-old widower who was married for 45 years, embodies both situations. During those 45 years, his wife was an alcoholic, suffered from schizoaffective symptoms, attempted suicide, was repeatedly unfaithful, and eventually developed dementia. Despite their tumultuous relationship, Patch served as his wife's primary caregiver before finally placing her in an inpatient geropsychology facility. While caregiving for his wife, he felt terribly isolated: "I had nobody. Maybe a neighbor would occasionally come by, but then they didn't want to because [his wife] would follow them home. I was just desperate to find somebody to sit down with and have a decent conversation." Patch also talked about what it was like after she finally died:

> Her death was actually kind of—you've heard the saying—a relief. The actual grief I had was the grief when I couldn't take care of her anymore. That was what really sunk in as the grief—that's when everything just kind of fell in on me.

Recent studies suggest that Patch is not alone. Bonanno, Wortman, and Nesse (2004) found that 10% of their older widowed sample had experienced significant symptoms of depression prior to their partner's death, but these symptoms lessened after the death. These individuals "had been in relatively unsatisfying marriages, and for most the spouse was ill prior to his or her death" (p. 268).

A psychotherapist may be the only person that a widowed person in this situation can talk to. A widower may believe he cannot express his relief after caregiving lest it be misinterpreted as hoping his partner would die. Likewise, he may have hid his troubled relationship from others and believes that expressing this after his partner's death may be viewed as disparaging the dead. In these situations it can be challenging to help the widower find a balance between honoring the positive aspects of the relationship while also acknowledging its painful aspects.

Deification

Although it is unlikely to be the primary reaction for a widower seeking grief counseling, psychotherapists should be ready for some widowers to idealize or deify their partners. This process of overlooking any negative qualities the deceased may have had or relationship problems the couple experienced appears to be common in widowed persons (Lopata, 1996; Parkes, 1996). Furthermore, cultural rules about not speaking ill of the dead can be quite powerful and help maintain and strengthen this viewpoint.

Deification or sanctification happens when the deceased is lionized to a point that he or she is no longer a real person with real flaws and imperfections. This can be harmful for a widower by impeding other grief reactions. For example, a widower who sanctifies his deceased wife after a long-term illness may be unable to give voice to his thoughts and feelings about being abandoned, his frustration that his wife did not seek medical attention more quickly, and other reactions. Furthermore, deification can impede future relationships as a new partner is compared to the flawless memory of the deceased partner (Tatelbaum, 1984).

Psychotherapists should only question the idealized version of the deceased partner after developing a strong relationship with the widower. I believe a tentative approach is best. One technique is to adapt Worden's (2009) questions for dealing with anger by beginning with asking the survivor what he misses about his partner and following up with what he does not miss. The goal is not to destroy the widower's view of his partner, but to develop a more realistic view.

Complicated Grief Responses

The impact of grief reactions fall on a continuum from mild to severe. As Bonanno and his colleagues (Bonanno, 2004; Bonanno et al., 2004) have noted, the majority of bereaved individuals will successfully adjust to life after their loss without professional intervention. However, it has been estimated that approximately 8% (Sanders, 1999) to 20% (Jacobs et al., 1990) of bereaved individuals will experience significant and/or long-term challenges after their loss. The term *complicated grief* is the most commonly used term to denote a variety of grief reactions that are particularly debilitating for the bereaved individual. Although the term is frequently used, there is not a consensus on the definition of complicated grief. Most prominent researchers and clinicians (e.g., Rando et al., 2012; Worden, 2009) conceptualize complicated grief or complicated mourning as an umbrella label for several specific complicated reactions. *Traumatic grief* and *abnormal grief* were previously used in place of complicated grief; these terms have fallen out of use because of their confusion with PTSD and an emphasis on not labeling grief reactions as abnormal (Lichtenthal, Cruess, & Prigerson, 2004). It is important to note that 'normal' grief is often complex and multifaceted, but this is different than all grief being *complicated*. In other words, just because a widower's situation is intricate does not mean it is inherently atypical or a type of complicated grief.

Generally speaking, complicated grief is defined as a group of reactions "associated with long-term functional impairments" (Prigerson, Maciejewski, et al., 1995, p. 66) including the bereaved's inability to return to his pre-loss capabilities and emotional status especially if significant manifestations of grief continue past 6 months post-loss (Prigerson, Frank, et al., 1995). Holly Prigerson has led many of the studies examining various definitions and methods of assessing complicated grief. Recently Prigerson has shifted from using the term *complicated grief* to *prolonged grief*; prolonged grief is recognized as one specific form of complicated grief.

It is useful for psychotherapists to have a general understanding of the various forms of complicated grief. There is some, but not complete, agreement in the various forms of complicated grief reactions. I conceptualize complicated

Table 6.1 Types of Complicated Grief Reactions

Troyer	Worden (2009)	Rando (1993)
Prolonged Grief	Chronic grief reactions	Chronic mourning
Distorted or Traumatic Grief	Exaggerated grief reactions	Distorted mourning
Inhibited or Absent Grief	Delayed grief reactions	Delayed mourning
Masked Grief	Masked grief reactions	—

reactions in terms of four clusters: (1) Prolonged grief, (2) Distorted or Traumatic grief, (3) Inhibited or Absent grief, and (4) Masked grief (see Table 6.1). My clusters are based on a combination of descriptions by Worden (2009) and Rando (1993) and my personal perspective.

Time and Complicated Grief

One of the difficult things about evaluating and defining various forms of complicated grief is that there is so little consensus on what is 'uncomplicated.' One critical factor, the time before a diagnosis of complicated grief, still has little consensus (Zisook & DeVaul, 1985). The issue of when an assessment of a widower for various types of complicated grief is made can significantly influence the result. As described in Chapter 4, the course of grief can vary widely by individual and there is empirical evidence to suggest that a significant portion of widowed individuals will feel worse before they get better (Zisook & Shuchter, 1985).

Given that a widower's grief reaction can vary widely within the first few months post-loss, it is important for a therapist not to diagnose complicated grief too early in the process. Furthermore, just because the widower reports feeling worse does not, in and of itself, constitute a form of complicated grief. How long should one wait before determining if a widower's grief response is atypical or maladaptive? Prigerson and her colleagues (Zhang, El-Jawahri, & Prigerson, 2006) suggest 6 months post-loss, while others suggest a year or more (Horowitz, 2005; Worden, 2009).

Factors Related to Complicated Grief

There are several situations and factors that are associated with complicated grief reactions. Two factors that often precede complicated grief are if the bereaved individual does not have strong social support and if he has previously experienced a complicated grief reaction. Another factor is if the relationship with the deceased was either highly dependent (Worden, 2009) or ambivalent (Parkes, 1996). Complicated grief is also more likely if the bereaved individual saw his loved one suffering or if he was engaged in caregiving that was particularly stressful (Doka, 1997).

There is no conclusive evidence that men or women experience complicated grief more frequently than the other. However, there are several factors related to the socialization and psychological development of men that may increase the likelihood of complicated grief in men. Wolfelt (1990) outlines several of these factors. Two factors are that men may experience a "need to remain independently self-sufficient" (p. 21) and an "inability to seek support" (p. 22). These factors are similar to Brannon's (1976) injunction for men to be a Sturdy Oak—that men should be autonomous. Another factor is that men are often unable to acknowledge the pain associated with their loss (similar to Brannon's No Sissy Stuff). Wolfelt also describes a man's "intolerance of turning inward and slowing down" (p. 22). This is similar to Brannon's injunctions to Give 'em Hell (focus on constant energy) and the Big Wheel (focus on achievements and status) and creates a drive for the widower to show that he has been largely unaffected by his loss. The most difficult factor is that men have a difficult time surmounting the social forces that created these 'rules.' As a result, a widower's complicated grief will not only be a product of the specific circumstances of his loss (e.g., the quality of his relationship, the cause of death, etc.), but also his view of himself and what it means to be a man.

Prolonged Grief

One of the most common complicated grief reactions, and one that has received considerable attention from researchers and grief therapists, is *prolonged grief*. Also called chronic grief or chronic mourning (e.g., Rando, 1993; Worden, 2009), it has been characterized by researchers as an ongoing yearning for the deceased that goes beyond the typical timeline of grief. As mentioned, a challenge in diagnosing complicated grief (and prolonged grief in particular) is determining what a 'typical timeline' is. Given that Western culture generally views grief as something that should be resolved quickly (i.e., in a few months), it is common for widowers to believe that they are not 'getting over' their grief quickly enough, when in fact they are quite normal (Rando, 1993). Worden (2009) suggests that prolonged grief can be diagnosed when the bereaved feels stuck in his grief and "the grieving has gone on for several years and the person is feeling unfinished" (p. 138). Prolonged grief refers not only to the duration of grief, but also to the intensity. Temporary upsurges of grief, as in those a widower might experience on significant dates (e.g., wife's birthday, wedding anniversary, anniversary of the death, etc.), are completely normal and would not, in and of themselves, constitute prolonged grief.

Distorted or Traumatic Grief

Distorted mourning is the development of severe psychological reactions that are associated with the bereaved person's grief (Rando, 1993; Raphael, 1983). Worden (2009) uses the term *exaggerated grief reactions* to describe a similar phenomenon. Raphael has focused on two specific distortions: extreme anger and extreme guilt. Rando and Worden include a much broader range of psychological problems including depression, anxiety, post-traumatic stress, and substance abuse. For example, a widower who developed an anxiety disorder near the time of his partner's death may be experiencing distorted or traumatic grief.

Individuals who have been bereaved by traumatic circumstances are predisposed to this type of complicated grief. Rando (1996) outlined the circumstances that may increase the likelihood of traumatic grief:

> Factors that make a specific death circumstance traumatic include (1) suddenness and lack of anticipation, (2) violence, mutilation, and destruction, (3) preventability, and/or randomness, (4) multiple deaths, or (5) the mourner's personal encounter with death, where there is either a significant threat to his or her own survival or a massive and/or shocking confrontation with the death of others. (pp. 143–144)

Unfortunately widowed individuals often develop significant psychological reactions following the death of their partner. Approximately 40% of spousally bereaved individuals in one study met criteria for an anxiety disorder during the first year post-bereavement (Jacobs et al., 1990). In a meta-analysis of 11 studies, Onrust and Cuijpers (2006) found that 22% of widowed individuals met criteria for Major Depressive Disorder and almost 11% met the criteria for PTSD within the first year post-loss.

Inhibited or Absent Grief

Inhibited grief and *absent grief* are also known as delayed grief (see Rando, 1993) or suppressed or postponed grief reactions (Worden, 2009). Inhibited grief and absent grief refer to the bereaved individual having a disproportionate response to his loss. This can occur several different ways. A man may have a very mild response to a loss early in his life (e.g., perhaps the death of a sibling or father) only to have the grief expressed more fully at a later loss (e.g., perhaps his wife's death). One could argue that the widower's grief was largely absent or inhibited during the first loss and was delayed until his later loss. Although some argue that absent grief can exist (e.g., Tatelbaum, 1984), both Worden and Rando argue that grief is rarely if ever completely absent in an earlier loss. Instead, it is merely delayed. Worden's research has found that approximately 8% of widowed individuals experienced delayed grief. It is critical that the psychotherapist is basing his or her assessment on the widower's public *and* private grief reaction. It is not uncommon for family and friends to worry about a widower's lack of grief only to discover that he is merely expressing his grief in private ways.

There are several factors that may influence delayed or inhibited grief. The widower may experience inhibited grief because he idealizes the deceased and avoids reflecting on aspects of his partner or their relationships that would cause anger or other reactions (Raphael, 1983). Other factors that may facilitate inhibited or delayed grief are situational conditions at the time of loss that hinder the bereaved person's grief reaction. Lack of social support is one common cause of delayed or inhibited grief (Worden, 2009). Widowers with young children who focus extensively on their new responsibilities as a single parent (to the exclusion of their own grief reaction) may also be at risk of inhibited grief.

Masked Grief

Masked grief is similar to distorted/traumatic grief in that it also involves the development of more severe psychological (and sometimes physical) reactions. However, the difference between these reactions is that in masked grief reactions the bereaved individual does not associate his symptoms with his loss (Worden, 2009). For example, a widower may seek a physician or mental health professional with complaints of physical ailments (pain, sleep disturbances, etc.) and/or psychological concerns (depressed mood, anxiety, etc.) although he does not attribute the cause to his reaction to the loss of his partner.

Although it is common for a bereaved individual to adopt traits and mannerisms of a deceased family member, in a minority of cases the bereaved person will go even further. In these situations a widower may begin to experience symptoms that mimic his partner's symptoms prior to death. Zisook and DeVaul (1985) designated this type of reaction as 'grief-related facsimile illness.'

Although I have presented these forms of complicated grief separately, it is common that a widower with complicated grief reactions would experience more than one form. Similarly, a widower's complicated grief may cycle through different forms. For example, he may first have a masked grief reaction, but may eventually see a connection between his loss and his symptoms which would result in distorted grief. If these grief reactions last long enough, he could also be viewed as having experienced prolonged grief.

7

PROCESSES AND TECHNIQUES OF COUNSELING WIDOWERS

In this chapter I review specific concepts and techniques of grief counseling for widowers. This includes a brief review of the efficacy of grief counseling, the goal of grief counseling, and avoiding common mistakes. I also describe a three-phase process of counseling widowers including a variety of techniques and how they may be adapted to widowers.

Grief Counseling Versus Grief Therapy

Most researchers and psychotherapists (e.g., Winokuer & Harris, 2012; Worden, 2009) make a distinction between grief counseling and grief therapy. Grief counseling is typically described as assisting the bereaved with making typical adjustments over a shorter period of time while therapy is almost always a longer process and assists the bereaved clients with complicated grief reactions. Personally, I believe the differences between therapy and counseling are much less clear than is typically described. Both are typically accomplished by mental health professionals and focus on assisting clients who feel stuck in their grief. Overall there are far more similarities than differences between counseling and therapy. I recognize that many bereaved individuals will not need professional support, some will benefit from short-term professional assistance, and some will require intensive and longer-term support. However, I rarely make a distinction between techniques that I use only for 'counseling' versus those reserved for 'therapy.' Hence, I use the terms interchangeably.

Throughout this book, but especially in this chapter, I have made the assumption that the reader has a solid foundation in basic counseling practices. There are several excellent sources for helping psychotherapists gain skills specific to bereaved clients. For counselors-in-training and others who need an introduction to using basic counseling skills with bereaved clients, Winokuer and Harris's (2012) *Principles and Practice of Grief Counseling* provides an excellent foundation. For psychotherapists with more experience and who are looking for more advanced techniques, Worden's (2009) *Grief Counseling and Grief Therapy* is a classic in the field.

Efficacy of Grief Counseling

Perhaps the most important question facing grief researchers and practitioners is: Is grief counseling effective? Over the last 15 years, a series of debates has sprung up regarding this question. A detailed review of this question is beyond the scope of this book. Briefly, the controversy began with a series of reports suggesting that grief counseling was less effective than other forms of psychotherapy and could potentially result in worse outcomes for subsets of bereaved individuals (see Jordan & Neimeyer, 2003; Neimeyer, 2000). Various meta-analyses of studies of bereavement interventions for adults have tentatively suggested that grief interventions were either generally efficacious (Allumbaugh & Hoyt, 1999) or not (Currier, Neimeyer, & Berman, 2008; Jordan & Neimeyer, 2003; Nseir & Larkey, 2013).

There are two reasons why the results of these meta-analyses are not particularly useful for determining if grief counseling is effective with widowers. For example, with the exception of Nseir and Larkey's (2013) study, these meta-analyses have included studies on bereaved individuals with a variety of losses (i.e., death of a child, sibling, parent, spouse, etc.). Furthermore, the studies included in the meta-analyses were representative of most grief studies; therefore, they oversampled female participants. For instance, the average study in Allumbaugh and Hoyt's (1999) meta-analyses comprised 84% female participants. Given that the vast majority of grief research is completed with female participants and includes a wide variety of relationships, the results of these meta-analyses are likely poor predictors of the effectiveness of counseling widowers.

Several other criticisms of these meta-analyses have been outlined; most of these critiques have focused on the ecological validity of the studies in the meta-analyses. That is, the studies included have characteristics that are significantly different from how grief counseling is typically practiced (Hoyt & Larson, 2010). For example, studies included in the meta-analyses have recruited participants who were not likely to seek out counseling on their own (Larson & Hoyt, 2007b) and focused exclusively on grief counseling techniques while ignoring other critical influences on counseling outcome such as the qualities of the counselor, the characteristics of the client, and the therapeutic relationship (Altmaier, 2011). Additionally, the interventions in most of the studies were so brief that they may not reach a therapeutic level for the participants and the majority of the interventions were based on strategies for intuitive grievers (Jordan & McMenamy, 2004). Furthermore, the interventions were often offered long after the loss. For example, the modal client in the studies reviewed by Allumbaugh and Hoyt (1999) was bereaved for 27 months before starting the intervention. Recently the discussion has shifted to focus less on whether or not grief counseling is effective, but instead on the specific factors that are related to positive outcomes (e.g., Association for Death Education and Counseling (ADEC), 2008; Larson & Hoyt, 2007b; Neimeyer, 2010).

What can psychotherapists do to improve the chances that their bereaved clients will benefit from grief counseling? Evidence from current research and client reports suggest three important things for grief therapists to keep in mind. First, counseling should be individualized to the widower (Worden, 2009). Psychotherapists should avoid relying unquestioningly on a single theory and set of interventions for bereaved clients. Second, clients should be self-referred. While it is important to remove barriers to counseling (especially for men who are less likely to use psychological services (Brooks, 1998; Parkes, 1996)), psychotherapists should not offer grief counseling as a preventative measure (Currier et al., 2008; Larson & Hoyt, 2007b; Schut & Stroebe, 2005). Larson and Hoyt summarize this perspective by suggesting a policy of "reach, but don't grab" (p. 163). Finally, psychotherapists should be welcoming and empathic toward bereaved clients, and they should seek first to understand the client's unique circumstances and presenting concerns before jumping in with interventions and explanations. All of these considerations are likely to enhance a widower's counseling experience.

Common Factors in Grief Counseling

A reminder is necessary before going further. When discussing counseling processes and techniques, it is easy to fall into the trap of believing that the right intervention or adhering to a systematic process is all that is necessary to help bereaved clients. This is understandable given that publications about processes and techniques of grief counseling tend to present a series of steps and lists of techniques to be employed (and this chapter is no exception). Unfortunately this leads to psychotherapists focusing too much on choosing the 'best' technique, and too little attention is paid to the therapeutic relationship and other common factors in counseling (see Frank & Frank, 1991). As Jordan and Neimeyer (2003) state:

> Although there is still debate about this point, there is convincing evidence that the non-specific, relational, and contextual aspects of psychotherapy are probably the most important "active ingredient" in the

treatment process, rather than specific techniques or procedures (see Deegear & Lawson, 2003, and Wampold, 2001, for recent reviews). (p. 780)

While specific techniques can be immensely helpful, psychotherapists should never use them without considering the client's entire circumstances and without tailoring them with the help of the client. Thomas Attig (1996, 2000) is one of the strongest advocates for viewing the care of the bereaved as a holistic process and avoiding the trap of deconstructing grief into meaningless parts. Similarly, Alan Wolfelt (2006) is an ardent champion of working *with* clients (a process he calls *companioning*) instead of treating bereaved individuals as in the medical model. I recommend psychotherapists working with bereaved clients should be familiar with the works of both authors.

Goals of Grief Counseling

I have not found a better definition of the overall goal of grief counseling than the one offered by Winokuer and Harris (2012):

> Counselors who work with bereaved individuals understand that although the grieving process may involve tremendous amounts of pain and adjustment, the goal of grief counseling is to facilitate the unfolding of the healthy and adaptive aspects of the process as it is manifested within each client, trusting that this unfolding will eventually help the bereaved individual to re-enter life in a way that is meaningful. (p. 15)

Not only is it important to help the client develop goals and work toward them, but it is also critical to help the client predict the various outcomes associated with achieving those goals including the benefits and drawbacks. For example, if a widower's stated goal for grief counseling is not to experience any sadness, it is appropriate to help the client see that an absence of sadness is likely only possible with completely forgetting his wife (which is likely impossible anyway). A careful balance must be struck between helping the widower with his goals and helping the client examine the likely outcomes, positive and negative, of achieving those outcomes. The client may find that his goals need to be adjusted to be realistic and ultimately beneficial. Because men are likely to have less experience with counseling and may have more misconceptions about the goals, practice, and outcomes of counseling, the counselor may need to spend more time educating the client about the typical process and outcomes of counseling. This can have the added benefit of dispelling myths about counseling early in the process.

Avoidance of Goals

As with clients with other presenting concerns, widowers may not actually want counseling to move forward for several reasons (Rando, 1993). One is because of the fear that he may forget or lose his connection to his partner. Rando suggests that this is why it is important to differentiate between healthy ongoing connections to the deceased and unhealthy pathological ties to the deceased. Another reason clients may fear improvement is the belief that they may be emotionally overwhelmed during the counseling process and suffer a complete 'breakdown.' A third reason is that the client believes he should be punished for real or imagined misgivings (see Grollman, 1996). In these situations, the client clings to the pain associated with the loss as penance for his misgivings. All of these potential factors mean that the psychotherapist may need to negotiate the reasons for seeking counseling and the possible inducements for the client to discourage progress. These roadblocks to counseling and therapy are more likely to come from individuals with more complicated grief situations.

Closure or Resolution as a Goal

Bereaved clients frequently cite 'closure,' 'resolution,' or 'recovery' as goals of grief counseling (Doka & Martin, 2010). I believe these are some of the trickiest terms in grief counseling. There is significant debate within the field regarding whether terms such as *closure*, *resolution*, or *recovery* should be used when discussing grief outcomes or goals. Some researchers, often those more sympathetic to grief work and cutting ties (e.g., Sanders, 1999; Tatelbaum, 1984), argue that these terms are appropriate if defined correctly because a resolution to grief can be achieved. Researchers who agree with this perspective are quick to point out that this resolution does not imply that the deceased is forgotten, nor that the bereaved will never again experience painful moments. Tatelbaum describes it this way:

> To recover fully from a loss means to finish or completely let go. Finishing with a dead loved one does not erase the love or the memories, but it does mean that we have accepted the death, that the pain and sorrow have lessened, and that we feel free to reinvest in our lives. . . . Finishing involves directly experiencing or expressing anew or again all the emotions connected with the unfinished situation, experiencing the full impact again in the now, until all the feelings are dissipated. The goal of finishing is to move feelings or experiences from foreground to background, to gain relief, and to attain some shift in perspective. (p. 107)

Generally speaking, these theorists suggest that grief has been resolved when the bereaved has finished his grief work and reinvested in living.

Theorists from the opposing perspective caution that using terms such as *closure*, *resolution*, or *recovery* promote misconceptions about the grief process. These misconceptions include the grief work assumption, the cutting ties perspective, and the belief that the bereaved can return to his or her previous worldview. For example, the term *recovery* is problematic because it suggests a return to previous functioning akin to recovery from a broken leg. Instead, these theorists argue that clients should be encouraged to think in terms of *readjustment* (Archer, 1999) or *accommodation* (Rando, 1993) to their loss given that it is impossible to return to a world where the deceased is living (Weiss, 1993). Rando suggests that terms like *accommodation* "captures more accurately the reality that the loss can be integrated appropriately into the rest of life but that a truly final closure usually cannot be obtained, nor is it even desirable" (p. 40). Theorists in this camp argue that implying or telling clients that closure or resolution is possible sets them up to expect reaching a point of never feeling sadness or pain associated with the loss (Shuchter & Zisook, 1993). In my own work I avoid terms like closure, resolution, or recovery. I believe that it is more helpful for widowers to begin thinking about life after their partner's death as being fundamentally different from what it was before.

As with the concepts of grief work and cutting ties, the disagreement between the two camps is generally a matter of degree. Contemporary theorists on both sides acknowledge aspects of the other. Those advocating for conceptualizing grief outcome in terms of resolution or recovery understand that resolution does not mean never experiencing painful reactions, but like the idea of providing hope to the bereaved by suggesting that this painful chapter will not continue indefinitely. Conversely, the other side recognizes that grief reactions lessen and that most grievers reach a point that is qualitatively different than their initial, acute grief. However, they do not want to provide a false perception that the bereaved person can return to the world as he previously knew it. Even more important than the use or avoidance of specific terms is that the counselor and client have a common understanding of what those terms mean and their implications for their work together.

Phases and Techniques of Counseling Widowers

I have adapted Doka and Martin's (2010) three phases of grief counseling to provide a context for the process and techniques of counseling widowers; these three phases include (1) the opening phase, (2) the intermediate phase, and (3) the final phase. In the opening phase, the counselor attempts to build an initial therapeutic relationship with the widower, to assess his current functioning, to learn about the widower and the effects of his loss, and to begin developing counseling goals. The intermediate phase is when the majority of work is done including the use of specific techniques. In the final phase the psychotherapist and the widower review the progress made, identify and prepare for ongoing topics of concern, and begin the process of termination. Throughout the description of the phases I will describe specific techniques that may be useful.

Before beginning to help others with their grief, therapists must engage in reflection about their own losses and their grief reactions. Similar to the reflection necessary before working with multicultural clients, therapists must examine their own assumptions about loss including how grief 'should' be expressed, the validity of various styles of grief, as well as cultural, familial, and class factors that influence grief (Doka & Martin, 2002; Worden, 2009). Psychotherapists may inadvertently disenfranchise their grieving clients if they fail to examine their own preconceptions about loss and grief reactions.

Opening Phase

Intake sessions and early counseling sessions can be deceptively difficult. As experienced therapists already know, the initial session with a client is challenging because of the numerous tasks that must be accomplished; furthermore, the demands of these tasks are often in conflict. For example, therapists need to: (1) communicate information to the client so he can make an informed decision about entering into psychotherapy, (2) assess the client's functioning and any emergency needs, (3) allow the client to discuss his presenting concerns, and (4) begin to establish a therapeutic relationship. Unfortunately the information the psychotherapist needs in the first session is not always the same information that the client is ready to share. It can be difficult to be as empathic and welcoming as one would like when you also need information for intake and reimbursement forms. However, it is critical to allow bereaved clients to tell their story during the first session. As Winokuer and Harris (2012) state,

> Much of grief counseling involves "bearing witness" to your client's story of loss—who he or she was before the loss, the relationship to the person who died if the loss was a death, or the nature of loss and its meaning, and what life has been since the loss occurred. (p. 91)

While challenging, the first sessions require balancing all of these components.

Therapists may need to provide more time for allaying widowers' concerns and misconceptions given that widowers, especially those with no previous counseling experience or who identify with traditional male gender norms, may be particularly suspicious and uneasy about entering psychotherapy. As I described in Chapter 2, therapists can take specific steps to be welcoming and empathic toward widowers seeking psychotherapy. Specifically, it can be useful to discuss the widower's path to therapy (including any pressure from others), answer his questions about the process of therapy, and depict his choice to pursue counseling as a courageous choice instead of a weakness (see Englar-Carlson & Stevens, 2006; Stevens & Englar-Carlson, 2006). For example, it may be necessary to talk explicitly about how therapy works, how your goal is not to 'mess with his mind,' and a promise to be open and genuine in your reactions (see Kiselica, 2006).

Widower Assessment

Along with the typical assessment questions covered during the first several sessions with a new client, psychotherapists should also ask widowers about bereavement-specific topics. In the "Widower Assessment" box, I have listed questions that may be pertinent as part of the assessment process. The questions are not provided in any specific order and psychotherapists should adapt the questions to the needs of their clients.

Widower Assessment

Early Experiences With Loss and Death
- Tell me about your previous losses (including death and non-death losses)
- Growing up, what 'rules' did you learn regarding loss and death?
  - Did you learn that men and women respond similarly or differently to loss?
- What were your early experiences with death and loss? How did adults react to death? What types of death rituals have you attended and what was your reaction to them? (Yalom, 2002)

Pre-Loss Factors
- Tell me about your partner and your relationship.
- Tell me about the cause of your partner's death.
- What changes did you make leading up to your partner's death (e.g., caregiving, etc.)?
- Tell me about the last time you saw your partner. Do you have any regrets related to that meeting?

Regarding the Death
- Where you present at the time of death? If so, what was it like to be there?
- Was your partner's death preventable?
- Was your partner's death expected or unexpected?

Thoughts and Reactions Post-Loss
- What is the meaning of the loss to you? (Neimeyer, 2006; Malkinson, 2007; Rando, 1993)
- Do you have any thoughts or images that you can't seem to let go of? (Malkinson, 2007)
- Are there any places you are afraid to go? (Malkinson, 2007)
- Do you feel guilty about anything related to your partner's death?
- Do you experience anger, fear, shame, or relief regarding your partner's death?
- Have you had thoughts about hurting yourself?
- What has surprised you about your reaction to your partner's death?
- Describe any 'moments of significance' or 'threshold experiences.'

Feelings Post-Loss
- Do you feel a need to express your feelings? Do you have opportunities to express your feelings?

Physical Health Post-Loss
- What physical changes have you experienced? (e.g., eating, sleeping, physical ailments, weight changes, etc.)
- Have you changed your consumption of alcohol? Has it caused a problem?
- Do you use any substances that influence your physical or mental health?
- How have you met your needs for intimacy?

Post-Loss Rituals and Acts of Remembrance
- What rituals or acts of remembrance were conducted? Did you participate in them? (Doka, 1993)
- What was your reaction during and following the rituals?
- Are there any acts of remembrance that you are still planning or have been left unfinished?

Continuing Bonds
- Are there times when you feel an ongoing connection to your partner? When/where?
- Have you had any unusual experiences following your partner's death?
- Do you visit the gravesite or other special places that are associated with your partner?

Spiritual/Religious Reaction
- Have your spiritual/religious views been challenged by your loss? Have your religious and spiritual views been a source of support? (Doka, 1993)

Post-Loss Benefits
- Is there anything about your partner that you don't miss? (Worden, 2009)
- Are there times when you feel relief that your partner has died?
- Do you have any reactions that you can't share with others because you don't think they would understand or you're afraid they would judge you?

Strengths
- What have you done that has really helped?
- What strengths (personally or in your support network) do you have that are helpful to you?

Family, Friends, and Social Support
- Do you feel supported in your grief? Do you feel like others recognize your loss and that you have a right to feel grief? (Doka, 2002a)
- Have you wanted to be around other people? Who are the people that mean the most to you now?
- How have your friends, family members, and co-workers responded to your situation?
- Do you have someone with whom you can share your deepest thoughts and reactions?

Presenting Concerns
- Tell me about what brought you to counseling? What is unfinished or stuck?
- Tell me about a typical day—please be specific (Yalom, 2002)

Direct Action and Experiments

Bereaved men, especially those who are instrumental grievers, often ask direct questions and want to engage in problem-solving (Doka & Martin, 2010). Given that most men come to psychotherapy reluctantly, it is often important for them to feel as if they are making progress quickly. This does not mean that psychotherapists must respond with direct advice, but they should recognize the importance of the widowers' questions and requests. I particularly like how Robertson (2006) describes his response to such direct requests for advice and action:

> I take the question, "What can I do about this?" seriously. When a man asks for an action plan, he generally is ready to act. So I talk about

creating "an experiment" to "see what might happen" if he were to change his approach. We might develop a plan and practice the new behavior in the consultation room itself (e.g., a stress-management exercise, a behavioral rehearsal). My role is to provide a "menu" of strategies that he might try and then to let him choose and shape his own experiment. (p. 130)

Men often respond well to this approach for several reasons. By implementing an experiment a widower can meet his goal of making quick and direct progress toward his goals while freeing the counselor from providing direct advice. Furthermore, experiments provide the widower with information which can be used to judge the usefulness of the adjustment. It can be reassuring to the client to emphasize that the experiment can be temporary. If it works, great; if it does not work the experiment can be cancelled and another option can be explored. Throughout this process, the counselor helps clarify the widower's concerns, enlists him to collaboratively develop a range of options and potential outcomes, and later helps evaluate the results.

Avoiding the Most Common Mistake

Counselors-in-training and psychotherapists with minimal experience counseling the bereaved can unintentionally make a common mistake: attempting to remove the client's suffering through reassurance and clichés. It is easy for therapists to fall into this trap and attempt to help clients feel better because therapists likely have entered the field for this very reason—to help alleviate another person's suffering (see Malkinson, 2007). Most therapists avoid this rookie mistake in other situations; they do not tell clients who are depressed to 'just cheer up' and would never tell a client suffering with an anxiety disorder to just 'calm down.' But for some reason (I suspect it is our discomfort with death and our death-denying culture), we forget this when talking with bereaved clients. Consequently we fall back on clichés and trying to help clients reframe their circumstances more positively when they primarily want to share their loss with a compassionate listener. Winokuer and Harris (2012) remind us that there is no magic wand for counselors:

The first rule of thumb is that you cannot "fix it" or make it better. There is no "ah hah" phrase or intervention that "works." You cannot bring back the deceased person. You cannot replace what is irreplaceable. A person cannot go back in time and "unknow" what is now known through a significant loss experience. (p. 90)

It is likely that bereaved clients have already heard unhelpful comments or clichés. In a study of almost 100 bereaved individuals, four 'support tactics' were identified that were consistently found to be unhelpful by the bereaved individuals: (1) providing unsolicited advice ("Do X and you'll feel better"); (2) minimizing their feelings or trying to be cheerful ("It can't be that bad"); (3) encouraging recovery ("You should feel better by now"); and (4) overly identifying with the bereaved's feelings ("I know how you're feeling") (Lehman, Ellard, & Wortman, 1986). Psychotherapists should be careful not to become yet another person in a widower's life who minimizes his concerns, offers premature optimism, or attempts to rush him through his grief.

Identifying and Exploring Common Reactions

In Chapter 6, I outlined many of the common grief reactions that widowers may experience including denial, shock and numbness, guilt, anger, shame, fear, helplessness, meaninglessness, loneliness, relief, and deification. An ongoing task for a psychotherapist is to help the widower identify and explore his reactions to his partner's death (Worden, 2009). This task begins immediately and continues throughout the counseling process. It is highly likely that the widower will experience more than one of these reactions and his reactions will change throughout his grief process.

Intermediate Phase

The intermediate phase is typically where the bulk of therapeutic work is done. For some widowers this may be a relatively short-term process where the client receives general support and clarification of thoughts and feelings within the context of a therapeutic relationship. For others this phase may be a longer process involving a deep examination of relationships, loss experiences, and serious psychological and physical reactions. In this section I provide a brief overview of how different theoretical orientations may approach grief counseling with widowers and several specific counseling techniques. My goal is to provide a thorough enough description of each technique that it could be incorporated into a psychotherapist's toolbox. Of course, each therapist must determine which techniques will fit within his or her theoretical orientation.

Specific Approaches to Grief Counseling

Most of the modern theories of grief allow for a large amount of individuality in how the goals of the theory are met. This is useful because no one grief counseling perspective has been demonstrated to be more efficacious than others (Neimeyer, 2000). This provides therapists and clients with a great deal of flexibility. For example, there are several different ways clients could fulfill Worden's (2009) second task: To process the pain of grief. This processing of pain could be accomplished by expressing feelings, thinking, or taking physical action (Doka & Martin, 2010).

Widowers use a wide variety of strategies to deal with their grief. Brabant, Forsyth, and Melancon (1992) conducted interviews with 20 widowers whose partners had used a hospice provider. Fifteen of the participants reported that they dealt with their grief alone and provided a variety of answers when asked what they did when they felt pain:

> Four prayed when they were in pain; four "kept busy" and one "worked around the house." Two concentrated on memories. For example, "I look at old pictures and remember the good things . . . I'm glad she was home to die." Two walked, one cried, and one screamed or hit things. One read or talked to a neighbor "if she has time," one got together with other people and one just kept to himself. (ellipses in original; p. 41)

Their responses suggest that widowers use spiritual, physical, cognitive, and affective strategies to deal with their grief-related pain. Given these results, psychotherapists should be knowledgeable about a wide variety of strategies and approaches to assisting widowers. In this section I will describe how different counseling approaches, including client-centered, affective, cognitive and cognitive-behavioral, constructivist/meaning reconstruction and existential, and spiritually focused perspectives can be used to assist widowers.

Client-Centered Focus

Winokuer and Harris (2012) suggest that "grief counseling at its heart is very person-centered in its approach" (p. 90). Using a client-centered focus, therapists can focus on the unique grief experience of the client and reduce the chance of overapplying grief models to the client's individual situation. Similarly, it is critical to communicate unconditional positive regard and acceptance. Bereaved individuals often report real or perceived lack of acceptance of their grief reactions, especially if their reactions are expressed beyond the artificially shortened time frame in which they are expected to grieve (Servaty-Seib, 2004). Therefore, widowers who are continuing to experience normal grief at six months post-loss may begin to experience disapproval from others who believe that their grief should be completed. The counselor's acceptance and normalizing of these grief behaviors can be incredibly powerful for clients who feel that they must now hide or inhibit their grief. Without question, an emphasis on acceptance, unconditional positive regard, and empathy (see Rogers, 1951) should be the foundation upon which more specific techniques are built.

Affective Strategies

Affective strategies include any theory or technique that focuses on sharing emotions. When the grief work assumption is paired with the fact that affective expression is generally valued over other counseling strategies (see Sue & Sue, 2013), it is easy to see why affective strategies have traditionally been the focus of grief counseling. While it is no longer assumed that grief must be expressed affectively for healing to occur, it can still be a helpful part of an individual's grieving process. Some widowers, particularly intuitive grievers, will find that expressing feelings can be helpful; however, many men struggle with the incompatibility of traditional male gender norms and sharing feelings. Psychotherapists can assist widowers by helping create an environment where they are comfortable and can choose to express their emotions. As mentioned in Chapter 5, widowers with an instrumental grieving style may still express their feelings, but are likely to be less comfortable doing this with others and will not use affective strategies as their primary adaptive strategy.

Widowers who are less comfortable expressing emotions may benefit from reframing their views of their feelings. For example, Robertson (2006) believes male clients can benefit from learning that emotions can be viewed as tools to gain more information about a situation.

> Conceptually, it makes sense to many men to think of emotions as having a purpose, a function. That is, emotions direct attention to a situation to resolve it. . . . This suggests to men that emotions are not something to avoid; they are realities that help people adapt more effectively to their worlds. In this way, a man does not have to think he must become "all emotional" or that he must "cry like my wife" to work effectively with me. (p. 130)

By pointing out the utility of emotions, psychotherapists can help widowers bring together their cognitive and affective traits to better understand their circumstances.

Psychotherapists should note two considerations regarding using affective strategies with bereaved men. First, for many men affective strategies should be gradually introduced. For example, emotionally focused counseling can be paired with other activities or topics such as physical actions or masculine metaphors. Second, it is important for psychotherapists to understand (and to help prepare their clients) that bereaved men who express their feelings outside of the therapy office may be met with resistance. While some family members and friends of widowers may welcome and support a widower who is more emotionally expressive, others will be very uncomfortable with a man expressing his grief in such a way (Doka & Martin, 2010). Widowers can benefit from affective strategies as long as the psychotherapist neither uses them exclusively nor dictates that expressing emotions is the only way to grieve adaptively.

Cognitive and Cognitive-Behavioral Strategies

Grief counselors and researchers have often overlooked the importance of cognitions in grief, especially when the circumstances of death were traumatic (Malkinson, 2007; Powers & Wampold, 1994; Rando, 1984). Doka and Martin (2010) warn that counselors who only endorse affective strategies can impair their work with clients who grieve instrumentally. Furthermore, these counselors will have more difficulty understanding the conflicts that instrumental widowers may be having with family and friends who grieve in a different style. Male clients often view cognitive and behavioral strategies as less threatening. Cognitive strategies can help with several specific aspects of loss for widowers including organizing their reaction, dealing with avoidance of reminders of the deceased, and engaging in problem-solving.

A cognitive approach to grief can help bereaved widowers organize their reaction and response to their loss. Thus, they gain a sense of agency and hope when facing the changes that have occurred. Furthermore, bereaved individuals who are able to moderate their grief reaction by alternating between their grief and non-grief needs may be better able to adjust to their loss (Powers & Wampold, 1994). This is similar to the process of oscillating between restoration-oriented coping and loss-oriented coping in the Dual Process Model (Stroebe & Schut, 1999).

Previous researchers (e.g., Ramsay, 1977) have hypothesized that taking extreme measures to avoid reminders of the deceased (e.g., never discussing the deceased, removing all reminders of the deceased, etc.) was analogous to a phobic response. Consequently, they used exposure techniques such as flooding and systematic desensitization to confront the bereaved individual with the feared stimulus (e.g., reminders of the deceased such as pictures and personal items). The goal was to decrease the bereaved individual's anxiety and cut ties with the deceased.

Malkinson (2007) argues that avoidance of the deceased in various forms of complicated grief is less like a phobia and more similar to the process and symptoms seen in PTSD. The major difference is that individuals with PTSD attempt to avoid any memories related to the traumatic event while bereaved individuals are avoiding specific reminders yet want to continue to maintain other memories of their loved one. For example, a widower may desperately want to remember his wife and their happy years together, yet may also avoid any thoughts related to her illness or death. Consequently, it is not uncommon for bereaved individuals to use avoidance as a way to maintain a sense of control, yet it often results in feeling out of control. For example, some bereaved individuals will

> avoid entering the deceased's room, or other reminders such as photos, certain food, music, or places that were of special interest to the deceased. For others any reminder of the circumstances of the loss is avoided because of the difficulty in confronting the finality of the loss; the belief that if one avoids certain reminders it is a way of not having to deal with the "knowing in the heart" that he or she is dead. (Malkinson, 2007, p. 107)

Malkinson (2007) has adapted exposure techniques to help bereaved individuals adjust their avoidance of reminders of the deceased to more adaptive responses. The process is similar to traditional flooding or systematic desensitization processes, yet the goal is on removing anxiety and avoidance behaviors as opposed to cutting ties with the deceased. For example, a widower who cannot walk into his deceased wife's room would be educated about the cognitive and physiological nature of fear and anxiety as well as taught anxiety reduction techniques. Next the psychotherapist would ask him to predict potential reactions and obstacles and construct a hierarchy of his fears. The widower would be asked to take the first step (imaginally or in vivo) and report his response. Ultimately the goal would be to have the widower be able to return to his wife's room and be able to enjoy reconnecting with his memories of her in that space.

Men's desire to solve problems and engage in action-empathy are two examples of strengths of traditional masculinity (Kiselica & Englar-Carlson, 2010; Levant, 1995). Widowers, especially instrumental grievers, may find solace in fulfilling daily tasks, solving problems, and gathering information. These tasks allow widowers "to 'do something,' reinforcing a sense of control in an otherwise helpless time" (Doka & Martin, 2010, p. 173). These efforts may be focused on a short-term task (e.g., planning the funeral), or may entail long-term endeavors (e.g., starting a foundation, raising money, etc.).

Cognitive strategies can resonate with many widowers, especially those who process their grief in an instrumental style. Given that many men are concerned about being asked to express their feelings and worry that they may become emotionally out-of-control in a therapy session, cognitive strategies can build from their strengths and be a more comfortable entry into counseling. Furthermore, cognitive therapy's educational nature, planned approach, and focus on specific results can provide widowers with a framework and process that matches their problem-solving style. While affective strategies can also be helpful, bereaved men may prefer to begin with more cognitive methods before eventually easing into more feelings-oriented strategies (Doka & Martin, 2010).

Constructivist / Meaning Reconstruction and Existential Approaches

In this section I have combined the meaning reconstruction and existential approaches; these two perspectives share many common elements. Both perspectives focus on meaning as defined by the client, and both place a strong emphasis on the therapist's collaboration and 'being' with the client instead of focusing on techniques (Servaty-Seib, 2004). Furthermore, both approaches focus on the client's need to develop new interpretations of his life, his responsibility as the author of his story, and his individual perception of reality (see Yalom, 1980; Neimeyer, 2000).

CONSTRUCTIVIST PSYCHOTHERAPY AND MEANING RECONSTRUCTION

Both constructivism and meaning reconstruction approaches focus on the meaning the individual constructs regarding his loss. Mahoney (2003) defines constructivism as:

> a view of humans as active, meaning-making individuals who are afloat on webs of relationships while they are moving along streams of life that relentlessly require new directions and connections. . . . A large part of what therapists and clients do together in constructive psychotherapy is to weave new possibilities for experiencing. This is much easier said than done. (p. xii)

Neimeyer (2000) describes *meaning reconstruction* as the bereaved individual's process of finding meaning in his own life as well as in the death of the loved one, integrating this meaning deep into his life, recognizing the interpersonal and cultural aspects of meaning making, and understanding that this is a process and not a destination or answer to be uncovered. Although research using constructivist perspectives has been criticized for imprecise definitions and assessment (see Park, 2008), therapists can avoid this pitfall because they can focus on learning the specific worldview and assumptions of an individual client. Works by Neimeyer (2001, 2006) and Mahoney (2003) are required reading for psychotherapists interested in incorporating these perspectives into their counseling process.

Constructivist perspectives argue that each person constructs his or her world based on a complex interaction among personal experiences, social interactions, and cultural influences (Neimeyer, 2000). Individuals will share some of these influences with others, yet will often have unique events and individual interpretations of those events; consequently, their reaction to events will be distinctive, although it certainly may have some commonalities with others. In constructivist therapy with the bereaved, the psychotherapist's goal is to learn about each client's distinctive worldview and how his loss fits and does not fit that worldview.

Following the death of a partner, a widower will need to adjust his current worldview (assimilation) or construct a completely new understanding of his situation. Or in other words:

> When events shake our sense of self and world, we respond by trying to interpret them in ways consistent with our overall theories and identities [assimilation]. When these attempts fail, and our most basic sense of self is assaulted, we lose our grip on familiar reality, and are forced to reestablish another [accommodation]. (Neimeyer, 2006, pp. 89–90)

An example of assimilation is an older man who has seen many friends and family members lose their partners. This man knows that his wife's family has a history of Alzheimer's disease; long ago he adjusted his perspective to expect that he would be taking care of his wife and would outlive her. Therefore, after a diagnosis and years of caregiving, he has already adjusted his expectations and the eventual death is still difficult, but does not require as much adjustment in his constructed worldview.

Conversely, accommodation occurs when an experience, such as the death of a loved one, forces an individual to create radically new ways of understanding his world. For example, I worked with a 19-year-old man whose fiancé had died in a car accident leaving him to care for their 3-year-old daughter. Although he knew that it was not uncommon for people to die in car accidents, he had to completely reorder his assumptive world to include the fact that not only do *some* people die, but *his* fiancée died. An additional challenge is that he had to face this new reality without any warning. Several researchers (e.g., Parkes, 1993; Rando, 1993; Redmond, 1996) have hypothesized that this lack of warning and challenge to one's worldview are why sudden and traumatic losses are more difficult to adjust to for the bereaved.

For all bereaved individuals there is a difference between the expectation or knowledge of a loss and the actual experience of a loss. This difference may be tremendously large or a small adjustment. Let me emphasize that simply because a loss is expected or requires a smaller reconstruction of personal meaning does not mean that the loss will be easy for the bereaved. I am simply acknowledging that those who are faced with a significant restructuring may struggle even more or longer as they reconcile their pre- and post-loss worlds.

EXISTENTIAL PERSPECTIVE

I believe it is impossible to work with widowers and not deal with existential themes. Yalom (2002) states that there are four fundamental concerns of existence: death, isolation, meaninglessness, and freedom. Although existential contributions can be difficult to study given the complexity of the concepts, research has supported the contribution of existential variables in grief. In a study of almost 100 older widowers, Fry (2001b) found that existential variables, including personal meaning, participation in organized religion, spiritual involvement, importance of religion, comfort from religion, sense of inner peace, accessibility to religious support, and optimistic outlook, were significantly correlated with the well-being of the participants.

Both constructivist and existential perspectives value the process of questioning and creating meaning in one's life. This process is common in bereaved individuals. Davis, Wortman, Lehman, and Silver (2000) found that 70% of their spousally bereaved participants had tried to find meaning in or make sense of their loss. Other studies have reported that widowers who were strongly dependent on their partners and whose partners experienced a sudden, traumatic, or premature death are more likely to have difficulty finding meaning in their loss (Davis et al., 2000). In some of these situations, the bereaved may be unable to develop an acceptable rationale for why the death occurred; instead, they are left with generating a personally relevant reason or response. For example, a 25-year-old widower whose pregnant wife dies after being hit by a drunk driver 18 months after their wedding may be unable to construct a satisfactory explanation for why her death occurred. His only option may be to focus on the meaning that comes from any strengths he develops as a result of his loss or the good he does for others in honor of his wife. As Davis and Nolen-Hoeksema (2001) suggest:

> Focusing on what good has come from the experience may not help one make sense of the loss as much as it distracts from it. Learning

something new about oneself or the value of relationships, for instance, does not explain why the loss happened or what purpose was served by it. But such lessons learned may take some of the pain of suffering away from not understanding why. (p. 734)

(For another example of this process, see the box regarding Viktor Frankl). However, psychotherapists should be careful not to engage in the process of finding benefits prematurely. The widower could easily interpret this as glossing over his loss to 'look on the sunny side' of life. Ideally the process of meaning reconstruction, including the recognition of any benefits, should be driven by the client.

Given that constructivist therapy involves constructing new meaning and is more extensive than simply changing one's thoughts, the techniques associated with meaning reconstruction are likewise deeper and seek to facilitate new understanding. A bereaved individual's new perspective would not only be a cognitive change, but also often a physical, emotional, philosophical, and spiritual change. Rituals are uniquely suited to helping individuals find meaning in their loss (Davis et al., 2000).

Viktor Frankl (1959/1984) provided one of my favorite descriptions of helping a widower. Frankl, a pioneer in existential therapy, emphasized that humans have personal responsibility and the power to choose one's own attitude even under the most desperate situations. He acknowledged that in unalterable situations (e.g., the death of a partner) the only option is to choose to find meaning. Frankl suggests this is a uniquely human process: "to transform a personal tragedy into a triumph, to turn one's predicament into a human achievement" (p. 135). What would this look like in practice? Frankl describes a time when he was approached by an elderly physician whose wife had died two years previously. The physician was deeply depressed.

> Now, how could I help him? What should I tell him? Well, I refrained from telling him anything but instead confronted him with the question, "What would have happened, Doctor, if you had died first, and your wife would have had to survive you?" "Oh," he said, "for her this would have been terrible; how she would have suffered!" Whereupon I replied, "You see, Doctor, such a suffering has been spared her, and it was you who have spared her this suffering—to be sure, at the price that now you have to survive and mourn her." He said no word but shook my hand and calmly left my office. In some way, suffering ceases to be suffering at the moment it finds a meaning, such as the meaning of a sacrifice. (p. 135)

Spiritually Focused Perspective

The death of a partner often causes the widower to try to make sense of the death and develop reasons for why life is still worth living. Sometimes his previous assumptions about life, religion, and spirituality can be swept away leaving "the bereaved feeling abandoned by God or cheated by fate" (Neimeyer & Jordan, 2002, pp. 108–109). This can lead the widower to a search for new religious and spiritual understandings or may cause him to abandon spiritual explanations for his loss. For example, C. S. Lewis, one of the most famous Christian writers of the 20th century, wrote about his new perspective on his faith after his wife died:

> From the rational point of view, what new factor has H.'s [his wife's] death introduced into the problem of the universe? What grounds has it given me for doubting all that I believe? I knew already that these things, and worse, happened daily. I would have said that I had taken them into account. I had been warned—I had warned myself—not to reckon on worldly happiness. We were even promised sufferings. They were part of the programme. We were even told, "Blessed are they that mourn," and I accepted it. I've got nothing that I hadn't bargained for. Of course it is different when the thing happens to oneself, not to others, and in reality, not in imagination. (pp. 36–37)

> Talk to me about the truth of religion and I'll listen gladly. Talk to me about the duty of religion and I'll listen submissively. But don't come talking to me about the consolations of religion or I shall suspect that you don't understand. (1961, p. 25)

Bereaved individuals often receive well-intentioned advice regarding spiritual and religious coping; this advice can viewed by the widower as positive or negative (Lehman et al., 1986). Anecdotally, many widowed individuals remember a comment or two from well-meaning individuals who suggest that taking a new perspective, having greater faith, or accepting the wisdom of a higher power could aid their grief. Kuhn (2002) explains the difficulties this may create for the bereaved:

> Well-intentioned people, trying to explain a loss to themselves as well as a griever, might suggest that a stronger faith would help the bereaved cope or that God intended to take the loved one or the relationship away in order to teach a lesson or achieve a greater purpose. This response is destructive to the psyche and the faith of the grieving person. It suggests not only that one has to deal with a loss, but

that one also must deal with a defective faith and a God that initiates loss in order to achieve God's own purposes. It also assumes that the comforter knows everything there is to know about the griever and about the will of the divine. (p. 125)

Psychotherapists must be careful not to join these voices in admonishing the widower for a lack of faith or trust in a higher power. Psychotherapists may be in a unique situation to be supportive of the widower who is spiritually disenfranchised.

Grief Counseling Techniques

I have not assigned these techniques to a specific theory because most counseling techniques can be used in conjunction with multiple theoretical approaches. For example, journaling can be used to help the client express his feelings or as a way to explore his cognitive response to loss. Psychotherapists should be mindful of how a technique can be used to match the widower's grief style and other relevant factors. Furthermore, psychotherapists should always use techniques within a larger model or theoretical orientation lest the techniques become a 'grief band-aid.'

Journaling and Letter Writing

Writing as a ritual or counseling technique can take a wide variety of formats and fulfill a variety of purposes. Writing as a therapeutic intervention can generally be categorized into writing for reflective purposes (e.g., journaling, memoirs, etc.) or writing for ritualistic purposes (e.g., writing to the deceased to say good-bye, ask or provide forgiveness, or express a shift in the bereaved's grief process, etc.). Pennebaker (1997) and his colleagues have completed a great deal of research on writing interventions with individuals who have experienced loss and trauma. Although writing interventions have not consistently received empirical support (e.g. Stroebe et al., 2002), many grief therapists advocate their use (e.g., Doka & Martin, 2010; Worden, 2009).

Some widowers have benefitted from writing about their grief journey. Likely the most famous memoir by a widower is *A Grief Observed* by C. S. Lewis (1961). Other famous individuals have published autobiographies with portions devoted to the death of their partners and their grief experience: George Burns (1976) wrote about the death of Gracie Allen and Gene Wilder (2005) wrote about the death of Gilda Radner. Neil Peart (2002), the acclaimed drummer of the rock band *Rush*, wrote about his motorcycle odyssey following the deaths of his wife and daughter.

Continuous letter writing is one form of writing as connected to grief therapy. In this technique, the client is asked to write to the deceased daily and express anything he or she wishes. The client can read the entire letter or portions of it to the therapist. Malkinson (2007) provides an example of using letter writing techniques with a 73-year-old widower, David, who was experiencing significant grief reactions and depression 10 months after his wife of 50 years had died. When presented with the idea of using continual letter writing, David asked for a rationale for the intervention. "He agreed, but he was afraid that he would be instructed to sever his emotional connections from his wife" (p. 168). Even after writing his very first letter, David reported feeling some relief. In addition to using the therapy sessions to recall and discuss an earlier traumatic memory regarding his presence at his grandfather's death when he was a young boy, David was able to go longer between therapy sessions due to feeling better. As his reactions and perspective on his grief improved, David began writing less and less frequently until he was able to terminate therapy.

Bibliotherapy

While some widowers benefit from writing about their own experience, others find consolation in reading about how their peers have faced similar challenges. The benefits of educating oneself and learning from the strategies and successes of others are widely supported. Instrumental widowers may especially benefit from reading about their concerns. Doka and Martin (2010) describe how reading:

> is by its very nature cognitive and active. It is solitary. It allows dosing, that is, if the griever finds something too painful or difficult, he or she can set it aside for a while. And certainly it offers control. Grievers can choose the time and place that they use it. (p. 189)

One of the most important considerations in using bibliotherapy with any bereaved individual is choosing books and articles that reflect recent research and avoids perpetuating myths about grief. Ideally the source would reflect the grieving style of the widower.

Exercise

Widowers can benefit from exercise and other physical activity. Exercise can improve widowers' physical functioning (Chen, Gill, & Prigerson, 2005), provide an outlet for restless energy, and promote sleep. Furthermore, physical activity can provide the bereaved individual with solitary time for reflection or an opportunity to socialize with others without a focus on grief (Doka & Martin, 2010).

A middle-aged widower I interviewed provides an example of how exercise can serve multiple purposes. Rusty would exercise very early in the morning and had developed a camaraderie with the other early-rising gym patrons. Each patron knew that Rusty had recently lost his wife; they balanced their support with also giving him space. Rusty would work out vigorously, but would also cry at various times throughout his workout. He explained, "I would be doing a set of bicep curls and the tears would just be flowing down my face." Rusty had found a place to release his feelings, feel supported and accepted, and gain the benefits of physical exercise.

Empty Chair

The Gestalt technique of *empty chair* is commonly cited as a useful technique to use with bereaved individuals (e.g., Rando, 1993; Worden, 2009). Gestalt therapy emphasizes the individual's present, integrated experience, avoids placing a great priority on any one emotion, action, or behavior over another, and recognizes that each individual will have a unique grief experience (Perls, 1973; Tatelbaum, 1984). Grief, especially complicated grief, is viewed through the Gestalt lens as being work that is unfinished or perhaps never started. Furthermore, bereaved individuals often focus on the past (or sometimes the future), but rarely on the present. Therefore Gestalt approaches and techniques, such as the empty chair, can be particularly effective with clients who are stuck in the past, feel they have unfinished business with the deceased, and could benefit from a shift from focusing on the past to focusing on the here-and-now (Clark, 1982; Sabar, 2000). The empty chair technique aids this process by helping the widower to naturally complete his grief by allowing him to express reactions and responses that have gone unsaid.

Although there are many variations, the empty chair technique usually proceeds in this order. After being prepared for the exercise, the widower sits across from an empty chair and takes a moment to imagine that his partner is sitting there. The widower should use the present tense and statements should be made directly to the deceased as if he or she were actually sitting there. When appropriate, the widower may switch to the deceased's chair and speak for him or her (Tatelbaum, 1984; Worden, 2009).

For example, a widower may begin with "'I have never been able to say goodbye to you,' or 'I have carried around my sorrow at losing you for years now' or 'I still feel angry at you' or 'I have never had any feelings or reactions to your death'" (Tatelbaum, 1984, p. 110). The client is encouraged to say what he feels is natural and relevant. The widower may include statements that reaffirm the loss ("I know I am not going to see you again") and recognize what was lost ("You were the most loving person I knew," "You were my best friend, my favorite person to talk with," adapted from p. 111). Similarly, the client may find it helpful to list all of the cherished qualities of the deceased as well as her or his faults. Statements to the deceased beginning with "I wish . . ." may help the widower uncover unfinished hopes that may be standing in the way of progress.

This process may initially feel artificial to the client, but it often brings out strong emotions. It may be helpful to place a picture of the deceased in the chair to make the conversation feel more real. Psychotherapists should prepare bereaved clients before using the empty chair technique. It may be helpful to allow the client time to consider what he would like to say. Given the potential for a strong emotional reaction, bereaved men may want to feel as prepared as possible before engaging in this technique. Furthermore, the therapist should take time to thoroughly discuss the widower's reaction following the exercise.

Creative Methods

Creative methods in grief counseling can include having the client write poetry, paint, sculpt, use sandtray/sandplay, play music, dance, carve or build things, and other expressions. The challenges for counselors who want to use creative activities with widowers include the initial reaction of the client and finding an option that interests him. While some clients are surprised by the benefits of previously untried activities, others are turned off by activities they feel are 'hokey' or childish.

Personally, I have had more success in talking with widowers about creative hobbies that they have given up or 'projects' that they would like to undertake. I interviewed John, a 72-year-old widower who had been married for over 50 years before his wife died from breast cancer (Troyer, in press). John began taking painting classes a year after his wife died. He had been an avid painter before his wife became ill, but had not painted since her diagnosis. I am frequently surprised by the number of men who already have a project in mind when asked, "Is there something you have thought about doing or building that might be important to you?" For example, widowers have described projects they have built, including an outdoor prayer garden, flower bed, fountain, and photo display stand (Troyer, 2011). Certainly not every client will have a project in mind. Widowers may be intrigued by the idea of creating or building something, but may not know what to do. They may find it helpful to hear about various projects or activities that could be adapted to be meaningful for them.

An advantage to using or discussing creative works with widowers is that instrumental, intuitive, and blended grievers can benefit (Doka & Martin, 2010). The intent of the creative project simply needs to match their counseling goals and grieving style. Intuitive grievers will likely use their projects as a way of venting their feelings; instrumental grievers will likely focus on the planning before and during the project, the meanings associated with the project, and cognitive and/or physical challenges involved. As mentioned previously, this does not mean that the intuitive griever will not benefit from the physical and cognitive challenges and instrumental grievers will not have an affective response. In fact, it is hoped that both will benefit from their secondary adaptive strategies. For instrumental grievers, this can be another way to dose their feelings over the course of a project. A further benefit of artistic projects related to grieving is that they can achieve multiple goals including acknowledging the loss, affirming a continuing bond, expressing unspoken messages, and others.

Rituals

A ritual is "specific behavior or activity which gives symbolic expression to certain feelings and thoughts of the actor(s) individually or as a group" (Rando, 1985, p. 236). They may be one-time events or recurring throughout the grief process and they involve preparation and reflection (Roberts, 2003). Almost any of the previously mentioned techniques can be a component within a ritual. Rituals, especially post-funeral rituals, may be especially helpful for bereaved individuals because most Americans are increasingly separated from death, have less direct contact with the deceased (Cable, 1998; Lundgren & Houseman, 2010), and use traditional death rituals (i.e., funerals) less frequently (Gadberry, 2000). It is important to note that rituals do not need to be associated with a religious or spiritual tradition, but they should resonate with the client's worldview and beliefs.

Moments of Significance and Threshold Experiences

'Moments of Significance' are similar to rituals in that a widower recognizes a change in meaning in his life, but is different in that they are typically unplanned events. Frequently, the first time a moment of significance happens may be especially important for the widower; Fulghum (1995) calls these events 'threshold experiences' and argues that they are often powerful events. A widower will have numerous threshold experiences. They can be recognized as an answer to the statement: "I will never forget the first time I ___ since my wife/partner died" (modified from Fulghum, 1995). For example, a widower may recognize that he

> is taking his first trip to the grocery store with a list to feed just one person or the first time he sleeps in his bed alone. Psychotherapists should help the widower explore these events, examine if they are impeding the widower (i.e., he won't sleep in his own bed because he is afraid of acknowledging the fact that his partner will not return), and discuss their meaning.

Rituals related to loss, whether public or private, assist the bereaved in several ways. First, death rituals help reinforce the reality of the death and combat denial (Corr, Nabe, & Corr, 1994), which is a key aspect of most models of healthy grieving (e.g., Parkes, 1996; Sanders, 1999; Rando, 1993; Worden, 2009) and may be especially difficult when the loss is sudden or violent (Rando, 1984; Weeks, 1996). Public death rituals bring together social support for the bereaved (O'Rourke, Spitzberg, & Hannawa, 2011), allow for a public recollection and celebration of the deceased's accomplishments (Rando, 1984), and give the bereaved a chance to 'do something' at a time when they are feeling helpless (Golden, 2000; Weeks, 1996). Rituals also provide an opportunity for the broader community to express its grief and support (Irion, 1999), as well as allow those who share a bond with the deceased (e.g., fellow firefighters, police officers, etc.) to share support with one another (Rando, 1984).

Support for the benefits of death rituals, including funerals, is typically based on personal experience and theoretical arguments. Unfortunately, little empirical work has examined funerals and post-funeral rituals (Gamino, Easterling, Stirman, & Sewell, 2000; Vale-Taylor, 2009), yet most studies have found that bereaved individuals are satisfied with them (Bosley & Cook, 1993; Doka, 1984). Conversely, funerals have been criticized for being too generic and impersonal (Elison & McGonigle, 2003; Romanoff & Terenzio, 1998) and being generally observational instead of participatory (Irion, 1999).

Given that funerals may happen too early to provide their full benefit (Parkes, 1996; Sanders, 1999), post-funeral rituals may be especially helpful for the widower. Most widowers use private, informal rituals even before entering counseling (Troyer, 2011). For example, a widower who takes care of his deceased wife's flower garden as a way to honor and remember her is engaging in a post-funeral ritual. Psychotherapists can build from these examples to examine the meaning associated with this ritual or to create new rituals for different purposes. The benefits of post-funeral rituals include the ability to be tailored to the widower's specific needs, the facilitation of continuing bonds with the deceased, the opportunity to be creative regarding the ritual's timing, location, and structure, as well as a planned way to express feelings. Furthermore, rituals do not need to be extravagant or complicated to be useful (Rando, 1985).

Post-funeral rituals may be the only type of death ritual afforded to disenfranchised widowers who are unable to attend funeral services (Doka, 2002d). For example, Blaine's partner committed suicide after his family discovered he was living with Blaine. The family instructed Blaine not to attend the funeral of his partner or any other public rituals. Blaine was forced to create his own post-funeral rituals that involved visiting the grave with flowers after dark to avoid interactions with Sam's family.

There are several reasons why rituals work especially well with grieving men. Rituals allow for men to use a planned and action-oriented approach (Doka & Martin, 2010) and provide a less-threatening, indirect way to express their emotions. Golden (2000) argues that rituals can be viewed as *containers* for one's grief and that men use rituals to help engender a sense of emotional control when expressing their grief. He defines containers as "anything that allows us to move from an ordinary state of awareness into the experience of pain, and then lets us move out of the pain again" (p. 135). In this way, rituals can provide a specific time and place for grief and can help the widower also avoid feeling as if his acute grief reaction may go on indefinitely (Rando, 1985).

Containers and Grief

Thomas Golden (2000) found that he had created his own 'container' when grieving his father:

> Only in retrospect have I realized how ironic it seems that one of the active containers I found for my grief that week [after his father died] was actually building a container. Joel [Golden's brother] and I decided to design and make the container for my father's ashes. . . . As we worked, my brother and I would share stories about my father. We used his tools and his wood. One of the most important aspects for us was the presence of my father's 80-year-old best friend, Charlie Beamen. Charlie was a retired minister who had been my father's woodworking buddy. As the three of us worked together we exchanged numerous tales of my father. Joel and I told Charlie of our experiences growing up with Dad, and Charlie told us of his exploits with my father in the recent past. As we worked and told stories, the tears and laughter flowed.
>
> We men had found a safe place to act as a "container" for our emotions. The workshop functioned in this manner to connect our pain and tears with a project. The project became a 'hook' for our pain. That week, the men who came to visit our family tended to be drawn to the workshop. They usually had ideas or comments about the work that was being done, and gladly chipped in to aid in making the container. (pp. 135–136)

PROCESS OF RITUALS

Borrowing from Roberts (2003) and others (Kollar, 1989; van der Hart, 1983), I believe rituals should follow a three-step process. I have labeled the steps as *preparation*, *performance*, and *pondering*. The preparation is critical because a ritual must be intentional. Furthermore, the ritual should arise naturally from the bereaved's concerns and needs (Doka & Martin, 2010). Or put another way, "ritual begins, not with the intention of formulating one but with the intention of responding to a given situation" (Irion, 1991, p. 162). At this point the bereaved must decide on the actions he wants to take and if he will use elements (real or symbolic) in the ritual (see Doka, 2002d). Fire and water have been used to symbolize purification and renewal in most societies throughout recorded history; likewise, the burial of the deceased's personal items is a common ritual. Bereaved individuals are often surprised to find that symbols can be just as powerful as 'real' items in rituals (van der Hart, 1988b).

The second step is performing the ritual. Rituals require action "for rituals work only if we do not remain the audience, but also become actors" (van der Hart, 1988a, p. 5). The widower may perform the ritual alone or with others (including the therapist). If possible, the ritual should be performed at a pace that allows for the bereaved to fully experience all of its components (Kollar, 1989).

Equally as important as the other steps, the widower should ponder or reflect following the ritual. Pondering includes the contemplation following a ritual and any new reactions, thoughts, or emotions regarding the survivor, the deceased, or the loss. These insights may be shared with others (e.g., family, friends, therapists, fellow group members, etc.) or can be a private reflection. Although this step is the most likely to be overlooked by therapists and survivors alike, it is impossible to not have some reaction to a ritual.

PURPOSES OF RITUALS

Rituals can serve a variety of purposes depending on the needs of the bereaved. While a ritual may serve multiple purposes, the bereaved are likely trying to achieve at least one of the following purposes: (1) honor the deceased; (2) express feelings; (3) recognize a transition; (4) recognition by a group; and (5) deal with unfinished business.

Honoring the deeceased Kollar (1989) described rituals designed to honor the deceased as opportunities for *regeneration* and *identification*, while van der Hart (1983) referred to similar goals as rituals of *continuity* and *affirmation*. A common example of a ritual to honor and remember the deceased is when a widower visits the gravesite. While there, he may choose to talk to his deceased wife about current events in his life and express how much he continues to care for her (Francis et al., 2005).

Expressing feelings Another goal is the expression of feelings related to the loss and the deceased partner. While feelings may be expressed during any ritual, sometimes the purpose of the ritual is primarily to set aside a special time and place to express feelings. As mentioned in Chapter 5, Doka and Martin (2010) relate the story of the widower who would sit in his car and cry while he played 'their song.' These rituals allow the widower to have a time and space devoted to focusing on his partner without distractions.

Recognizing a transition Examples of transitional rituals include removing a wedding ring, moving from the house a widower shared with his wife, beginning to date, and disposing of the deceased's personal items. One type of transitional ritual is the symbolic 'letting go' of some aspect of the deceased or a specific item (van der Hart, 1988c). While earlier grief theorists and therapists overemphasized letting go of the deceased (Romanoff & Terenzio, 1998), some forms of symbolic good-byes can be adaptive. These types of rituals can take a variety of forms:

> Over the years we have asked people to burn, freeze, bury, flush, or send up in balloons a variety of symbolic items, such as photographs, rings, letters, written memories, psychiatric records, and clothes. Such ritual actions have assisted people in moving beyond traumatic events and meanings that have interfered with their living in the present. (Whiting, 2003, p. 98)

A ritual of letting go may be easier and more adaptive if the bereaved also recognizes that he can continue to hold on (Whiting, 2003). For example, a widower may decide that it is time to give his wife's clothes away, but may choose a symbolic piece or two to keep so as not to feel as if he is trying to remove all traces of his wife from his life.

Group recognition Sometimes a ritual is designed to recognize the grief of a broader community beyond the widower and immediate family. Kollar (1989) describes two similar opportunities for rituals: *communal awareness* and *confirmation of community values*. These rituals emphasize the many roles the deceased fulfilled and allows those affected by the death to honor the contributions of the deceased. Group recognition can be rituals or memorial services which include extended family members, co-workers, neighbors, club/association members,

> ## Letting Go—Removing Wedding Rings
>
> One example of a ritual related to the transition from married/partnered to widowed/single is the removing of a wedding band. Although widowers may not think of it as such, this act has all the components of a ritual. For many widowers the decision to remove their ring may come over a long period of reflection and recognition of the changing relationship with their deceased wife. Doka and Martin (2010) describe a widow's poignant and meaningful ritual for removing her wedding ring.
>
>> Mary is a widow in her 40s, whose husband died 7 years ago after a 5-year debilitating struggle with multiple sclerosis (MS). Mary is at a point where she would like to take off her wedding ring and begin dating, but she seems unable to do so. In discussing her relationship with her counselor, it becomes clear that the ring has great meaning. Though the illness was very difficult for both every night, after a long day's struggle, when they lay in bed, they would put their ring fingers together and repeat their vows "in sickness and in health." The counselor acknowledged that she had put on the ring in a ritual that had great value, and both he and Mary agreed that it should be removed in another meaningful ritual. It was arranged that on a Sunday afternoon, Mary and her friends and family gathered in the church where she and her husband exchanged vows. The priest met her at the altar. There he repeated the vows, now in the past tense. "Were you faithful in sickness and in health, in good times and in bad?" he intoned. Mary could, in the presence of these witnesses, affirm that she had been. The priest then asked for the ring. As Mary later described, it came off "as if by magic." As planned the priest arranged to have both rings interlocked and welded to her wedding picture. He returned it to her in a brief ritual of continuity. (p. 194)
>
> This example illustrates many of the concepts that have been discussed thus far. The ceremony naturally arose based on a specific grief-related concern of the widow. The location and choice to include loved ones in the ceremony reflected her need to share this with others. The vignette mentions that "Mary later described" which suggests that she had an opportunity to reflect on the ritual, its usefulness, and likely future implications. While not every widowed person needs a ritual this elaborate and public to remove his or her wedding ring, this ceremony fits Mary's particular needs.

and others. For example, Bob, a young widower, described how he scattered some of his wife's ashes at a camp where they had met and worked. One of their favorite events at the camp had been the weekly bonfires just before the campers would return home. Bob decided to invite their friends (many of whom had also worked at the camp) to the camp and have another bonfire and sing camp songs. He placed the ashes in the bonfire to be spread throughout the camp. When many people are involved in a ritual, it is important to remember that the rituals are most beneficial if they are personalized and participatory (Doka, 1993).

Unfinished business   A fifth goal of rituals involves dealing with various aspects of 'unfinished business' with the deceased. Van der Hart (1983) refers to these as *rituals of reconciliation*. This type of ritual may be especially helpful in situations where the widower is experiencing guilt, asking for forgiveness, or seeking to communicate things that were left unsaid (Doka, 2002d). The core of the ritual can include actual or symbolic ways of expressing messages such as: "I'm sorry," "I forgive you," "I'm so angry," and "I need you to know . . ." A widower that writes a letter to his wife confessing his anger at her for committing suicide would be an example of using a ritual for this type of goal. The empty chair technique can be quite useful as part of rituals dealing with unfinished business.

CAUTIONS REGARDING THERAPEUTIC RITUALS

Psychotherapists should always ensure that rituals are relevant to the widower's grief experience and are developed collaboratively. Rituals are not drugs or band-aids; they should not be the equivalent of "write two letters, burn a candle, and let's debrief in the morning." Furthermore, rituals should complement, not replace, the psychotherapy process. As van der Hart (1988b) states, "We must be keenly aware that a ritual works not only because it is a ritual, but primarily because it acts as a *vehicle*, as a suitable framework for the necessary processes of change" (p. 22).

Recognizing Milestones and Anniversaries

It is important for psychotherapists to assist their bereaved clients as they cope with significant milestones and anniversaries. Significant days for a widower may include the partner's or his birthday, their anniversary or other important days related to their relationship, holidays, the date of his partner's death or funeral, the date of his partner's diagnosis, and others (see Brabant et al., 1992; Yalom, 2002). Other important milestones may include when a widower moves out of a home he shared with his partner, going on a first date, as well as significant milestones for their children (e.g., graduations, weddings, moving out, etc.).

Psychotherapists should regularly ask their bereaved clients if there are any significant dates or events in the near future.

Psychotherapists should assist widowers with preparing for significant dates and events. Of course, it is up to the widower himself to determine which events and dates are noteworthy. It may be helpful to assist the widower with a plan for the day. Rituals may be particularly useful on anniversaries because they can provide structure for days and events that the widower may dread.

Final Phase

The final phase of the counseling process with widowers includes a review of the client's progress, identification of ongoing and future concerns, and preparation for termination. First, it is important to review the changes and adaptations made by the widower since beginning psychotherapy and acknowledge the improvements he has made. I have adapted the concept of 'survivor's pride' (see Wolin & Wolin, 1993) as a way to reframe the difficult lessons the widower has had to learn (Bennett, 2007). For example, a widower should take pride in learning how to manage tasks for which he may have had to rely on his wife (e.g., housekeeping, financial record-keeping, maintaining relationships with family members, etc.). Although he likely wishes that he did not have to learn new skills that his partner previously completed, he can take pride in his achievement. Furthermore, he should take pride in developing a mindset of being able to face life's challenges without his partner's assistance.

Psychotherapy never ends with the resolution of all the client's problems. Psychotherapists should help the widower explore the concerns that will continue to challenge him in the future. Ideally, the widower and psychotherapist should preview future concerns, develop a plan to deal with them, and discuss indicators that may be a sign that he should return to counseling. These 'red flags' will be specific to the widower and his presenting concerns.

Finally, sensitively managing termination is especially important when working with bereaved clients. The widower may interpret the end of the counseling relationship as yet another loss. Termination should be planned well in advance. It may be helpful for the client and therapist to develop their own ritual of goodbye; ideally something meaningful for both individuals.

8

WIDOWERS IN GROUPS

Grief groups are one of the most popular options for bereaved individuals to receive support. A wide variety of different institutions and organizations (e.g., religious organizations, hospices and medical facilities, and non-profit organizations) sponsor grief groups. In this chapter I will describe several different types of grief groups, review the empirical research on the efficacy of grief groups, and describe why men have been reluctant to join them. Furthermore, I will describe the characteristics of groups that may be well suited to widowers, and outline the practical concerns related to starting a grief group.

Throughout this chapter I will be discussing the types and formats of groups that work well with widowers with an instrumental grieving style. Widowers with an intuitive style will often benefit from traditional grief groups which focus on self-disclosure and the expression of feelings. Conversely, widowers with an instrumental grieving style will likely benefit from groups that emphasize structure, psycho-educational topics, and a stronger focus on cognitive processes and problem-solving.

Types of Grief Groups

In this section I will outline the various types and formats of grief groups. In particular I will emphasize how different characteristics of groups will influence a widower's experience.

Self-Help Versus Professionally Led Groups

Most grief groups are self-help groups that operate independently from professional therapists (Yalom & Vinogradov, 1988). By definition, self-help groups are led by peers who have experienced the same loss or challenge. Most grief groups use previously widowed individuals as group facilitators; these peer group leaders (as well as professional therapists) can have varying degrees of experience in facilitating groups. One benefit of having a group led by a widowed person is that some group members may be looking for a leader who has experienced the same loss (Tedeschi & Calhoun, 1993); this may result in immediate credibility for the group leader as someone who has 'been there.' Furthermore, limited research suggests no difference in outcomes for grief groups who are led by professionals versus widowed peers (Lund & Caserta, 1992).

However, there are several concerns related to groups with lay leaders. Without the advantages of professional training, lay group leaders may be more likely to violate ethical guidelines regarding confidentiality, dual relationships, and crisis referrals. Furthermore, lay leaders may be more prone to perpetuating myths about the grieving process. For example, Francis (1997) described a group leader that insisted on evoking anger from the members as a supposedly critical part of the process by portraying the deceased as a perpetrator of their pain: "They left you! They abandoned you! What's going on here? Let's be real clear about that. That's what you're feeling right now. That's what you were crying about in the cemetery. That's what hurts" (p. 162). Professional training does not guarantee that psychotherapists are necessarily more knowledgeable about modern grief theories and practices, but it does mean that they would have at least some knowledge and experience dealing with common ethical pitfalls.

Structured or Psycho-Educational Versus Unstructured or Process-Oriented

Leaders (lay or professional) of psycho-educational grief groups typically focus on educating bereaved adults or children about grief and loss, dispelling myths, and providing structured activities. In general, psycho-educational groups tend to meet for fewer sessions and are more structured than counseling or self-help groups. Psycho-educational groups for widowed individuals focus on dispelling myths of grief and loss (e.g., grief models, common reactions, etc.), but may also emphasize self-care and daily living tasks (e.g., Caserta, Lund, & Rice, 1999). Bereaved men may prefer the structure and didactic nature of psycho-educational groups. Some psycho-educational groups include opportunities for voluntary self-disclosure. One way to encourage mutual support as part of a psycho-educational group is to pair the group experience with a meal; this combination provides the group members with an opportunity to socialize.

Conversely, unstructured or process-oriented groups operate without structured topics or activities. Process-oriented groups are more common in formal psychotherapy groups where the group leaders (psychotherapists) are often trained to focus on group dynamics, group cohesion, and other variables (e.g.,

Corey, 2000; Yalom & Leszcz, 2005). Process-oriented grief groups may frustrate some widowers with an instrumental style of grieving due to their focus on self-disclosure and affective sharing (Doka & Martin, 2010).

Kiselica and Kiselica (in press) suggest that a hybrid approach of structured and unstructured activities may be the best fit for all-male groups. Structured activities in early group meetings can assuage group members' concerns about the need to share spontaneously (Rabinowitz, 2001). After group members have become more comfortable with one another and group norms have been established, the group leader can shift to more unstructured activities.

Single-Sex Versus Mixed Groups

Most therapists who express an opinion regarding whether men should be in mixed or single-sex groups advocate for single-sex groups (e.g., Worden, 2009) (for an exception, see Lund & Caserta, 1992). One concern of mixed groups is that men may fall into a pattern of allowing women to express emotions and opinions for them (Brooks, 1998; Barusch & Peak, 1997; Sternbach, 1990), and self-monitoring the topics they discuss in front of women (Jolliff & Horne, 1996; Staudacher, 1991). When women are not present, men often react differently to one another. Staudacher (1991) quoted a facilitator of an all-male grief group regarding how the group members responded differently to a member's tears:

> This seems to be one of the major ways in which men's and women's groups differ. Women would have more of a tendency to take care of and to want to comfort and support, which is real valuable at times. But [with] men it's almost as if they're saying, "I know you have the strength and I'm there for you." There was respect for each other's strength. (p. 175)

The topics discussed and the nature of the discussion will also likely change depending on the presence of women in the group (including the therapist). For example, men are more comfortable discussing sexual and relationship needs more freely in an all-male group. Widowers report that they avoid these topics in mixed groups out of respect for the women in the group (Staudacher, 1991). Furthermore, men in groups are more likely to confront other members who are avoiding problems and ask difficult questions (Brooks, 1998), to use humor (Anderson, 2001), and to openly express anger and frustration (Jolliff & Horne, 1996). In his study of group norms, Lieberman (1989) found these same behaviors as being the most likely to be judged by widowed members of support groups as inappropriate. These factors can cause a male group member to feel isolated and misunderstood—the exact opposite reasons for joining a group.

Given the fewer numbers of widowers and their hesitancy to seek and attend grief groups, it may be impossible to have a sufficient number of members for an all-male group. In these circumstances it is important for group leaders to be aware of the tendency for males in mixed-gender groups to be more passive, to desire structure, to be less comfortable with being forced to share their feelings.

Specific Loss Versus Multiple Types of Losses

Grief groups can include a variety of types of losses or relationships or can be restricted to only one type of loss or relationship. For example, some groups include bereaved individuals with any type of death-related loss (spouse/partner, prenatal, child, parent, sibling, friend, etc.) while others restrict the membership to only one type of loss (commonly the death of a spouse or child). Other groups may only include individuals who have died from a specific cause (e.g., long-term illness, suicide, AIDS, etc.).

Some grief therapists (e.g., Worden, 2009) specifically recommend groups that have a common connection. In these groups members relate to one another more easily, are more likely to socialize outside the group, and are more likely to share a sense of 'we-ness' (see Yalom & Leszcz, 2005). Another benefit of a homogenous group (in terms of the type or cause of death) is the reduction in comparing losses by group members. A common impediment to group cohesion and trust in groups that include heterogeneous types of losses or causes of death is the ongoing determination of who has experienced the 'worst loss' (Rognlie, 1989). For example, widowers whose partners have died may view their loss as much more painful than the group members who have lost a sibling. I strongly recommend against mixing group members who have suffered a death (e.g., spousal death) with those who have experienced a non-death loss (e.g., divorce). Comparisons among the group members are inevitable and can irrevocably harm the group's cohesiveness.

Nevertheless, even in homogenous groups these comparisons can arise. In terms of the widowed, younger widowed individuals may feel their loss is worse than older widowed individuals given that they had comparatively less time with their partner ("at least you had 40 years together"); conversely, older widowed individuals may believe that their loss is more difficult because they knew their partner for such a long time and have little opportunity to remarry ("you hardly knew her and you have plenty of time to get remarried").

Open Versus Closed Membership

There are both advantages and disadvantages to closed and open group formats. Open groups allow for new members to begin attending at any time and this makes it more likely that the group will maintain an ideal size (Yalom & Leszcz, 2005). Conversely, closed groups maintain the same membership throughout their duration. This consistency in membership allows for a stronger sense of cohesion among the group members and removes the need to repeat information for new members (Corey, 2000). Some group leaders (e.g., Mosely, Davies, & Priddy, 1988) have argued that groups for men should be closed or 'semi-closed' because men may be slower to develop cohesion and trust within a group setting. Another option is to occasionally bring in new members, but only with the consent of the original members of the group.

Time-Limited Versus Open-Ended Duration

Grief groups vary in their overall duration depending on several factors. Groups focusing on education tend to be the shortest—often having 4 to 8 sessions. Groups that focus on providing ongoing support may last for 8 to 16 sessions or longer. Self-help groups tend to last longer and some that continually allow new members may last for years. Grief groups led by professionals typically last 8–10 sessions (Staudacher, 1991), but may vary. Limiting the number of group meetings at the outset can help some men feel more comfortable joining a group because it allays their concerns about open-endedness or long-term commitment to the group (Sternbach, 1990). Several reports of all-male groups have shown that men can and will choose to continue a group (formally or informally) if they find it helpful (e.g., Mosely et al., 1988).

Social Groups of Widowed Persons

Although not a traditional type of psychotherapy or self-help group, social groups of widowed persons are one of the most popular options. When I interviewed Dilbert, an older widower who had been referred to be a participant in one of my studies, I was surprised to discover that his 'grief group' did not discuss their losses: "Never about grief, never about the deceased. Just what we're doing day by day." One benefits of these social groups for widowed persons is that they provide an opportunity for interaction with others while removing the stigma of attending a social function alone. Everyone in attendance already knows why everyone else is there alone. For example, a local funeral home has one of the largest regular meetings of widowed persons in my area. The organizer of the group found that attendance was highest and the most consistent after switching from a focus on grief and loss topics to providing a lunch and presentations about non-grief related topics (i.e., educational programs related to personal finances, car maintenance, etc.).

Benefits of Grief Groups

Individuals who attend groups benefit from the recognition of the universality of their experiences, the opportunity to help others, the comfort drawn from consistent meetings, and the opportunity to learn new coping methods from others (Yalom & Leszcz, 2005). Furthermore, groups have the potential to be especially helpful for bereaved individuals (Steiner, 2006) and men (Andronico, 1996; Jolliff, 1994).

In addition to the general benefits of groups, grief group members also benefit from support from those who genuinely understand the implications of a loved ones' death. Given the tendency for our culture to deny and avoid death, bereaved individuals often view their reactions, thoughts, and feelings as unique. Grief groups can provide first-hand evidence of the universality of grief reactions. When I asked John, an older widower, what had been particularly helpful about attending a grief group, he said, "You felt like you could relax. You could just be yourself there because they were just like you. They were hurting and so you just felt at home, you know. . . . Because you didn't feel you'd be judged." Furthermore, grief groups are one of the few places where bereaved individuals can share embarrassing or taboo topics and where humor and laughing can be experienced without feeling judged (Schneider, 2006; Tedeschi & Calhoun, 1993).

Grief groups also provide frequent opportunities for members to provide and receive help from one another. After asking older spousally bereaved individuals what advice they had for others, Lund (1999) reported a common theme: "By helping others, bereaved persons can find meaningful ways to remain socially connected and ultimately facilitate their own coping. This is particularly true of those for whom it represents the continuation of an important part of their own identity" (p. 209). Addis and Mahalik (2003) reported that men may be less likely to seek professional help if they cannot reciprocate the assistance. Because men frequently participate in professional and social all-male groups (e.g., sports teams, fraternal organizations, etc.), men are often more comfortable in all-male counseling groups than in individual therapy (Andronico, 1996). All-male groups can also help men learn to become more comfortable receiving assistance from other men (Kiselica & Kiselica, in press). In my experience, widowers particularly enjoy being able to provide support to fellow group members especially by helping them think through problems and providing physical assistance. Although there is little empirical research on all-widower's groups, there is significant support for single-sex counseling groups for men facing other challenges (for an overview see Kiselica & Kiselica, in press).

Widowers' Reluctance to Join Grief Groups

Given the numerous benefits of group support, it can be difficult to understand why widowers are so hesitant to attend them. Mastrogianis and Lumley (2002) surveyed widowers who had access to a free grief support group through the funeral home they used. They found that only 15% of the widowers attended the grief support group; but, of those who did attend, 63% reported that it was helpful. Moore and Stratton (2002) reported that only 6 of the 51 older widowers they interviewed attended a grief group, and most did not attend more than the first few sessions.

The reasons why widowers are less likely to join and continue attending a grief group are similar to the same factors that are associated with men being less likely to seek individual counseling (see Addis & Mahalik, 2003; Robertson & Fitzgerald, 1992) and medical help (Courtenay, 2011). Several general concerns for widowed men and women include the stigma associated with seeking help, a fear of 'breaking down' in a group, and concerns about sharing their concerns with strangers (Levy & Derby, 1992). In addition to these general factors, conflicts between the practices and norms in traditional grief groups and the preferences of most men generally fall into two areas: the differences related to intuitive versus instrumental grieving styles (Doka & Martin, 2010) and differences related to a stronger focus on loss-oriented coping versus restoration-oriented coping (Stroebe & Schut, 1999, 2010).

Conflicts Related to Grieving Style

The expectations of group leaders and norms of most grief groups (and most counseling and self-help groups, in general) emphasize the discussion and expression of feelings of loss and a high level of self-disclosure (Barusch & Peak, 1997). This is one reason why women, who are more likely to be intuitive grievers, are more likely to attend and persist in most grief groups. These 'traditional' grief groups are a poor fit with men with an instrumental style of grief (Doka & Martin, 2010). Grieving men in traditional grief groups often complain that the group expects them to share quickly and beyond their comfort level.

Not only are men less comfortable with the type of sharing that typically occurs, they can also feel misunderstood and may also feel attacked when they attempt to share. Leaders and co-members of traditional grief groups may interpret men's efforts to problem-solve or express their grief in more cognitive or physical ways as attempts to hide or minimize their 'true' feelings about their loss. This can be especially true for male instrumental grievers. Doka and Martin (2010) state:

> Instrumental grievers tend to be uncomfortable with self-disclosure and their tempered affect may be perceived as cold or resistant by other grievers. And instrumental grievers may look to utilize such groups for problem-solving approaches, striking facilitators and other group members as inappropriate or premature. For example, they may see such groups as opportunities for respite or socialization. (p. 197)

For instance, a well-meaning group leader that endorses an intuitive style and the grief work perspective may admonish a widower who wants practical advice about living alone as someone who is not fully 'speaking from the heart' and 'releasing the feelings that are locked inside.' It is important to remember that not all men are instrumental grievers. The goals and methods of traditional grief groups match well with the style of male *intuitive* grievers. Male intuitive grievers and dissonant grievers (at least those whose natural grieving style is intuitive) may find traditional grief groups to be a safe haven where their natural process of grieving is supported and encouraged (Doka & Martin, 2010).

Groups and Loss-Orientation Versus Restoration-Orientation

Another characteristic of traditional grief groups that is poorly suited to most grieving men is the extensive focus on the loss (including remembering the deceased and expressing and discussing painful feelings) while avoiding the examination of current and future problems. This discrepancy is largely similar to the differences in loss-oriented coping versus restoration-oriented coping as described by Stroebe and Schut (1999, 2010) in the Dual Process Model of Coping with Bereavement (DPM). As summarized in Chapter 3, the DPM describes the process of grief as alternating between two types of coping: loss-oriented and restoration-oriented. Loss-oriented coping focuses on the loss including confronting the loss, dealing with the emotional pain of the loss, concentrating on reminders of the deceased, and other aspects of grief work. Restoration-oriented coping deals with the problems and challenges that result from the loss including fulfilling new roles, developing skills, and distracting oneself from the loss. A key feature of the DPM is the process of oscillating between loss- and restoration-oriented coping so that the bereaved individual does not focus exclusively on either aspect of coping (Stroebe & Schut, 1999, 2010). To put it another way, men are more likely to focus on restoration-oriented coping methods, yet traditional grief groups emphasize loss-oriented aspects of grief.

At first glance, this mismatch is similar to the discrepancy between grief groups that match Doka and Martin's (2010) intuitive style versus the fact that most men display an instrumental style of grieving. However, there are several important differences. Stroebe and Schut (2010) assert that physical, cognitive, or emotion-based coping styles can be used for either loss- or restoration-oriented coping. For example, addressing the needs of being a single parent for young children would clearly fall within restoration-oriented coping, and widowers may choose emotion-based methods (e.g., discussing their fears about being a newly single parent with a therapist or friend) or cognitive methods (reading books about how to be a single parent). The former would be an example of grieving intuitively while the latter would be an example of instrumentally grieving this secondary loss (i.e., the loss of the mother of his children).

How would this discrepancy play out in grief groups? For example, Jerry, a widower who participated in research by Moore and Stratton (2002), reported that many of the members of the grief group he attended (but quickly left) appeared to be stuck in their grief; he feared that the same fate would befall him. He specifically mentioned a woman that had been actively grieving for six years. "If I'm still where that woman is in six years, somebody ought to put a gun to my head" (p. 91). Bob also did not return after his first grief group session for similar reasons:

> The group experience was really depressing.... As part of me being new to the group everyone introduced themselves and explained who they had lost and how. Many of the people had been there longer than a year and they forgot part of their story. Other group members would chime in and tell some of the sad aspects, and I just felt like that wasn't what I wanted. I didn't want people helping me to remember sad aspects of [my wife's] passing. I wanted to try to focus more about what was good.

Generally speaking, grieving men tend to want to focus on active steps they can take to improve their situation and solve their current problems. While it is possible that widowers may benefit from engaging in more loss-oriented coping (see Schut et al., 1997; Stroebe, 1998), they may not stay in the group long enough to see these benefits.

Characteristics of Groups That Work for Widowers

There are several principles and strategies for organizing and conducting a group so as to attract and retain widowers. These principles include emphasizing acceptance and safety, beginning with strengths, being open to emotional expression, and using rituals.

Emphasize Acceptance and Safety

All groups for widowers should begin with emphasizing a welcoming environment and safety. Men are often afraid that personal information will be used to belittle or attack them. This does not preclude having disagreements or confronting one another, but simply allowing group members (or leaders) to recognize that revealing personal thoughts, reactions, and feelings is not unmasculine. Jolliff and Horne (1996) summarized it this way:

> When men are sure that they are not going to be shamed or blamed, they are eager to share openly. Observing such openness in a men's group is exciting to behold because the men communicate honestly, and often very directly, with each other. Feedback goes directly to the heart of the matter, honesty comes before niceness, genuine emotions such as anger and frustration are communicated openly, tears are not only accepted but encouraged, and profanity is not shamed. (p. 57)

Groups should be constructed and supervised in a way that allows widowed men to feel safe and demonstrate acceptance. From this foundation, widowers continue to receive support as they seek to solve problems, express their grief in ways that are congruent, and may explore emotions.

Begin With Strengths: Encouraging Problem-Solving and Behavior Change

As described in Chapter 2, the Positive Psychology/Positive Masculinity (PPPM) perspective emphasizes building from the strengths of male development, male socialization, and masculinity. By using the PPPM perspective, the group leader can recognize and affirm instances when group members have exhibited strengths (e.g., taken risks, sacrificed for others, worked with other men toward a noble goal, been self-sufficient, etc.) (Kiselica & Kiselica, in press). Although they were not writing in terms of grieving style or particular coping strategies, Barusch and Peak (1997) offered an excellent description of how an all-male group of widowers might work best:

> The key to effective involvement of older men in support groups is designing an experience that builds on their strengths and is compatible

with their relationship styles. Traditional male strengths include the capacity to "play by the rules" and to accomplish discrete, objective goals. Group formats that are well structured and that emphasize task achievement build on this strength. (p. 274)

As men will often focus on tangible outcomes, it can be helpful to incorporate this into the purpose and goals of a men's grief group. Doka and Martin (2010) provide some examples of groups where male grievers focused the group process on solving practical problems and developing a specific, physical product. For example, they describe a cooking class for widowers sponsored by a hospice group. At the end of the class the men decided to publish a cookbook for men. The book included their wives' favorite recipes and stories about their lives. Davies, Priddy, and Tinkleberg (1986) described a group of men who were caregivers for their wives who suffered from Alzheimer's disease. Initially, the researchers had difficulty recruiting a sufficient number of group members. They were finally able to secure enough participants when they reframed the group's purpose as a pilot study for creating a new intervention for other male caregivers. This shift in focus incorporated their desire to help others and took the focus off the assistance that they were receiving. Anderson (2001) convened a long-term group of men to learn more about the death and non-death losses in men's life: "my plan to use the group for conducting research and writing a book gave the group viability, and lent credibility to their participating in it. Their work will have an end product which will be useful to society" (p. 319).

A word of caution is necessary. I do not mean to suggest that widowers will only attend groups that involve fishing, hunting, and attending monster truck rallies. Do not plan your grief group with a view toward some mythical hyper-masculine ideal. I am suggesting that groups should begin where men are comfortable by allowing them to interact in social patterns and practices that are familiar to them.

Be Open to Emotional Expression

Men return to groups where they are allowed to be themselves and begin with their strengths and many men reach the point where they are comfortable sharing deeper emotions. When given the opportunity in a safe and empathic environment, men can become quite comfortable sharing their concerns. Anderson (2001), a female therapist, reported being quite surprised by the extent to which the men in her all-male grief group shared their concerns:

> While I had expected that all men felt some loss and pain, I had no idea that they had experienced so much of it. One man would tell his story

and another would follow and another and another. It seems that being invited to share loss, grief, and pain was the catalyst for these men to recount many aspects of their life histories that had not previously been told or shared, except perhaps with a spouse or partner. To share these facts and the feelings unleashed by them with other men was unrehearsed and unusual. (p. 315)

Men can reach the point of sharing more personal information, doubts, sadness, fears, and other intimate information. Given that this is a rare experience for most men, men may initially be less comfortable, but also have the most to gain (Brooks, 1996). Psychotherapists should assist the group members as they experiment with discussing emotional topics and expressing feelings.

Use Rituals

As described in Chapter 7, rituals can be especially helpful for men; using rituals in men's grief groups can also be effective (Barusch & Peak, 1997). Just as in individual counseling, rituals can be useful in groups because they allow for planning and preparation (as opposed to spontaneous disclosure) and structure and predictability. Ideally the group members will help plan and shape the ritual and individual variations should be encouraged to make the ritual as meaningful as possible for each member. Men's friendships have frequently been described as 'side-by-side' (while women's friendships are face-to-face; Wright, 1982); this approach to friendships emphasizes physical activity and problem-solving instead of sharing and emotional disclosure. Consequently, rituals involving physical activity and side-by-side work may be especially preferred.

An example of a ritual in a widower's grief group may be as simple as everyone shaking hands and expressing a positive sentiment to each member of the group. A more complex ritual could include the entire group taking a trip to a local cemetery to support a group member who has been unable to visit his wife's grave.

Practical Matters When Starting a Group

There are a variety of different decisions that a group leader must make when formulating a group. As mentioned at the beginning of the chapter, groups can vary based on the following choices: self-help versus professionally led, single-sex versus mixed groups, specific loss versus variety of losses, open versus closed membership, time-limited versus open-ended, and structured/psycho-educational versus process-oriented. There are also a large number of other practical matters regarding the start of a grief group for widowers. These include advertising for the group, pre-screening potential group members, and determining how soon after a loss a widower can join the group. Given the hesitancy of widowers to join groups, being mindful of these practical matters can increase the potential number of group participants, can better prepare widowers for the group experience, and reduce disruptions related to having widowers in the group before they can take full advantage of the experience.

Advertising

Effectively publicizing a grief group to men begins with the advertisements. Widowed men are often quite aware of (or strongly suspect) the gender disparity in most grief groups, and many worry that they will be the only man in attendance. Small details like including pictures of men on the advertisements may help encourage men to attend and sends the message that they are welcome (Barusch & Peak, 1997). Labeling the support group as a 'workshop' or 'seminar' may also increase the number of male attendees (Barusch & Peak, 1997; Robertson & Fitzgerald, 1992; Russell, 2004); however, it is critical to deliver the program as advertised and not use the name of the group as a bait-and-switch technique (Doka & Martin, 2010).

Pre-Screening Group Members

Although time-consuming, pre-screening potential group members can be immensely helpful before a group begins or before adding new members to an existing group. Therapists should usually exclude individuals with serious psychological pathology (Worden, 2009) as well as individuals who are unwilling to self-disclose, unable to review their own thoughts and behaviors, and averse to engaging with others (Yalom & Leszcz, 2005). In relation to grief groups, reasons for possible exclusion include individuals who have suffered multiple losses and individuals suffering losses that may be difficult for other group members to talk about (Worden, 2009). Furthermore, it is especially important to rule out any individuals (widowers or widows) who are simply attending the group as a way to find a new partner and have little interest in participating in the group process. Therefore, one of the most important benefits of pre-screening is determining if the group is a good fit for a particular widower *before* he joins, thereby minimizing any disruption to the group process. Another benefit of pre-screening is the opportunity for the therapist to educate the potential group member about the norms and processes of the group and dispel any myths and misconceptions.

Group leaders should avoid including bereaved individuals whose loss was quite recent. The length of time after which a bereaved individual could benefit from a grief group varies from at least six weeks to six months (Worden, 2009); bereaved individuals have reported significant benefits from grief groups within three months after their loss (Picton, Cooper, Close, & Tobin, 2001). Furthermore Allumbaugh and Hoyt (1999) reported that bereaved individuals who begin counseling approximately three to four months after their loss could expect greater improvements from individual and group counseling. By not including a widower in a counseling group during the first few days or weeks after his loss makes it much more likely that he has moved past the initial, often debilitating, shock that accompanies a loss (especially if the loss is sudden and unexpected). During this initial period of shock and disbelief, a group experience is unlikely to be helpful for the widower and may impair the group process for the other members. In setting the exclusionary period before allowing new members to join a group, it is important to consider the type of group (psychoeducational vs. process).

Socializing Outside of Group Counseling

In his classic book on group therapy, Yalom (Yalom & Leszcz, 2005) warns that one of the most serious threats to group cohesiveness is the development of subgroups. A common cause of subgrouping is having some of the group members meet socially outside of the group setting. As a result this subgroup of members will have more information about one another, may begin to share thoughts and reactions about group members who are not present, and may begin to limit their participation during group sessions. Conversely, several grief group leaders (e.g., Staudacher, 1991; Rognlie, 1989) have not only recognized that extra-group meetings are likely to happen, but they encourage these meetings. Some even create opportunities for group members to meet socially at other times (e.g., Schneider, 2006). Because social isolation is such a common concern of widowed individuals and these extra-group social meetings are already common in grief groups (Caserta & Lund, 1996), they are viewed as an additional benefit of the grief group experience (Worden, 2009). Certainly, group leaders should continue to be aware of subgroups within the group and how they may influence group dynamics, but extra-group meetings of widowed individuals (especially associated with self-help groups) are less concerning than when they occur in process-oriented counseling groups.

9

UNDERSTUDIED AND MINORITY WIDOWERS

Given that widowers, as a group, are understudied (Thompson, 1998), it should come as little surprise that many subgroups of widowers have received little attention from researchers. In this chapter I will examine widowers who belong to understudied groups. I have categorized these widowers into four groups based on a key characteristic: age, sexual orientation, minority status/identity, and marital status. It can be easy to get caught up in the differences between various minority and understudied groups and widowers from various majority groups. However, I believe there are many more similarities than differences among widowers from different groups. Nonetheless, therapists will be more effective if they are aware of the challenges and strengths associated with widowers from these groups.

Understudied Widowers: Younger and Very Old Widowers

Younger Widowers and Widowers With Dependent Children

Younger adult and middle-aged widowers constitute a smaller, but significant portion of the widowed population in the US. In 2010, the US Census reported that there were approximately 84,000 widowers between 18 and 39 years of age (4% of all widowers) and 760,000 between 40 and 64 (36% of all widowers). Of course, statistics based on census results only identify those who are currently widowed and have not remarried; it is difficult to accurately estimate how many widowers have remarried. Using 2004 data from the US Census, there were almost 4 million men who had been widowed at some point in their life. This was 44% more than the number of 'current' widowers at that time. These statistics should be viewed conservatively because census records do not include any widower who was not legally married including same-sex couples (legally married or not), cohabiting couples, and fiancés.

Despite the fact that approximately 40% of widowers in the US are under 65 years of age (US Census Bureau, 2010), researchers focus overwhelmingly on older (65+) widowers. This is troubling considering that some studies have found that younger widowers may suffer more serious health problems and greater severity of grief (Gamino et al., 1998; Stroebe & Schut, 2001). These differences may be due to the fact that younger widowers' partners are more likely to die from sudden and traumatic causes (Archer, 1999).

Research on younger widowers with dependent children has been rare; widowers are often included with single or divorced fathers with the assumption that the experiences are largely similar (O'Neill & Mendelsohn, 2001). One widower with young children expressed his frustration at family members who equated his loss to divorce this way: "My father always irritated me when he said that he knew what I was going through and then related my loss to his divorce. No one knows your grief like you do" (p. 200).

O'Neill and Mendelsohn (2001) conducted one of the few studies focusing on widowers with dependent children. Their study included 46 widowers with school-aged children; the majority (76%) of the participants' wives had died from cancer. The widowers in the study reported being socially isolated and feeling as if they were a unique category of single men. They believed this unique status was a reason why they were more likely to be sought out by potential female partners. The participants also reported problems with several roles conflicting with one another, including the socialization role (instilling values, habits, skills for their children), child care role, provider role, housekeeper role, and therapeutic role (listening, sympathizing, solving problems, and giving reassurance). Overall, most of the widowers had a difficult time adjusting to various domestic chores and having more than two children was related to a more difficult transition. The participants' education level had a mixed relationship with the widowers' post-loss reactions. Widowers with a bachelor's degree or higher had a better overall adjustment to their loss. However, these widowers had more difficultly than widowers with less than a bachelor's degree in terms of adjusting to the responsibilities of a single parent. Despite largely relying on extended family members for child care support, the participants reported a general lack of positive support from in-laws. One said, "My in-laws tried to be uplifting but mostly cared about their loss. My friends cared for me" (p. 201).

Some of the best research on single-parent widowers has come from studies that focus on parentally bereaved children. One of the most frequently cited studies is the Harvard Child Bereavement Study conducted by Worden, Silverman, and their colleagues (Silverman, Nickman, & Worden, 1992; Silverman & Worden, 1992; Worden & Silverman, 1996). They studied 125 parentally bereaved children between the ages of 6 and 17 from 70 different families. Of the 70 families in the study, 20 of them involved the loss of the mother/wife. Results from the study suggest that widowers with dependent children may have more difficult challenges than widows. For example, with the exception of preteen boys, most children exhibited more behavioral and emotional problems if their mother, instead of their father, had died. Children whose mother had died were also more anxious about losing the remaining parent at one year post-loss. Widowed fathers were more likely to say that they were not prepared for being a single parent and had difficulty negotiating time between work and parenting. Furthermore, widowed fathers were found to be less sensitive to their children's needs than widowed mothers (Worden & Silverman, 1993, 1996). Worden (1996a) reported that one father said, "It took me almost a year before I realized that they lost *their* mother. It wasn't only that I lost my wife" (p. 38). But the fathers also began to realize that they were needed: "I try to be home for supper every night. I told my oldest boy he was not his kid brother's father, that was my job and I was here to do it" (p. 39). This research supports some aspects of popular assumptions that widows are better able to adjust to caring for children as a single parent, although the Harvard Study researchers do not suggest that widowers inherently make poor parents or are incapable of successfully parenting their dependent children.

Psychotherapists should be prepared to help widowers with children deal with practical questions regarding parenting strategies and how to explain death and loss to children. Because of children's developmental differences in understanding that death is irreversible and permanent (Smilansky, 1987), the surviving parent will often be forced to explain the death and the circumstances of the death over and over. While this is exactly what the child needs to move toward a more thorough understanding of death and its consequences, it can be emotionally taxing on the widowed parent. For example, Kaslow (2004) described a 39-year-old widower with twin 3-year-old daughters who had successfully ended grief counseling only to call back months later when he was unsure how to respond to his daughters' requests to 'make mommy come back.' Widowers with children are often concerned about what is normal for grieving children. They may be especially concerned when children ask questions or grief resurfaces months or years after they seem to have adjusted to the loss. Furthermore, each instance of a child revisiting the loss also reminds the widower of the long-standing effects of grief on his children and himself.

Oldest Widowers

Gerontologists have subdivided individuals near the end of the lifespan into several specific categories; these designations help recognize the vast differences between individuals who are 65 versus 105. The categories include *older adults* (65+), *young-old* (65–75), *old-old* (75+ or 75–84), and *oldest-old* (85+) (Bee & Bjorkland, 2004). Research on widowers generally focuses on men in the young-old age range. This makes sense given that there are enough widowers in their late 60s and early 70s for researchers to find. Furthermore, they have time to participate in research projects, are in better health, and are more likely to be able to drive or travel. Widowers in the old-old and oldest-old categories are less likely to be included in research. Part of the difficulty in studying widowers over 75 is that it can be difficult to reach widowers who live in assisted living and skilled-nursing facilities; widowers who live in their own homes or apartments are easier to contact by mail and telephone.

While some research has suggested that age of the bereaved is not significantly associated with negative grief outcomes (e.g., Lund et al., 1993; Sanders, 1999), others have found significant differences based on the age of the widowed person (Archer, 1999; Gamino et al., 1998). Sometimes these differences show an advantage for older widowed persons (health and mortality rates; Stroebe & Schut, 2001) while others show a benefit to being younger (rates of suicide, McIntosh et al., 1997). Widowers over the age of 75 may have different grief experiences than younger widowers based on their view of their own mortality, health, and suitability for remarriage. Worden (2009) suggests that "some elderly, particularly the 'old-old,' may be at a stage in their lives at which it is best for them to consolidate their memories and draw on them for sustenance throughout their remaining years" (p. 244). For example, every day, twice a day, William Petroff, age 91, visits his wife's grave. He was married to Jeanne for 68 years. William makes the short trip to his wife's grave, sets up his camping chair and turns on some big band music while he talks to his wife. If it is rainy, windy, or cold, he sets up a large umbrella to shield himself from the elements. "I love her and I'm used to being with her and I'm not going to stay away if I can help it," Petroff said. "I'm going to try and be here every day for the rest of my life" (Fogarty, 2010).

Another concern related to older widowers is that their grief may be disenfranchised because of their age and the age of their deceased partner. Moss and Moss (1989) argue that older widowed individuals may receive less support simply because their partner was also (usually) older and therefore the loss is more expected and less threatening to others. When this is combined with the tendency to avoid the very old because their age reminds us of our own mortality and the multiple losses that older adults often experience, it can lead to widowers receiving less care by loved ones and therapists.

Challenges related to daily living may also be more difficult for the oldest widowers. In a study in England with widowers who averaged 75 years of age,

Bennett, Hughes, and Smith (2003) found that both older widows and widowers agreed that older widowed men face greater challenges in dealing with household tasks—most notably cooking healthy meals and housekeeping. Some widowers are more comfortable with these tasks, especially if they had to tackle them as part of the caregiving process for their partner. However, others may have little or no experience with some household tasks. For example, in a study (Lund, Caserta, Dimond, & Shaffer, 1989) which involved interviews with widowers in their homes, Lund (1999) later reported that following the interviews "several widowers reluctantly asked a female interviewer to show them how to use their dishwashers" (p. 205).

Another concern for older widowers is the choice to remain in their homes (Worden, 2009) and whether or not to remain in the same geographical area. Although this decision must be made by widowers of any age, it has special ramifications for older widowers. Several factors may influence his decision including the widower's view of his home and the availability of social support. For example, bereaved spouses who associate their homes with traumatic relationships or other traumatic memories might be quick to move out and possibly away from such a large reminder of a painful chapter in their life (Elison & McGonigle, 2003). Another issue is the availability of social, medical, spiritual, and psychological resources. Depending on the older adult's available transportation options, even moving a short distance within a community may effectively disconnect him from important resources such as religious organizations, easy access to medical care, and friends and family members. These concerns are even more important if the older widowed person is moving a long distance. A common pattern is for widowed adults to move closer to adult children. While this can be a great option for some, for others it may take them away from their well-established social support network to a place where they are only connected to one family.

I am not suggesting that older widowers (and especially widowers over 75+) necessarily have a more difficult grief experience; there is not conclusive research to support that conclusion. However, I am concerned about the lack of information regarding the oldest widowers. In some ways, widowers the age of Mr. Petroff may have a completely different grief experience than younger widowers. Unfortunately we can only speculate on the differences due to the lack of research on widowers over the age of 75.

Gay Widowers

As I mentioned at the beginning of the chapter, the most important thing to remember about widowers from minority and understudied groups is that there are far more similarities than differences; this is also true for widowers who have lost a male partner. However, gay widowers face several challenges that heterosexual widowers do not. Two primary challenges include a lack of role models and various ways that gay widowers may be disenfranchised. To my knowledge, there has not been a book focusing exclusively on the experiences of gay widowers since Michael Shernoff's (1997a) *Gay Widowers: Life after the Death of a Spouse*. Consequently, much of this section is adapted from his work. In this section I refer to all bereaved men whose male partners have died as gay widowers. Given the lack of published empirical research on bisexual widowers, we can only speculate about the similarities between bisexual and gay widowers.

Grief and Gay Identity

Shernoff (1997b) suggests that coming to terms with being a gay widower is similar to the 'coming out' process in that acknowledging, accepting, and embracing one's status (as gay or as a widower) takes time. Furthermore, if a gay man has fully integrated his sexual orientation into his sense of self, it will make the grieving process easier. Conversely, gay widowers who are still wrestling with their gay identity will likely have more challenges dealing with the death of a partner. Much of this can be attributed to the social support the gay widower will receive.

Shernoff (1997b) uses Cass's (1979) stages of homosexual identity formation as the template for how a gay male moves through stages to fully integrate his sexual orientation into his overall sense of self. This template can also be adapted to understanding how a gay widower recognizes and integrates his new status as a widower into his overall sense of self. Cass's (1979) stages include identity confusion, identity comparison, identity tolerance, identity acceptance, identity pride, and identity synthesis. In the first three stages, Cass focused on the man's feelings of uniqueness, alienation, and desire to reduce his isolation in terms of his homosexual identity. Shernoff believes that gay widowers experience similar emotions after their loss. Cass's later stages focus on the gay man's ongoing recognition, acceptance, and comfort with his sexual identity which eventually deepens and becomes an integrated part of his identity. Shernoff sees a similar pattern in gay widowers as they become more comfortable with their status as widowers including recognition of the variety of credible paths and reactions to being widowed. Just as a gay man mourns the losses associated with being heterosexual before he can celebrate the positive aspects of being gay, the gay widower must mourn his loss before he can acknowledge the new opportunities that being single provides. In most cases the acknowledgment of the positive aspects of being a widower takes some time before they can be recognized and accepted as benefits and can be enjoyed without feeling guilty. Certainly for most widowers (heterosexual or homosexual), any benefits are recognized much later in the process and many would argue that they are not worth the cost. Cass's model is not perfect; its primary weakness is that most individuals do not follow clear, predictable stages in their coming out process. This is also true for the self-identification and acceptance as a widower.

Social Support and Positive Role Models for Gay Widowers

Shernoff (1997b) argues that gay identity development is best done with social support and positive role models; gay widowers also need this support. Unfortunately, most gay widowers have few role models. Picano, in his forward to Shernoff's (1997a) book, describes how this influences a gay widower's experience:

> Our heterosexual grandmothers and grandfathers had been handed down certain traditional rules for how to be a widow, how to be a widower. And along with those rules, a certain status, a place in society to compensate for their loss. Our parents have taken this and modified and updated it somewhat, retaining the status. But grieving gay men—some of whom have only recently come to think of themselves as adults even though they've gone through so much already—have no rules to follow, no advice, no models—and certainly no compensations of status. Without the approval, or even the recognition of our plight by most of society, we seem doomed to individually thrash our way through our individual darkness. We and thousands like us. (pp. xvi–xvii)

Consequently, gay widowers are faced with the loss of their partner and the added burden of blazing a new trail without knowing the destination. Several other challenges for gay widowers include the different ways that gay widowers and their grief can be disenfranchised.

Gay Widowers and Disenfranchised Grief

Doka (1989a, 2002a) has described five ways in which a bereaved individual and his response to loss can be disenfranchised. Three of the five ways often apply to gay widowers including when the relationship is not recognized, when the circumstances of the death influence the bereaved's support, and the ways in which the widower grieves. (The other two types of disenfranchisement can also apply, but not as frequently.)

Lack of Recognition of the Relationship

It is still common for gay widowers to not have their role as partner be fully recognized by others. Upon the death of his partner, the widower's status may not be acknowledged by his own family, his partner's family, funeral professionals, clergy, his employer and co-workers, and government institutions. This may result in the widower being left out of planning death rituals (e.g., funerals, scattering of ashes, etc.), not receiving the support typically afforded to a bereaved spouse, not receiving bereavement leave from his workplace, and not receiving financial and legal death benefits (Shernoff, 1997b). These aspects of disenfranchisement are most likely for widowers who have not disclosed their sexual orientation and relationship to their families, friends, or community. However, even men who are 'out' often struggle to have their relationship and status fully accepted by friends and family members (Hornjatkevyc & Alderson, 2011; Shernoff, 1997b).

One reaction to these types of disenfranchised grief is the widower's need to defend his relationship and attempt to prove the relationship's validity to unsympathetic individuals. Examples of this include disagreements with funeral professionals about his right to plan the service or arguments with his partner's family about where to bury his partner. This may result in the widower being distracted from his grief as he deals with the disenfranchisement. These distractions may delay his grief and provide excuses and opportunities to downplay the significance and reality of his loss (Shernoff, 1997b).

In addition to struggling with lack of recognition from others, gay widowers may also struggle with internalized homophobia. Shernoff (1997b) suggests that the death of a partner may be distressing enough to bring up feelings of internalized homophobia that may have been dormant for years. Gay widowers may even feel that somehow "they did something to deserve the pain they are in the midst of experiencing. Another way blame is internalized and becomes merged with homophobia is in thinking if 'I were not gay perhaps then I would not be feeling this way'" (p. 146). This internalized homophobia may be surprising to the widower; counseling can provide an ideal setting for him to explore these thoughts and feelings.

Circumstances of the Death: AIDS

Some gay widowers have lost their male partner due to complications related to AIDS though there are many other causes too. When AIDS is the cause of death the widower often experiences dual disenfranchisement; his loss is less recognized due to the nature of the relationship and he receives less support as a result of the cause of death. Unfortunately, for a large portion of the public being gay is still equated synonymously with AIDS. Therefore some gay widowers whose partners die from other causes may make a special effort to communicate that their partners did not die from AIDS (Hornjatkevyc & Alderson, 2011). In cases where the partner died from AIDS, the surviving partner may have either escaped being infected with HIV or may not develop AIDS despite being HIV positive. A widower in these circumstances may experience significant guilt and "the concept of being 'blameworthy' can complicate his bereavement as he struggles with 'Why am I still alive while my spouse died from this disease?'" (Shernoff, 1997b, p. 146).

Widowers whose partners have died from AIDS will likely have been long-term caregivers for their partners. As such, they may suffer the effects of long-term stress related to caregiving especially if their partner needed extensive care or was in pain. They may also be experiencing relief, yet also guilt, at not having to continue the caregiving. Some widowers are thoroughly supported throughout this process while others face it alone.

Given that gay men are more likely than heterosexual men to seek psychotherapy (American Psychological Association, 2000) and that gay widowers are more likely to experience disenfranchised grief, psychotherapists are in a unique position to provide empathy and a safe place to discuss their losses. The psychotherapist must have a thorough understanding of the individual widower's needs and sources of support while also not jumping to conclusions about the similarities and differences between the experiences of heterosexual and homosexual widowers.

Ex-Partners and Cohabitating Widowers

Divorced Widowers

In 2010 there were approximately 10 million divorced men in the United States (US Census Bureau, 2010), and this does not include men who had remarried or did not have the legal status of being previously married (i.e., same-sex couples and men who were long-term cohabitators). Ex-partners are often tied to one another after divorce or separation by their prior relationship, children, financial arrangements, and other connections. Furthermore, it is not uncommon that one of the partners never wanted to divorce and continued to feel romantically connected to the other. As Doka (2002e) states, "divorce, then, ends a marriage, not a relationship" (p. 156). Consequently, there are millions of men who have a relationship and common history with a previous partner, even if this relationship is not legally recognized.

Despite these ties to the deceased ex-spouse, the status of ex-partners as having a right to grieve is often either reduced or denied entirely. For example, an ex-spouse may not be welcomed at the funeral or visitation, is not given time off from work, and does not receive the social support typically afforded to those suffering a significant loss. The ambivalence in Western culture regarding how to view the ex-partner was reflected in a study that asked participants to rate the intensity and duration of grief of a fictitious case by various family and friend relationships. Ex-spouses of the deceased received a wide range of responses (from the least affected of 15 different relationships, to the second-most affected) while the still-married partner was consistently ranked as the primary griever (Robson & Walter, 2012–13).

In a study of 79 divorced individuals whose ex-spouses had died, Scott (2000) found that over 75% reported some grief related to their ex-partners' deaths. Approximately half of the individuals who had a grief reaction indicated that their family and friends did not acknowledge their loss. This lack of acknowledgment is a clear example of disenfranchised grief in that their losses were not socially recognized nor were they supported (see Doka, 2002e).

In their studies of divorcees whose ex-partner died, Doka (1986) and Scott (1987) found that the bereaved could be classified into two patterns: those who had resolved the loss of the marriage and those who had not resolved the loss of the divorce and were now faced with the death of the ex-spouse. As might be expected, the first group generally handled the death of their ex-spouse well; those in the latter group reported strong grief reactions. Guilt was evident in some of responses of the 'unresolved' group:

> Respondents felt that they may have contributed to the death by the stresses that the relationship and its dissolution created. They sometimes felt that if they hadn't gone through with the divorce, their ex-spouses might still be alive. . . . There was often much unfinished business. . . . And many respondents in this pattern felt a deep sense of anger. (Doka, 2002e, p. 158)

Other problems and frustrations described by the ex-spouses at the time of the death included frustration at not being included in obituaries, uncertainty at how to act and where to sit at funeral, and unease at how others reacted to their presence. For example, in her study of bereaved ex-spouses, Scott (2000) found that while 60% of the respondents attended their ex-partner's funeral, only 56% percent reported feeling comfortable while there.

After the death, other concerns surfaced including lack of social support, hesitancy to seek assistance due to the ambiguity of their situation, and lack of leave time from work. If they had children in common with the deceased, the ex-spouse sometimes became the target of the children's anger (Doka, 2002e). If they had remarried, their new partners often responded with resentment and jealousy, especially if their grief lasted more than a few weeks (Scott, 2000).

Due to the ambiguous nature of the relationship, men who experience the death of their ex-partners may be especially sensitive to a psychotherapist's recognition of the seriousness of their loss (Doka, 1989b). The key is appreciating what the relationship meant to the bereaved client. For example, at first glance it might seem unusual that a grieving client is having such a strong reaction to the death of an ex-wife from whom he has been divorced for 25 years. Despite the divorce, the ex-wife may have continued to play several important roles in the client's life, including the mother/co-parent of his children, his first love, someone from whom he learned a great deal, someone who stood with him during a difficult challenge, and so on. Furthermore, the loss of a spouse (or ex-spouse) likely brings up concerns about the client's own mortality. Given this and the likelihood that his grief is largely unrecognized by others, and it becomes much easier to find empathy for the client's reaction.

Unfortunately, the ex-partners may not have the insight to identify and express why the loss is painful; they may only know that they are experiencing some uncomfortable reactions. As Doka (1989b) states, "bereaved ex-spouses may internalize a belief that they have no right, role, or reason to grieve" (pp. 108–109). An ex-partner may self-disenfranchise his grief by assuming he 'shouldn't' experience grief regarding someone with whom he does not have frequent contact (i.e., his ex-partner). Furthermore, he may have created a pattern of self-disenfranchisement by convincing himself that he does not need to express grief because it goes against male gender norms (Kauffman, 2002). Given this, a key role of the psychotherapist is helping the client recognize that his grief for the death of his ex-partner is normal and reasonable. This in itself will likely bring relief. In fact, counseling may be one of the few safe havens for the bereaved man to express his reaction to his ex-spouse's death without fear of judgment or condemnation (Doka, 1989b, 2002e). Counselors should be sensitive to the likelihood that grieving ex-spouses often have limited social support and may struggle to believe that they have a right to their grief.

Cohabitating Widowers

Accurate statistics on unmarried cohabitating couples are difficult to collect. The 2010 US Census reported that almost 5 million households included unmarried opposite sex partners. (For comparison, this is more than the number of households that include a stepchild; Lofquist et al., 2012) This suggests that at any given time a significant number of men are living with an unmarried romantic partner. If these men's partners die, they often experience a similar grief reaction as widowers who were married.

There are several parallels between the status of widowers who had been cohabitating and men whose ex-partner has died. Men in neither group typically receive full acknowledgment of their loss by family members, friends, or employers. Furthermore they may not be included in funeral rituals, and they typically have few legal rights. A significant factor for widowers who were cohabitating is the recognition of the relationship by the deceased's family and friends. (This is also true for widowers who were 'only' engaged to be married to their partner. See the box "Bereaved Fiancés.") Some family members may not acknowledge any significant relationship, while others may see the widower as a full-fledged member of the family. The level of recognition by the deceased's family before and after the loss will have a significant impact on how the cohabitating widower will be supported and included (Doka, 1989b). Of particular importance to cohabitating couples, as with same-sex partners, is the degree to which the relationship has been shared with others. Doka (1989b) suggests that the "more open the relationship, the more opportunity there is to acknowledge grief and receive social support" (p. 69).

The cohabitating widower's reactions to his loss will be influenced by the same factors as a married widower: the quality, length, closeness, and other important relationship factors. It would be a mistake to assume that a cohabitating widower will have less grief simply because he was not married to his partner, just as it is a mistake to assume that all married widowers will have a strong grief response simply because their relationship was legally sanctioned. Factors that may add stress to a cohabitating widower's grief include guilt related to not getting legally married, the lack of social support, and legal problems associated with not being married to a person with whom you shared a home and other resources (Doka, 1989b). One of the biggest challenges for cohabitating widowers may be determining custody of children they were actively co-parenting but whom they were not recognized as the legal guardian.

As with widowers who are ex-spouses, counseling can provide previously cohabitating widowers one of the few refuges to express their reactions without fear of judgment or condemnation. Counselors should be sensitive to the likelihood that these widowers have limited social support and may self-disenfranchise their own grief. I believe that counselors should approach men who experience the loss of a cohabitating partner as they would a widower who was legally married until the client suggests differently. Therefore, the techniques and topics of exploration recommended for married widowers are a good starting point for these clients.

> ## Bereaved Fiancés
>
> Men whose partners die before they are legally married may experience many of the same challenges as men who were cohabitating with their partners. The most important factor is the level of acceptance by the family of the deceased. Ideally, the bereaved partner will be treated as a full-fledged member of the family and be able to participate fully in any death rituals. Roberts (2010) describes a situation where a widowed fiancé's partner died a week before their planned wedding. Against the wishes of the deceased and the fiancé, a sister had the body buried. In response the fiancé created his own 'ashes' by taking a few meaningful items including "little pictures, little photographs, a page or two from some of her favorite books . . . perfume, a fish hook" (p. 7). The fiancé decided to scatter these ashes in a bay and take pictures of the process to remember and share the event with those who supported him. When widowers are not recognized as legitimate grievers by the family and have no legal standing, they may be left with no alternative but to come up with their own meaningful rituals.

Ethnic Minority Widowers

There are several general principles to follow when working with widowers from minority ethnic groups. Some of these are general principles regardless of the client's presenting problem, while others are specific to grief counseling. In regard to multicultural grief counseling, the psychotherapist should begin by being aware of his or her own assumptions about death and grief. This includes the therapist's views on the afterlife (including if he or she believes in some form of life after death), grief rituals, and methods of disposition (e.g., burial, cremation, etc.) (Sue & Sue, 2013). These perspectives are likely to be based on the counselor's own experiences with grief. Counselors should be aware of their own preconceptions and assumptions about grief and death just as they should be cognizant of other critical topics that may be the focus of counseling (e.g., views on life purpose, partner and family dynamics, religion/spirituality, how lasting change is achieved, substance use and abuse, etc.).

Counselors who frequently counsel bereaved individuals should also educate themselves about various grief rituals, practices, and beliefs. The goal is not to become an expert on the death practices and beliefs of every ethnic group, but to have a general knowledge of a variety of practices that can serve as scaffolding for learning about new practices. The counselor can learn from books, articles, and documentaries about grief and death in specific cultures. Of course not all members of a group share the same views or practices related to death, grief, or rituals. General knowledge about a group is a good start, but specific knowledge regarding how your client accepts, interprets, and finds meaning in those traditions (or does not) is best gained from the client himself.

In this section, I will discuss some considerations when working with widowers who identify with the three largest ethnic minority groups in the United States: African Americans, Latinos, and Asian Americans. Because almost all research on grief in the US is based on Euro-Americans, a discussion of grief in minority cultures is often based on a comparison to the dominant culture. This can be useful as long as the practices of the dominant culture are not viewed as the standard against which others are judged (Rosenblatt & Wallace, 2005). Given that research on widowers is relatively sparse, research on widowers from minority ethnic groups is even scarcer. In many cases, the best option is to take previous research on grief as related to specific groups and try to adapt it to widowers of that group. Of course this is not ideal given that widowers of various groups do not necessarily think and behave like members of the larger group. However, until more research is completed on minority widowers, it is the only option. I hope this book, along with previous research on widowers, can serve as a starting point for more research on widowers who belong to various minority groups.

African American Widowers

Individuals who self-identify as Black or African American represent over 13% of the US population (not including those who identify as bi- or multiracial; US Census Bureau, 2012). Although African Americans are less likely than Caucasians to seek mental health services (Churn, 2003), psychotherapists may still work with African American widowers given that they are part of the second-largest ethnic minority group in the US.

There are several general differences in the grief and death rituals in African American culture. Generally speaking African Americans view the funeral as a critical ritual. The funeral is a religious (usually Christian) event (Barrett, 1998; Churn, 2003). Attendance and participation at a funeral, which may be three to five hours in length, is expected for family, friends, and other members of the community. The presence and viewing of the body is very important; African Americans are less likely than European Americans to use cremation. Many African American funerals involve strong expressions of emotions (e.g., 'whooping and hollering') although there is also a compelling social imperative to 'be strong' after the funeral (Rosenblatt & Wallace, 2005).

There are several factors that may make the grief experience for African Americans more difficult. African Americans are more likely to face violent, sudden, and unexpected deaths. Furthermore, they are also more likely to deal with a combination of situational variables that may make grieving more difficult, including lower socioeconomic status and accumulated loss/bereavement overload (Meagher & Bell, 1993).

Conversely, African Americans have several strengths from which to draw. African Americans have a larger number of family members in their social networks and tend to have more frequent contact with them (Ajrouch, Antonucci, & Janevic, 2001; Sue & Sue, 2013). By having larger social networks, widowers may be less likely to rely exclusively on their partners for support. African American grievers may be especially likely to use their religious beliefs as a source of support. In a study of bereaved African Americans, over 70% spoke about the importance of Biblical scripture in their grief adjustment (Rosenblatt & Wallace, 2005). If the widower is affiliated with a religious institution, this will likely be a significant aspect of his social network.

Research that includes large samples of widowed African Americans is relatively rare. Carr (2004a) used the longitudinal CLOC study of older married couples to examine differences between African American and European American widowed persons. Based on previous research that suggests that African Americans share housework more evenly, have broader social networks, rate their marriages as having more conflict, and attend religious services more frequently, Carr hypothesized that older African American widowed persons may experience fewer grief reactions than Whites. Although the two groups had no significant differences in terms of grief reactions related to intrusive thoughts, yearning, shock, or overall grief, they did significantly differ in terms of African American widowed persons having less despair and anger. Carr (2004a) attributes the differences to the higher social connectivity of African Americans.

For counselors who are not African American, there are several reminders for working with grieving African Americans. It is critical to understand the religious and spiritual views of the client as well as his conceptualization of family (which may be broader than European American grievers). Furthermore, the counselor should recognize the long history of discrimination including access to health services (Meagher & Bell, 1993). Finally, Barrett (1998) reminds counselors to be sensitive to differences, but not to forget the commonalities of human experience and basic counseling processes:

> While race, culture and ethnicity should not be taken lightly, they should not be perceived as insurmountable barriers. Be yourself, be honest, be real, and be open to and teachable about those aspects of Black experience that may be a bit different from your own. Have faith

in our common humanity to connect and support one another in our experiences of loss, grief, and pain in spite of our separateness and apparent differences. (pp. 95–96)

I believe this advice is equally valid in all cross-cultural counseling situations.

Latino Widowers

Given that no common consensus has been established regarding the use of *Latino/a* or *Hispanic*, I have decided to follow Sue and Sue (2013) and Vazquez and Rosa (2011) in using the term *Latino/a* while recognizing that this is an imperfect term and that others may prefer different ones. For clarification, I will use *Latino/a* when referring to men and women and will use *Latino* when only talking about men. While terminology is important, it is even more important for the counselor to learn about how each individual widower conceptualizes his racial and ethnic identity. In many cases, the widower may feel that a much more specific designation (Mexican American, Cuban American, etc.) is the best reflection of his identity. Furthermore, the client's level of acculturation will significantly influence his views of cultural identity.

Individuals who self-identify as Latino/a or Hispanic represent almost 17% of the US population (US Census Bureau, 2012). As with all large ethnic groups, individual differences among subgroups can be significant. However, there are several generally recognized common aspects for Latinas/os including an emphasis on family privacy, a commitment to religious faith, a strong sense of maintaining cultural traditions, and tight-knit families and a respect for older family members (Casas, Raley, & Vasquez, 2008; Sue & Sue, 2013).

Vazquez and Rosa (2011) suggest that there are several key cultural values to be knowledgeable of when working with Latinos. I believe three of these values are particularly relevant when counseling Latino widowers: *tradicionalismo*, *machismo*, and *orgullo*. Tradicionalismo refers to an overall sense of adhering to and passing down traditions. A widower's desire to maintain traditions may include avoiding assistance from anyone besides family and close friends (see Casas, Raley, & Vasquez, 2008; Sue & Sue, 2013).

I (and I should point out I am Caucasian American) interpret machismo as the Latino equivalent of Brannon's (1976) injunctions; they are socially and culturally derived male gender role expectations for Latinos. Just as traditional masculinity has positive and negative aspects, so does machismo. One aspect of machismo is a sense of protection (and sometimes overprotection) for a man's property and family as well as being a good provider (Vazquez & Rosa, 2011).

Given that a Latino husband is expected to be dominant and strong (Sue & Sue, 2013), it may be difficult for him to accept assistance following the death of his partner. It is too simplistic to view machismo simply as a barrier to grief in widowers. As described in Chapter 5, grief can be expressed in cognitive and physically active ways including taking care of others. As Vazquez and Rosa (2011) state, "Many times, components of *machismo* can hinder the process of healing and adaptation, while at other times it can facilitate it" (p. 43).

A third value that may be important to Latino widowers is orgullo. Orgullo refers to a sense of cultural pride and is related to machismo (Vazquez & Rosa, 2011). While this sense of pride may provide the widower with a sense of strength, it can also hinder a widower from seeking outside assistance. For example, he may fear that seeking professional help may be interpreted as reflecting poorly on his family.

Counselors working with Latino widowers should learn about the client's perspective on cultural influences on his grief. This may include how comfortable he is asking for and receiving assistance as well as if he feels he needs to restrain or hide any thoughts, behaviors, or feelings. Psychotherapists should adapt the positive and empathic model described in Chapter 2 for Latino widowers by recognizing the strengths that come from adhering to machismo-related standards while also helping them identify when these cultural and gender norms may be hurting them and others.

Asian American Widowers

Approximately 5% of Americans identify as Asian American (US Census Bureau, 2012). As with Latinos, Asian Americans are typically conceptualized as a homogenous group when there are actually considerable variations among subgroups (e.g., Japanese Americans, Filipino Americans, Indian Americans, Chinese Americans, Korean Americans, etc.; Braun & Nichols, 1997). As Klass and Goss (1998) state, "There is no 'Eastern' way of grieving or of coming to terms with death, just as there is no 'Western' way" (p. 13). However, other researchers have noted several common values generally shared by most Asian American cultures. For example, Leong, Lee, and Chang (2008) state that the

> Asian American worldview emphasizes humility, modesty, treating oneself strictly while treating others more leniently, obligation to family, conformity, obedience, and subordination to authority. Other factors that contextualize the cultural context of Asian Americans include familial relations, interpersonal harmony versus honesty emphasis, role hierarchy versus egalitarianism, and self-restraint versus self-disclosure (W.W. Chien & Banerjee, 2002, p. 114)

Perhaps due to the popular perception of high rates of educational and occupational success as well as social adjustment, Asian Americans are often viewed as a 'model' minority that experience little prejudice and discrimination. Unfortunately this perception reinforces several stereotypes that impede the use of counseling services by Asian Americans and ignores long-standing discrimination (Sue & Sue, 2013).

There are some common components of Asian American grief rituals and traditions. In many Asian cultures funeral rituals last at least 40 days after the death; some Asian Americans maintain these traditions of grief rituals that continue for a significant time after the death. Furthermore, many cultures have yearly rituals associated with deceased family members that may last up to 50 years after the death. Asian Americans are also more likely than Caucasian Americans to believe that their deceased family members may be close by, watching over the living, or may return to visit the living (Braun & Nichols, 1997). These beliefs and practices may be the reason for a common misconception that Asians (and by extension, Asian Americans) 'worship' their deceased ancestors when it could be better explained by long-term rituals and a strong sense of continuing bonds (Klass & Goss, 1998). Other aspects of death rituals among Asian cultures may be quite different. For example Chinese Americans tend to prefer to bury the deceased's body intact while other Asian American groups prefer cremation.

One significant difference among the various Asian American subgroups that influences death rituals is the dominant religious and spiritual views within a given culture. For example, the grief reactions and death rituals for the majority of Filipino Americans are influenced by their Catholic beliefs, while Chinese Americans may be influenced by Confucianism, Taoism, Buddhism, or other belief systems (Braun & Nichols, 1997). It is critical that psychotherapists who work with grieving Asian American clients learn about the client's specific belief system and not make assumptions based on belonging to a specific group.

Cultural practices and beliefs can influence the grief of Asian American widowers; likewise it can also influence the counseling practices they perceive as most welcoming and culturally sensitive. For example, Asian American widowers may be especially hesitant to express emotions. They may also view the act of seeking assistance as an admission of failure and may view seeking counseling as a sign of severe mental illness (Leong, Lee, & Chang, 2008; Sue & Sue, 2013). Park (2006) suggests that avoiding 'losing face' is one of the most important values in Asian American culture. Park differentiates 'losing face' from shame by stating that losing face has a strong social component—often resulting in disgrace for the family as well as the individual. Asian American widowers may be particularly focused on their presenting problem; counselors should help the client set specific goals related to the concerns that brought him to counseling.

Generally speaking, Asian American widowers may be more comfortable with counseling sessions that are more structured and counselors who use a more directive style. Counselors can help Asian American widowers by thoroughly explaining and educating the client about the counseling process.

Caucasian Subgroups

I believe that Euro-American groups are often overlooked when examining minority ethnic groups. Although it is impossible to even briefly examine them in this book, it is important for psychotherapists to be aware that some Caucasians strongly identify with their European heritage. More important, each of these groups has particular customs and values that may affect a widower's grief experience and may be relevant in counseling. For example, Campbell and Silverman (1987) interviewed Jan, a younger widower whose wife was murdered. Jan strongly identified with his Finnish heritage and argued that his lack of desire to talk about his loss was influenced by his cultural values:

> I ride to work every day with a Dane, and he can sympathize with my apparent lack of emotion. He thinks it's something that's genetic in us Scandinavians, and that the trouble with the world is, at least for us Scandinavians, that all the therapists in the world are nice Jewish ladies and Italians and Irishmen. And nice Jewish ladies and Italians and Irishmen really love to cry. There's nothing better than a good cry. But for Finns and Danes, it's not the heritage. One just doesn't cry. . . . That's his theory, anyway. I thought it sounded pretty good. So I'm scouting around for a good Scandinavian therapist who'll say, "Aha! That's the way it is! You bet! That's it, sure enough!" (pp. 43–44)

Jan was not interested in attending a support group for single parents or a widowed persons group. Instead he was able to draw support from his family and friends through a culturally-relevant practice:

> There are a lot of people around me, very caring people. I get what I need from them. Every Saturday at 3:00, there's a sauna bath at my uncle's house. People come from miles around. They have, ever since I was little. We have births, we have deaths, we have weddings and wakes, but nothing interrupts the bath. Every Saturday at 3:00, ever since I was little. The sauna is very important to me. The people there have all had hard times. They've all had bad things happen to them one way or another, as all of us have, I guess. But they aren't there to say, "Oh, I feel so badly for you, I cried for a week." They are there just to be there. I know that they've had trouble, they know I've had troubles, and we've shared experiences. I don't go to them and say, "Oh, I have

> problems, I feel so bad," and they'll say, "Well tell me about it." It's simply that they're there. (pp. 44–45)
>
> In my opinion Jan had been attending a grief group since before his wife was murdered—he just didn't call it that. For him, it was the perfect group. It fit his cultural and family identity, met regularly, provided unconditional support for him, and allowed him to provide support for others. I wish all bereaved individuals had a support system as culturally and personally relevant as Jan's.

Empathy and Understudied and Minority Widowers

At times it can be overwhelming for counselors to work with clients from different backgrounds than their own. These differences may include sexual orientation, ethnicity, age, sex, and other factors. Regardless of the differences, it is important that counselors approach their clients empathically. When counselors begin with a desire to learn about widowers from different backgrounds, they are less likely to make assumptions and counsel based on stereotypes. It is also important for counselors to have a broad base of knowledge and to educate themselves when working with a client from a different background, but empathy and a desire to learn about a widower's unique circumstances is the most critical starting point. The details may be different, but there are far more commonalities among men who lose a partner.

REFERENCES

Addis, M. E., & Mahalik, J. R. (2003). Men, masculinity, and the contexts of help seeking. *American Psychologist, 58*, 5–14.

Ajdacic-Gross, V., Ring, M., Gadola, E., Lauber, C., Bopp, M., Gutzwiller, F., & Rossler, W. (2008). Suicide after bereavement: An overlooked problem. *Psychological Medicine, 38*, 673–676.

Ajrouch, K. J., Antonucci, T. C., & Janevic, M. R. (2001). Social networks among Blacks and Whites: The interaction between race and age. *Journal of Gerontology: Social Sciences, 56B*, S112–S118.

Allumbaugh, D. L., & Hoyt, W. T. (1999). Effectiveness of grief therapy: A meta-analysis. *Journal of Counseling Psychology, 46*, 370–380.

Altmaier, E. M. (2011). Best practices in counseling grief and loss: Finding benefit from trauma. *Journal of Mental Health Counseling, 33*, 33–45.

American Psychological Association. (2000). Guidelines for psychotherapy with lesbian, gay, and bisexual clients. *American Psychologist, 55*, 1440–1451.

Anderson, P. M. L. (2001). A grief unheard: A woman's reflection on a men's grief group. In D. Lund (Ed.), *Men coping with grief* (pp. 309–325). Amityville, NY: Baywood.

Andronico, M. P. (1996). Introduction. In M. P. Andronico (Ed.), *Men in groups: Insights, interventions, and psychoeducational work* (pp. xvii–xxiv). Washington, DC: American Psychological Association.

Arbuckle, N. W., & de Vries, B. (1995). The long-term effects of later life spousal and parental bereavement on personal functioning. *The Gerontologist, 35*, 637–647.

Archer, J. (1999). *The nature of grief: The evolution and psychology of reactions to loss*. London, England: Routledge.

Assar, A., & Bobinski, G. S., Jr. (1991). Financial decision making of baby boomer couples. *Advances in Consumer Research, 18*, 657–665.

Association for Death Education and Counseling (ADEC). (2008). *Researching efficacy and finding deterioration*. Retrieved from www.adec.org/documents/Grief_Counseling_Helpful_or_Harmful_Revision.pdf

Attig, T. (1991). The importance of conceiving of grief as an active process. *Death Studies, 15*, 385–393.

Attig, T. (1996). *How we grieve: Relearning the world*. New York, NY: Oxford University Press.

Attig, T. (2000). *The heart of grief: Death and the search for lasting love*. New York, NY: Oxford University Press.

REFERENCES

Balaswamy, S., Richardson, V., & Price, C.A. (2004). Investigating patterns of social support use by widowers during bereavement. *Journal of Men's Studies, 13*, 67–84.

Barrett, R.K. (1998). Sociocultural considerations for working with blacks experiencing loss and grief. In K.J. Doka & J.D. Davidson (Eds.), *Living with grief: Who we are, how we grieve* (pp. 83–96). Washington, DC: Hospice Foundation of America.

Barrett, T.W., & Scott, T.B. (1990). Suicide bereavement and recovery patterns compared with nonsuicide bereavement patterns. *Suicide and Life-Threatening Behavior, 20*, 1–15.

Bartholomew, K. (1990). Avoidance of intimacy: An attachment perspective. *Journal of Social and Personal Relationships, 7*, 147–178.

Barusch, A.S., & Peak, T. (1997). Support groups for older men: Building on strengths and facilitating relationships. In J.I. Kosberg & L.W. Kaye (Eds.), *Elderly men: Special problems and professional challenges* (pp. 262–278). New York, NY: Springer.

Bee, H.L., & Bjorkland, B.R. (2004). *The journey of adulthood* (5th ed.). Upper Saddle River, NJ: Pearson.

Bennett, K.M. (1998). Longitudinal changes in mental and physical health among elderly, recently widowed men. *Mortality, 3*, 265–273.

Bennett, K.M. (2002). Low level of social engagement as a precursor of mortality among people in later life. *Age and Ageing, 31*, 165–168.

Bennett, K.M. (2007). "No sissy stuff": Towards a theory of masculinity and emotional expression in older widowed men. *Journal of Aging Studies, 21*, 347–356.

Bennett, K.M. (2009). Gender difference in bereavement support for older widowed people. *Bereavement Care, 28*(3), 5–9.

Bennett, K.M., Hughes, G.M., & Smith, P.T. (2003). "I think a woman can take it": Widowed men's views and experiences of gender differences in bereavement. *Ageing International, 28*, 408–424.

Bennett, K.M., Hughes, G.M., & Smith, P.T. (2005). Psychological response to later life widowhood: Coping and the effects of gender. *Omega: Journal of Death and Dying, 51*, 33–52.

Bergman, S.J. (1995). Men's psychological development: A relational perspective. In R.F. Levant & W.S. Pollack (Eds.), *A new psychology of men* (pp. 68–90). New York, NY: Basic Books.

Bierhals, A.J., Frank, E., Prigerson, H.G., Miller, M., Fasiczkaf, A., & Reynolds, C.F. (1995). Gender differences in complicated grief among the elderly. *Omega: Journal of Death and Dying, 32*, 303–317.

Blando, J. (2011). *Counseling older adults*. New York, NY: Routledge.

Bly, R. (1990). *Iron John: A book about men*. New York, NY: Vintage Books.

Boerner, K., & Heckhausen, J. (2003). To have and have not: Adaptive bereavement by transforming mental ties to the deceased. *Death Studies, 27*, 199–226.

Bonanno, G.A. (2004). Loss, trauma, and human resilience: Have we underestimated the human capacity to thrive after extremely aversive events? *American Psychologist, 59*, 20–28.

Bonanno, G.A., & Boerner, K. (2007). Letters—the stage theory of grief. *Journal of the American Medical Association, 297*, 2693.

Bonanno, G.A., & Field, N.P. (2001). Examining the delayed grief hypothesis across 5 years of bereavement. *American Behavioral Scientist, 44*, 798–816.

Bonanno, G.A., & Keltner, D. (1999). Facial expressions of emotion and the course of conjugal bereavement. *Journal of Abnormal Psychology, 106*, 126–137.

Bonanno, G.A., Papa, A., Lalande, K., Zhang, N., & Noll, J.G. (2005). Grief processing and deliberate grief avoidance: A prospective comparison of bereaved spouses and parents in the United States and the People's Republic of China. *Journal of Consulting and Clinical Psychology, 73*, 86–98.

REFERENCES

Bonanno, G. A., Wortman, C. B., Lehman, D. R., Tweed, R. G., Haring, M., Sonnega, J., Carr, D., & Nesse, R. M. (2002). Resilience to loss and chronic grief: A prospective study from preloss to 18-months postloss. *Journal of Personality and Social Psychology, 83*, 1150–1164.

Bonanno, G. A., Wortman, C. B., & Nesse, R. M. (2004). Prospective patterns of resilience and maladjustment during widowhood. *Psychology and Aging, 19*, 260–271.

Bosley, G. M., & Cook, A. S. (1993). Therapeutic aspects of funeral ritual: A thematic analysis. *Journal of Family Psychotherapy, 4*, 69–83.

Boss, P. (1999). *Ambiguous loss: Learning to live with unresolved grief*. Cambridge, MA: Harvard University Press.

Boss, P. (2006). *Loss, trauma, and resilience: Therapeutic work with ambiguous loss*. New York, NY: W.W. Norton.

Bowen, M. (1976). Family reaction to death. In P. Guerin (Ed.), *Family therapy: Theory and practice* (pp. 335–348). New York, NY: Gardner.

Bowlby, J. (1980). *Attachment and loss: Loss, sadness, and depression*. (Vol. III). New York, NY: Basic Books.

Bowling, A., & Windsor, J. (1995). Death after widow(er)hood: An analysis of mortality rates up to 13 years after bereavement. *Omega: Journal of Death and Dying, 31*, 35–49.

Brabant, S. (2002). A closer look at Doka's grieving rules. In K. J. Doka (Ed.), *Disenfranchised grief: New directions, challenges, and strategies for practice* (pp. 23–60). Champaign, IL: Research Press.

Brabant, S., Forsyth, C. J., & Melancon, C. (1992). Grieving men: Thoughts, feelings, and behaviors following deaths of wives. *The Hospice Journal, 8*(4), 33–47.

Brannon, R. (1976). The male sex role: Our culture's blueprint of manhood and what it's done for us lately. In D. S. David & R. Brannon (Eds.), *The forty-nine percent majority: The male sex role* (pp. 1–45). Reading, MA: Addison-Wesley.

Braun, K. L., & Nichols, R. (1997). Death and dying in four Asian American cultures. *Death Studies, 21*, 327–359.

Brooks, G. R. (1996). Treatment for therapy-resistant men. In M. Andronico (Ed.), *Men in groups: Insights, interventions, and psychoeducational work* (pp. 7–19). Washington, DC: American Psychological Association.

Brooks, G. R. (1998). *A new psychotherapy for traditional men*. San Francisco, CA: Jossey-Bass.

Bureau of Justice Statistics. (2011). *Homicide trends in the U.S.: Intimate homicide (1980–2008)*. Retrieved from http://bjs.ojp.usdoj.gov/content/pub/pdf/htus8008.pdf

Burns, G. (1976). *Living it up*. New York, NY: Putnam's Sons.

Byrne, G. J. A., & Raphael, B. (1994). A longitudinal study of bereavement phenomena in recently widowed elderly men. *Psychological Medicine, 24*, 411–421.

Byrne, G. J. A., Raphael, B., & Arnold, E. (1999). Alcohol consumption and psychological distress in recently widowed older men. *Australian and New Zealand Journal of Psychiatry, 33*, 740–747.

Cable, D. G. (1998). Grief in the American culture. In K. J. Doka & J. D. Davidson (Eds.), *Living with grief: Who we are, how we grieve* (pp. 61–70). Washington, DC: Hospice Foundation of America.

Campbell, S., & Silverman, P. R. (1987). *Widower: When men are left alone*. Amityville, NY: Baywood.

Canetto, S. S. (1992). Gender and suicide in the elderly. *Suicide and Life-Threatening Behavior, 22*, 80–97.

Carr, D. (2003). A 'good death' for whom? Quality of spouses' death and psychological distress among older widowed persons. *Journal of Health and Social Behavior, 44*, 215–232.

Carr, D. (2004a). Black/White differences in psychological adjustment to spousal loss among older adults. *Research on Aging, 26*, 591–622.

REFERENCES

Carr, D. (2004b). Desire to date and remarry among older widows and widowers. *Journal of Marriage and Family, 66*, 1051–1068.

Carr, D. (2004c). Gender, preloss marital dependence, and older adults' adjustment to widowhood. *Journal of Marriage and Family, 66*, 220–235.

Carr, D. (2006). Methodological issues in studying late life bereavement. In D. Carr, R. Nesse, & C. B. Wortman (Eds.), *Spousal bereavement in late life* (pp. 19–47). New York, NY: Springer.

Carr, D., & Boerner, K. (2009). Do spousal discrepancies in marital quality assessments affect psychological adjustment to widowhood? *Journal of Marriage and Family, 71*, 495–509.

Carr, D., House, J. S., Kessler, R. C., Nesse, R. M., Sonnega, J., & Wortman, C. (2000). Marital quality and psychological adjustment to widowhood among older adults: A longitudinal analysis. *Journal of Gerontology, 55B*, S197–S207.

Carr, D., House, J. S., Wortman, C., Nesse, R., & Kessler, R. C. (2001). Psychological adjustment to sudden and anticipated spousal loss among older widowed persons. *Journal of Gerontology, 56B*, S237-S238.

Casas, J. M., Raley, J. D., & Vasquez, M. J.T. (2008). Adelante! Counseling the Latina/o from guiding theory to practice. In P. B. Pedersen, J. G. Draguns, W. J. Lonner, & J. E. Trimble (Eds.), *Counseling across cultures* (6th ed., pp. 129–146). Thousand Oaks, CA: Sage.

Caserta, M. S., & Lund, D.A. (1996). Beyond bereavement support group meetings: Exploring outside contact among members. *Death Studies, 20*, 537–556.

Caserta, M. S., Lund, D.A., & Rice, S. J. (1999). Pathfinders: A self-care and health education program for older widows and widowers. *American Journal of Health Education, 32*, 229–236.

Cass, V. (1979). Homosexual identity formation: A theoretical model. *Journal of Homosexuality, 4*, 219–235.

Centers for Disease Control and Prevention. (2004, October 12). *National Vital Statistics Reports: Deaths: Final Data for 2002* (Vol. 53 (5)).

Centers for Disease Control and Prevention. (2012, January 11). *National Vital Statistics Reports: Deaths: Preliminary Data for 2010* (Vol. 60 (4)).

Chen, J. H., Gill, T. M., & Prigerson, H. G. (2005). Health behaviors associated with better quality of life for older bereaved persons. *Journal of Palliative Medicine, 8*, 96–106.

Churn, A. (2003). *The end is just the beginning: Lessons in grieving for African Americans*. New York, NY: Broadway Books.

Clark, A. (1982). Grief and Gestalt therapy. *The Gestalt Journal, 5*, 49–63.

Cleiren, M., Diekstra, R., Kerkhof, A., & van der Wal, J. (1994). Mode of death and kinship in bereavement: Focusing on "who" rather than "how." *Crisis, 15*, 22–36.

Colgrove, M., Bloomfield, H. H., & McWilliams, P. (1991). *How to survive the loss of a love*. Los Angeles, CA: Prelude Press. (Original work published 1976).

Coombs, R. H. (1991). Marital status and personal well-being: A literature review. *Family Relations, 40*, 97–102.

Corey, G. (2000). *Theory and practice of group counseling* (5th ed.). Belmont, CA: Brooks/Cole.

Corr, C.A. (1993). Coping with dying: Lessons that we should and should not learn from the work of Elisabeth Kübler-Ross. *Death Studies, 17*, 69–83.

Corr, C., & Doka, K. (2001). Master concepts in the field of death, dying and bereavement: Coping vs. adaptive strategies. *Omega: Journal of Death and Dying, 43*, 183–199.

Corr, C.A., Nabe, C. M., & Corr, D. M. (1994). A task-based approach for understanding and evaluating funeral practices. *Thanatos, 19*(2), 10–15.

Courtenay, W. H. (2011). *Dying to be men: Psychosocial, environmental, and biobehavioral directions in promoting the health of men and boys*. New York, NY: Routledge.

REFERENCES

Currier, J. M., Neimeyer, R. A., & Berman, J. S. (2008). The effectiveness of psychotherapeutic interventions for bereaved persons: A comprehensive quantitative review. *Psychological Bulletin, 134*, 648–661.

Davidson, K. (2002). Gender differences in new partnership choices and constraints for older widows and widowers. *Ageing International, 27*, 43–60.

Davidson, K. (2004). "Why can't a man be more like a woman?": Marital status and social networking of older men. *Journal of Men's Studies, 13*, 25–43.

Davies, H., Priddy, J. M., & Tinkleberg, J. R. (1986). Support groups for male caregivers of Alzheimer's patients. *Clinical Gerontologist, 5*, 385–395.

Davis, C. G., & Nolen-Hoeksema, S. (2001). Loss and meaning: How do people make sense of loss? *The American Behavioral Scientist, 44*, 726–741.

Davis, C. G., Wortman, C. B., Lehman, D. R., & Silver, R. C. (2000). Searching for meaning in loss: Are clinical assumptions correct? *Death Studies, 24*, 497–540.

Dickinson, G. E. (2007). End-of-life and palliative care issues in medical and nursing schools in the United States. *American Journal of Hospice and Palliative Care, 19*, 181–186.

Dimond, M., Lund, D. A., & Caserta, M. S. (1987). The role of social support in the first two years of bereavement in an elderly sample. *The Gerontologist, 27*, 559–604.

Doka, K. J. (1984). Expectation of death, participation in planning funeral rituals, and grief adjustment. *Omega: Journal of Death and Dying, 15*, 119–129.

Doka, K. J. (1986). Loss upon loss: The impact of death after divorce. *Death Studies, 10*, 441–449.

Doka, K. J. (Ed.). (1989a). *Disenfranchised grief: Recognizing hidden sorrow*. Lexington, MA: Lexington Books.

Doka, K. J. (1989b). The left lover: Grief in extramarital affairs and cohabitation. In K. J. Doka (Ed.), *Disenfranchised grief: Recognizing hidden sorrow* (pp. 67–76). Lexington, MA: Lexington Books.

Doka, K. J. (1993). The spiritual crises of bereavement. In K. J. Doka with J. Morgan (Eds.), *Death and spirituality* (pp. 185–193). Amityville, NY: Baywood.

Doka, K. J. (1997). When illness is prolonged: Implications for grief. In K. J. Doka (Ed.), *Living with grief: When illness is prolonged* (pp. 5–15). Washington, DC: Hospice Foundation of America.

Doka, K. J. (Ed.). (2002a). *Disenfranchised grief: New directions, challenges, and strategies for practice*. Champaign, IL: Research Press.

Doka, K. J. (2002b). Introduction. In K. J. Doka (Ed.), *Disenfranchised grief: New directions, challenges, and strategies for practice* (pp. 5–22). Champaign, IL: Research Press.

Doka, K. J. (2002c). How we die: Stigmatized death and disenfranchised grief. In K. J. Doka (Ed.), *Disenfranchised grief: New directions, challenges, and strategies for practice* (pp. 323–336). Champaign, IL: Research Press.

Doka, K. J. (2002d). The role of ritual in the treatment of disenfranchised grief. In K. J. Doka (Ed.), *Disenfranchised grief: New directions, challenges, and strategies for practice* (pp. 135–147). Champaign, IL: Research Press.

Doka, K. J. (2002e). A later loss: The grief of ex-spouses. In K. J. Doka (Ed.), *Disenfranchised grief: New directions, challenges, and strategies for practice* (pp. 155–166). Champaign, IL: Research Press.

Doka, K. J., & Aber, R. A. (2002). Psychosocial loss and grief. In K. J. Doka (Ed.), *Disenfranchised grief: New directions, challenges, and strategies for practice* (pp. 217–231). Champaign, IL: Research Press.

Doka, K. J., & Martin, T. L. (2001). Take it like a man: Masculine response to loss. In D. Lund (Ed.), *Men coping with grief* (pp. 37–47). Amityville, NY: Baywood.

Doka, K. J., & Martin, T. L. (2002). How we grieve: Culture, class, and gender. In K. J. Doka (Ed.), *Disenfranchised grief: New directions, challenges, and strategies for practice* (pp. 337–347). Champaign, IL: Research Press.

REFERENCES

Doka, K. J., & Martin, T. L. (2010). *Grieving beyond gender: Understanding the ways men and women mourn.* New York, NY: Routledge.

Doughty, E. A., & Hoskins, W. J. (2011). Death education: An internationally relevant approach to grief counseling. *Journal for International Counselor Education, 3,* 25–38.

Downe-Wambolt, B., & Tamlyn, D. (1997). An international survey of death education trends in faculties of nursing and medicine. *Death Studies, 21,* 177–188.

Easterling, L. W., Gamino, L. A., Sewell, K. W., & Stirman, L. S. (2000). Spiritual experience, church attendance, and bereavement. *Journal of Pastoral Care, 54,* 263–275.

Echelbarger, D. (1993). Spirituality and suicide. In K. J. Doka & J. D. Morgan (Eds.), *Death and spirituality* (pp. 217–226). Amityville, NY: Baywood.

Elison, J., & McGonigle, C. (2003). *Liberating losses: When death brings relief.* Cambridge, MA: De Capo Lifelong.

Elwert, F., & Christakis, N. A. (2008). The effect of widowhood on mortality by the causes of death of both spouses. *American Journal of Public Health, 98,* 2092–2098.

Eng, P. M., Kawachi, I., Fitzmaurice, G., & Rimm, E. B. (2005). Effects of marital transitions on changes in dietary and other health behaviors in US male health professionals. *Journal of Epidemiology and Community Health, 59,* 56–62.

Englar-Carlson, M., & Stevens, M. A. (Eds.). (2006). *In the room with men: A casebook of therapeutic change.* Washington, DC: American Psychological Association.

Farberow, N. L., Gallagher-Thompson, D. E., Gilewski, M. J., & Thompson, L. W. (1992). Changes in grief and mental health of bereaved spouses of older suicides. *Journal of Gerontology, 47,* 357–366.

Farrell, W. (1993). *The myth of male power.* New York, NY: Simon & Schuster.

Field, N. P., Gal-Oz, E., & Bonanno, G. A. (2003). Continuing bonds and adjustment at 5 years after the death of a spouse. *Journal of Consulting and Clinical Psychology, 71,* 110–117.

Fitzgerald, H. (1994). *The mourning handbook: A complete guide for the bereaved.* New York, NY: Simon & Schuster.

Fogarty, S. (2010, Nov. 21). Till death and beyond for the Petroffs. *The Chronicle Telegram.* Retrieved from http://chronicle.northcoastnow.com/2010/11/21/till-death-and-beyond-for-the-petroffs

Francis, D., Kellaher, L., & Neophytou, G. (2005). *The secret cemetery.* Oxford, England: Berg.

Francis, L. E. (1997). Ideology and interpersonal emotional management: Redefining identity in two support groups. *Social Psychology Quarterly, 60,* 153–171.

Frank, J. D., & Frank, J. B. (1991). *Persuasion and healing: A comparative study of psychotherapy* (3rd ed.). Baltimore, MD: John Hopkins University Press.

Frankl, V. E. (1984). *Man's search for meaning.* New York, NY: Simon & Schuster. (Original work published 1959).

Frantz, T. T., Trolley, B. C., & Johll, M. P. (1996). Religious aspects of bereavement. *Pastoral Psychology, 44,* 151–163.

Freeman, S. J., & Ward, S. (1998). Death and bereavement: What counselors should know. *Journal of Mental Health Counseling, 20,* 216–226.

Freud, E. L. (1963). *Letters of Sigmund Freud.* New York, NY: Basic Books.

Freud, S. (1917). Mourning and melancholia. In *Collected papers* (Vol. 4., pp. 152–170). London, England: Hogarth Press.

Fry, P. S. (2001a). Predictors of health-related quality of life perspectives, self-esteem, and life satisfactions of older adults following spousal loss: An 18-month follow-up study of widows and widowers. *Gerontologist, 41,* 787–798.

REFERENCES

Fry, P. S. (2001b). The unique contribution of key existential factors to the prediction of psychological well-being of older adults following spousal loss. *Gerontologist, 41*, 69–81.

Fulghum, R. (1995). *From beginning to end: The rituals of our lives.* New York, NY: Villard Books.

Gadberry, J. H. (2000). When is a funeral not a funeral? *Illness, Crisis, and Loss, 8*, 166–180.

Gamino, L. A., Easterling, L. W., Stirman, K. W., & Sewell, K. W. (2000). Grief adjustment as influenced by funeral participation and occurrence of adverse funeral effects. *Omega: Journal of Death and Dying, 41*, 79–92.

Gamino, L. A., Sewell, K. W., & Easterling, L. W. (1998). Scott & White grief study: An empirical test of predictors of intensified mourning. *Death Studies, 22*, 333–355.

Gamino, L. A., Sewell, K. W., & Easterling, L. W. (2000). Scott & White grief study—phase 2: Toward an adaptive model of grief. *Death Studies, 24*, 633–660.

Glick, I. O., Weiss, R. S., & Parkes, C. M. (1974). *The first year of bereavement.* New York, NY: John Wiley & Sons.

Golden, T. (2000). *Swallowed by the snake: The gift of the masculine side of healing* (2nd ed.). Kensington, MD: Golden Healing.

Good, G. E., Dell, D. M., & Mintz, L. B. (1989). Male role and gender role conflict: Relations to help seeking in men. *Journal of Counseling Psychology, 36*, 295–300.

Goodkin, K., Baldewicz, T.T., Blaney, N.T., Asthana, D., Kumar, M., Shapshak, P., ... Zheng, W. L. (2001). Physiological effects of bereavement and bereavement support group interventions. In M. S. Stroebe, R. O. Hansson, W. Stroebe, & H. Schut (Eds.), *Handbook of bereavement research: Consequences, coping, and care* (pp. 671–704). Washington, DC: American Psychological Association.

Granek, L. (2010). Grief as pathology: The evolution of grief theory in psychology from Freud to the present. *History of Psychology, 13*, 46–73.

Grimby, A. (1998). Hallucinations following the loss of a spouse: Common and normal events among the elderly. *Journal of Clinical Geropsychiatry, 4*, 65–74.

Grollman, E. A. (1996). Spiritual support after sudden loss. In K. J. Doka (Ed.), *Living with grief after sudden loss: Suicide, homicide, accident, heart attack, stroke* (pp. 185–190). Washington, DC: Hospice Foundation of America.

Guarnaccia, C., Hayslip, B., & Landy, L. P. (1999). Influence of perceived preventability of the death and emotional closeness to the deceased: A test of Bugen's model. *Omega: Journal of Death and Dying, 39*, 261–276.

Guggenheim, B., & Guggenheim, J. (1995). *Hello from heaven.* New York, NY: Bantam.

Hansson, R. O., & Stroebe, M. S. (2007). *Bereavement in late life: Coping, adaptation, and developmental influences.* Washington, DC: American Psychological Association.

Harris, D. (2010). Oppression of the bereaved: A critical analysis of grief in western society. *Omega: Journal of Death and Dying, 60*, 241–253.

Helsing, K. J., Szklo, M., & Comstock, G. N. (1981). Factors associated with mortality after widowhood. *American Journal of Public Health, 71*, 802–809.

Hersh, S. P. (1996). After heart attack and stroke. In K. J. Doka (Ed.), *Living with grief after sudden loss: Suicide, homicide, accident, heart attack, stroke* (pp. 17–24). Washington, DC: Hospice Foundation of America.

Hershberger, P. J., & Walsh, W. B. (1990). Multiple role involvements and the adjustment to conjugal bereavement: An exploratory study. *Omega: Journal of Death and Dying, 21*, 91–102.

Holmes, T. H., & Rahe, R. H. (1967). The social readjustment rating scale. *Journal of Psychosomatic Research, 11*, 213–218.

Hornjatkevyc, N. L., & Alderson, K. G. (2011). With and without: The bereavement experiences of gay men who have lost a partner to non-AIDS-related causes. *Death Studies, 35*, 801–823.

Horowitz, M. J. (2005). Meditating on complicated grief disorder as a diagnosis. *Omega: Journal of Death and Dying, 52*, 87–89.

Howell, R. (2013). I'm not the man I was: Reflections on becoming a widower. *Illness, Crisis, and Loss, 21*, 3–13.

Hoyt, W.T., & Larson, D. G. (2010). What have we learned from research on grief counseling? A response to Schut and Neimeyer. *Bereavement Care, 29*(1), 10–13.

Hughes, C., & Fleming, D. (1991). Grief casualties on skid row. *Omega: Journal of Death and Dying, 23*, 109–118.

Hughes, G., Bennett, K. M., & Hetherington, M. M. (2004). Old and alone: Barriers to healthy eating in older men living on their own. *Appetite, 43*, 269–276.

Humphries, D. (2012). *Goodnight dear: The unsentimental diary of a bereaved husband*. Retrieved from www.amazon.com/Goodnight-Dear-Unsentimental-Bereaved-ebook/dp/B007OMTFAI/

Irion, P. E. (1991). Changing patterns of ritual responses to death. *Omega: Journal of Death and Dying, 22*, 159–172.

Irion, P. E. (1999). Ritual responses to death. In J. D. Davidson & K. J. Doka (Eds.), *Living with grief: At work, at school, at worship* (pp. 157–165). Levittown, PA: Hospice Foundation of America.

Jacobs, S., Hansen, F., Kasl, S., Ostfeld, A., Berkman, L., & Kim, K. (1990). Anxiety disorders during acute bereavement: Risk and risk factors. *Journal of Clinical Psychiatry, 51*, 269–274.

Jolliff, D. (1994). Guest editorial: Group work with men. *Journal for Specialists in Group Work, 19*, 50–51.

Jolliff, D. L., & Horne, A. M. (1996). Group counseling for middle-class men. In M. Andronico (Ed.), *Men in groups: Insights, interventions, and psychoeducational work* (pp. 51–68). Washington, DC: American Psychological Association.

Jordan, J. R., & McMenamy, J. (2004). Interventions for suicide survivors: A review of the literature. *Suicide and Life-Threatening Behavior, 34*, 337–349.

Jordan, J. R., & Neimeyer, R. A. (2003). Does grief counseling work? *Death Studies, 27*, 765–786.

Kaslow, F. W. (2004). Death of one's partner: The anticipation and the reality. *Professional Psychology: Research and Practice, 35*, 227–233.

Kastenbaum, R. J. (1969). Death and bereavement in later life. In A. H. Kutscher (Ed.), *Death and bereavement* (pp. 28–54). Springfield, IL: Charles C. Thomas.

Kauffman, J. (2002). The psychology of disenfranchised grief: Liberation, shame, and self-disenfranchisement. In K. J. Doka (Ed.), *Disenfranchised grief: New directions, challenges, and strategies for practice* (pp. 61–77). Champaign, IL: Research Press.

Keen, S. (1991). *Fire in the belly*. New York, NY: Bantam.

Kelly, L. (2000). *Don't ask for the dead man's golf clubs: What to do and say (and what not to) when a friend loses a loved one*. New York, NY: Workman.

Kilmartin, C.T. (2000). *The masculine self* (2nd ed.). Boston, MA: McGraw-Hill.

Kiselica, A. M., & Kiselica, M. S. (in press). Gender-sensitive group counseling and psychotherapy with men. In J. DeLucia-Waack, C. Kalodner, & M. Riva (Eds.), *The handbook of group counseling and psychotherapy* (2nd ed.). Thousand Oaks, CA: Sage.

Kiselica, M. S. (2006). Helping a boy become a parent: Male-sensitive psychotherapy with a teenage father. In M. Englar-Carlson & M. A. Stevens (Eds.), *In the room with men: A casebook of therapeutic change* (pp. 225–240). Washington, DC: American Psychological Association.

Kiselica, M. S. (2011). Promoting positive masculinity while addressing gender role conflicts: A balanced theoretical approach to clinical work with boys and men. In C. Blazina & D. Shen-Miller (Eds.), *An international psychology of men: Theoretical advances, case studies, and clinical innovations* (pp. 127–156). New York, NY: Routledge.

REFERENCES

Kiselica, M.S., & Englar-Carlson, M. (2010). Identifying, affirming, and building upon male strengths: The positive psychology/positive masculinity model of psychotherapy with boys and men. *Psychotherapy Theory, Research, Practice, Training, 47*, 276–287.

Kiselica, M.S., Englar-Carlson, M., Horne, A.M., & Fisher, M. (2008). A positive psychological perspective on helping boys. In M.S. Kiselica, M. Englar-Carlson, & A.M. Horne (Eds.), *Counseling troubled boys: A guidebook for professionals* (pp. 31–48). New York, NY: Routledge.

Klass, D. (2006). Continuing conversations about continuing bonds. *Death Studies, 30*, 843–858.

Klass, D., & Chow, A.Y.M. (2011). Culture and ethnicity in experiencing, policing, and handling grief. In R.A. Neimeyer, D.L. Harris, H.R. Winokuer, & G.F. Thornton (Eds.), *Grief and bereavement in contemporary society: Bridging research and practice* (pp. 341–353). New York, NY: Routledge.

Klass, D., & Goss, R.E. (1998). Asian ways of grief. In K.J. Doka & J.D. Davidson (Eds.), *Living with grief: Who we are, how we grieve* (pp. 13–26). Washington, DC: Hospice Foundation of America.

Klass, D., Silverman, P.R., & Nickman, S.L. (Eds.). (1996). *Continuing bonds: New understandings of grief*. Washington, DC: Taylor & Francis.

Klicker, R.L. (2007). *Funeral service psychology and counseling*. Buffalo, NY: Thanos Institute.

Klugman, C.M. (2006). Dead men talking: Evidence of post death contact and continuing bonds. *Omega: Journal of Death and Dying, 53*, 249–262.

Kollar, N.R. (1989). Rituals and the disenfranchised griever. In K.J. Doka (Ed.), *Disenfranchised grief: Recognizing hidden sorrow* (pp. 271–285). Lexington, MA: Lexington Books.

Krugman, S. (1995). Male development and the transformation of shame. In R.F. Levant & W.S. Pollack (Eds.), *A new psychology of men* (pp. 91–126). New York, NY: Basic Books.

Kubitz, N., Thornton, G., & Robertson, D.U. (1989). Expectations about grief and evaluation of the griever. *Death Studies, 13*, 39–47.

Kübler-Ross, E. (1969). *On death and dying*. New York, NY: MacMillan.

Kübler-Ross, E., & Kessler, D. (2005). *On grief and grieving: Finding the meaning of grief through the five stages of loss*. New York, NY: Scribner.

Kuhn, D.R. (2002). A pastoral counselor looks at silence as a factor in disenfranchised grief. In K.J. Doka (Ed.), *Disenfranchised grief: New directions, challenges, and strategies for practice* (pp. 119–126). Champaign, IL: Research Press.

LaGrand, L.E. (2005). The nature and therapeutic implications of the extraordinary experiences of the bereaved. *Journal of Near-Death Studies, 24*, 3–20.

Lamers, W.M. (2002). Disenfranchised grief in caregivers. In K.J. Doka (Ed.), *Disenfranchised grief: New directions, challenges, and strategies for practice* (pp. 181–196). Champaign, IL: Research Press.

Larson, D.G., & Hoyt, W.T. (2007a). What has become of grief counseling? An evaluation of the empirical foundations of the new pessimism. *Professional Psychology: Research and Practice, 38*, 347–355.

Larson, D.G., & Hoyt, W.T. (2007b). The bright side of grief counseling: Deconstructing the new pessimism. In K.J. Doka (Ed.), *Living with grief: Before and after the death* (pp. 157–174). Washington, DC: Hospice Foundation of America.

Lazarus, R.S., & Folkman, S. (1984). *Stress, appraisal, and coping*. New York, NY: Springer.

Lee, G., Willetts, M.C., & Seccombe, K. (1998). Widowhood and depression: Gender differences. *Research on Aging, 20*, 611–630.

Lehman, D.R., Ellard, J.H., & Wortman, C.B. (1986). Social support for the bereaved: Recipients' and providers' perspectives on what is helpful. *Journal of Consulting and Clinical Psychology, 54*, 438–446.

REFERENCES

Lehman, D. R., Wortman, C. B., & Williams, A. F. (1987). Long-term effects of losing a spouse or child in a motor vehicle crash. *Journal of Personality and Social Psychology, 52*, 218–231.

Leong, F.T. L., Lee, S., & Chang, D. (2008). Counseling Asian Americans. In P. B. Pedersen, J. G. Draguns, W. J. Lonner, & J. E. Trimble (Eds.), *Counseling across cultures* (6th ed., pp. 113–128). Thousand Oaks, CA: Sage.

Levang, E. (1998). *When men grieve: Why men grieve differently and how you can help*. Minneapolis, MN: Fairview Press.

Levant, R. F. (1990). Psychological services designed for men: A psychoeducational approach. *Psychotherapy, 27*, 309–315.

Levant, R. F. (1992). Toward the reconstruction of masculinity. *Journal of Family Psychology, 5*, 379–402.

Levant, R. F. (1995). Toward the reconstruction of masculinity. In R. F. Levant & W. S. Pollack (Eds.), *A new psychology of men* (pp. 229–251). New York, NY: Basic Books.

Levant, R. F. (1996). The new psychology of men. *Professional Psychology: Research and Practice, 27*, 259–265.

Levant, R. F., & Pollack, W. S. (Eds.). (1995). *The new psychology of men*. New York, NY: Basic Books.

Levy, L. H., & Derby, J. F. (1992). Bereavement support groups: Who joins; who does not; and why. *American Journal of Community Psychology, 20*, 649–662.

Levy, L., Martinkowski, K., & Derby, J. (1994). Differences in patterns of adaptation in conjugal bereavement: Their sources and potential significance. *Omega: Journal of Death and Dying, 29*, 71–87.

Lewis, C. S. (1961). *A grief observed*. New York, NY: Harper Collins.

Li, G. (1995). The interaction effect of bereavement and sex on the risk or suicide in the elderly: An historical cohort study. *Social Science Medicine, 40*, 825–828.

Lichtenthal, W. G., Cruess, D. G., & Prigerson, H. G. (2004). A case for establishing complicated grief as a distinct mental disorder in *DSM-V*. *Clinical Psychology Review, 24*, 637–62.

Lieberman, M. (1996). *Doors close, doors open: Widows, grieving and growing*. New York, NY: Grosset/Putnam.

Lieberman, M. A. (1989). Group properties and outcomes: A study of group norms in self-help groups for widows and widowers. *International Journal of Group Psychotherapy, 39*, 191–208.

Lindamood, S., & Hanna, S. D. (2005, October). *Determinants of the wife being the financially responsible spouse*. Paper presented at the Academy of Financial Services Meeting, Chicago, IL.

Lindemann, E. (1944). The symptomatology and management of acute grief. *American Journal of Psychiatry, 101*, 141–148.

Liu, W. M. (2005). The study of men and masculinity as an important multicultural competency consideration. *Journal of Clinical Psychology, 61*, 685–697.

Lofquist, D., Lugaila, T., O'Connell, M., & Feliz, S. (2012). *Households and families: 2010*. (2010 Census Briefs No. C2010BR-14). Washington, DC: Census Bureau. Retrieved from www.census.gov

Lopata, H. Z. (1996). Widowhood and husband sanctification. In D. Klass, P. R. Silverman, & S. L. Nickman (Eds.), *Continuing bonds: New understandings of grief* (pp. 149–162). Washington, DC: Taylor & Francis.

Lord, J. H. (1996). America's number one killer: Vehicular crashes. In K. J. Doka (Ed.), *Living with grief after sudden loss: Suicide, homicide, accident, heart attack, stroke* (pp. 25–39). Washington, DC: Hospice Foundation of America.

Lukas, C., & Seiden, H. M. (2007). *Silent grief: Living in the wake of suicide*. Philadelphia, PA: Jessica Kingsley.

Lund, D. A. (1999). Giving and receiving help during later life spousal bereavement. In J. D. Davidson & K. J. Doka (Eds.), *Living with grief: At work, at school, at worship* (pp. 203–212). Levittown, PA: Hospice Foundation of America.

REFERENCES

Lund, D.A., & Caserta, M.S. (1992). Older bereaved spouses' participation in self-help groups. *Omega: Journal of Death and Dying, 25*, 47–61.

Lund, D.A., & Caserta, M.S. (2001). When the unexpected happens: Husbands coping with the deaths of their wives. In D. Lund (Ed.), *Men coping with grief* (pp. 147–167). Amityville, NY: Baywood.

Lund, D.A., Caserta, M.S., & Dimond, M.F. (1986). Gender differences through two years of bereavement among the elderly. *The Gerontologist, 26*, 314–320.

Lund, D.A., Caserta, M.S., & Dimond, M.F. (1989). Impact of spousal bereavement on the subjective well-being of older adults. In D.A. Lund (Ed.), *Older bereaved spouses: Research with practical applications* (pp. 3–15). New York: Taylor & Francis/Hemisphere.

Lund, D.A., Caserta, M.S., & Dimond, M.F. (1993). The course of spousal bereavement in later life. In M.S. Stroebe, W. Stroebe, & R.O. Hansson (Eds.), *Handbook of bereavement: Theory, research, and intervention* (pp. 240–254). New York, NY: Cambridge University Press.

Lund, D.A., Caserta, M.S., Dimond, M.F., & Shaffer, S.K. (1989). Competencies: Tasks of daily living and adjustments to spousal bereavement in later life. In D.A. Lund (Ed.), *Older bereaved spouses: Research with practical applications* (pp. 135–156). New York, NY: Hemisphere.

Lund, D.A., Caserta, M.S., Utz, R., & de Vries, B. (2010). Experiences and early coping of bereaved spouses/partners in an intervention based on the dual process model (DPM). *Omega: Journal of Death and Dying, 61*, 291–313.

Lundgren, B.S., & Houseman, C.A. (2010). Banishing death: The disappearance of the appreciation of mortality. *Omega: Journal of Death and Dying, 61*, 223–249.

Luoma, J.B., & Pearson, J.L. (2002). Suicide and marital status in the United States, 1991–1996: Is widowhood a risk factor? *American Journal of Public Health, 92*, 1518–1522.

Maciejewski, P.K., Zhang, B., Block, S.D., & Prigerson, H.G. (2007). An empirical examination of the stage theory of grief. *Journal of the American Medical Association, 297*, 716–723.

Mahalik, J.R., Good, G.E., & Englar-Carlson, M. (2003). Masculinity scripts, presenting concerns, and help seeking: Implications for practice and training. *Professional Psychology: Research and Practice, 34*, 123–131.

Mahoney, M.J. (2003). *Constructive psychotherapy: A practical guide.* New York, NY: Guildford Press.

Malkinson, R. (2007). *Cognitive grief therapy: Constructing a rational meaning to life following loss.* New York, NY: W.W. Norton.

Martin, T.L., & Doka, K.J. (1996). Masculine grief. In K.J. Doka (Ed.), *Living with grief after sudden loss: Suicide, homicide, accident, heart attack, stroke* (pp. 161–171). Washington, DC: Hospice Foundation of America.

Martin, T.L., & Doka, K.J. (1998). Revisiting masculine grief. In K.J. Doka & J.D. Davidson (Eds.), *Living with grief: Who we are, how we grieve* (pp. 133–142). Washington, DC: Hospice Foundation of America.

Martin, T.L., & Doka, K.J. (2000). *Men don't cry ... women do: Transcending stereotypes of grief.* Philadelphia, PA: Bruner/Mazel.

Mastrogianis, L., & Lumley, M.A. (2002). Aftercare services from funeral directors to bereaved men: Surveys of both providers and recipients. *Omega: Journal of Death and Dying, 45*, 167–185.

McCarthy, J., & Holliday, E.L. (2004). Help-seeking and counseling within a traditional male gender role: An examination from a multicultural perspective. *Journal of Counseling and Development, 82*, 25–30.

McDonald, J., Quandt, S.A., Arcury, T.A., Bell, R.A., & Vitolins, M.Z. (2000). On their own: Nutritional self-management strategies of rural widowers. *The Gerontologist, 40*, 480–491.

REFERENCES

McGill, M. E. (1985). *The McGill report on male intimacy*. New York, NY: Holt, Rinehart, and Winston.

McIntosh, J. L., Pearson, J. L., & Lebowitz, B. D. (1997). Mental disorders of elderly men. In J. I. Kosberg & L. W. Kaye (Eds.), *Elderly men: Special problems and professional challenges* (pp. 193–215). New York, NY: Springer.

Meagher, D. K., & Bell, C. P. (1993). Perspectives on death in the African-American community. In K. J. Doka & J. D. Morgan (Eds.), *Death and spirituality* (pp. 113–130). Amityville, NY: Baywood.

Mineau, G. P., Smith, K. R., & Bean, L. L. (2002). Historical trends of survival among widows and widowers. *Social Science and Medicine, 54*, 245–254.

Moen, P., Robison, J., & Dempster-McClain, D. (1995). Caregiving and women's well-being: A life course approach. *Journal of Health and Social Behavior, 36*, 259–273.

Moore, A. J., & Stratton, D. C. (2002). *Resilient widowers: Older men speak for themselves*. New York, NY: Springer.

Mosely, P. W., Davies, H. D., & Priddy, J. M. (1988). Support groups for male caregivers of Alzheimer's patients: A followup. *Clinical Gerontologist, 7*, 127–136.

Moss, M. S., & Moss, S. Z. (1989). Death of the very old. In K. J. Doka (Ed.), *Disenfranchised grief: Recognizing hidden sorrow* (pp. 213–227). Lexington, MA: Lexington Books.

Murphy, S. L., Xu, J. Q., & Kochanek, K. D. (2013). Final data for 2010. *National Vital Statistics Reports, 61*(4). Hyattsville, MD: National Center for Health Statistics.

Neimeyer, R. A. (2000). Searching for the meaning of meaning: Grief therapy and the process of reconstruction. *Death Studies, 24*, 541–548.

Neimeyer, R. A. (Ed). (2001). *Meaning reconstruction and the experience of loss*. Washington, DC: American Psychological Association.

Neimeyer, R. A. (2006). *Lessons of loss: A guide to coping*. Memphis, TN: Center for the Study of Loss and Transition.

Neimeyer, R. A. (2010). Grief counseling and therapy: The case for hope. *Bereavement Care, 29*(2), 13–16.

Neimeyer, R. A., & Jordan, J. R. (2002). Disenfranchisement as empathic failure: Grief therapy and the co-construction of meaning. In K. J. Doka (Ed.), *Disenfranchised grief: New directions, challenges, and strategies for practice* (pp. 95–117). Champaign, IL: Research Press.

Nickman, S. (1996). Retroactive loss in adopted persons. In D. Klass, P. R. Silverman, & S. L. Nickman (Eds.), *Continuing bonds: New understandings of grief* (pp. 257–272). Washington, DC: Taylor & Francis.

NIDA InfoFacts. (2012). *Drug facts: Nationwide trends*. Retrieved from www.drugabuse.gov

Nowatzki, N., & Grant Kalischuk, R. (2009). Post-death encounters: Grieving, mourning, and healing. *Omega: Journal of Death and Dying, 59*, 91–111.

Nseir, S., & Larkey, L. K. (2013). Interventions for spousal bereavement in the older adult: An evidence review. *Death Studies, 37*, 495–512.

Ober, A. M., Granello, D. H., & Wheaton, J. E. (2012). Grief counseling: An investigation of counselors' training, experience, and competencies. *Journal of Counseling and Development, 90*, 150–159.

Olson, P. R., Suddeth, J. A., Peterson, P. J., & Egelhoff, C. (1985). Hallucinations of widowhood. *Journal of the American Geriatrics Society, 33*, 541–549.

O'Neal, J. M. (1981). Male sex-role conflict, sexism, and masculinity: Implications for men, women, and the counseling psychologist. *Counseling Psychologist, 9*, 61–80.

O'Neil, J. M. (2008). Summarizing 25 years of research on men's gender role conflict using the gender role conflict scale: New research paradigms and clinical implications. *Counseling Psychologist, 36*, 358–445.

REFERENCES

O'Neill, D. E., & Mendelsohn, R. (2001). American widowers with school-age children: An exploratory study of role change and role conflict. In D. Lund (Ed.), *Men coping with grief* (pp. 169–206). Amityville, NY: Baywood.

Onrust, S. A., & Cuijpers, P. (2006). Mood and anxiety disorders in widowhood: A systematic review. *Aging and Mental Health, 10*, 327–334.

O'Rourke, T., Spitzberg, B. H., & Hannawa, A. F. (2011). The good funeral: Toward an understanding of funeral participation and satisfaction. *Death Studies, 35*, 729–750.

Osherson, S., & Krugman, S. (1990). Men, shame, and psychotherapy. *Psychotherapy, 27*, 327–339.

Park, C. L. (2008). Testing the meaning-making model of coping with loss. *Journal of Social and Clinical Psychology, 27*, 970–994.

Park, S. (2006). Facing fear without losing face: Working with Asian American men. In M. Englar-Carlson & M. A. Stevens (Eds.), *In the room with men: A casebook of therapeutic change* (pp. 151–173). Washington, DC: American Psychological Association.

Parkes, C. M. (1993). Psychiatric problems following bereavement by murder or manslaughter. *British Journal of Psychiatry, 162*, 49–54.

Parkes, C. M. (1996). *Bereavement: Studies in grief in adult life* (3rd ed.). Madison, CT: International Universities Press.

Parkes, C. M., Benjamin, B., & Fitzgerald, R. G. (1969). Broken heart: A statistical study of increased mortality among widowers. *British Medical Journal, 1*, 740–743.

Peart, N. (2002). *Ghost rider: Travels on the healing road*. Toronto: ECW Press.

Pennebaker, J. W. (1997). Writing about emotional experiences as a therapeutic process. *American Psychological Society, 8*, 162–166.

Perls, F. (1973). *The Gestalt approach and eyewitness to therapy*. Palo Alto, CA: Science & Behavior Books.

Peters, A., & Liefbroer, A. C. (1997). Beyond marital status: Partner history and well-being in old age. *Journal of Marriage and the Family, 59*, 687–699.

Petrie, R. G. (2001). *Into the cave: When men grieve*. Portland, OR: One to Another.

Picton, C., Cooper, B. K., Close, D., & Tobin, J. (2001). Bereavement support groups: Timing of participation and reasons for joining. *Omega: Journal of Death and Dying, 43*, 247–258.

Pleck, J. H. (1980). Men's power with women, other men, and society: A men's movement analysis. In E. H. Pleck & J. H. Pleck (Eds.), *The American man* (pp. 417–433). Englewood Cliffs, NJ: Prentice Hall.

Pleck, J. H. (1981). *The myth of masculinity*. Cambridge, MA: MIT Press.

Pleck, J. H. (1995). The gender role strain paradigm: An update. In R. F. Levant & W. S. Pollack (Eds.), *A new psychology of men* (pp. 11–32). New York, NY: Basic Books.

Pollack, W. S. (1995). No man is an island: Toward a new psychoanalytic psychology of men. In R. F. Levant & W. S. Pollack (Eds.), *A new psychology of men* (pp. 33–67). New York, NY: Basic Books.

Pollack, W. S. (1998). *Real boys: Rescuing our sons from the myths of boyhood*. New York, NY: Henry Holt.

Powers, L., & Wampold, B. (1994). Cognitive behavioral factors in adjustment to adult bereavement. *Death Studies, 18*, 1–24.

Prigerson, H. G., Frank, E., Kasl, S. V., Reynolds, C. F., Anderson, B., Zubenko, ... Kupfer, D. J. (1995). Complicated grief and bereavement-related depression as distinct disorders: Preliminary empirical validation in elderly bereaved spouses. *American Journal of Psychiatry, 152*, 22–30.

Prigerson, H. G., Maciejewski, P. K., Reynolds, C. F., Bierhals, A. J., Newsom, J. T., Fasiczka, ... Miller, M. (1995). Inventory of complicated grief: A scale to measure maladaptive symptoms of loss. *Psychiatry Research, 59*, 65–79.

REFERENCES

Rabinowitz, F. E. (2001). Group therapy for men. In G. R. Brooks & G. E. Good (Eds.), *The new handbook of psychotherapy and counseling with men* (pp. 603–621). San Francisco, CA: Jossey-Bass.

Ramsay, R.W. (1977). Behavioral approaches to bereavement. *Behavioral Research and Therapy, 15*, 131–135.

Rando, T.A. (1984). *Grief, dying, and death: Clinical interventions for caregivers.* Champaign, IL: Research Press.

Rando, T.A. (1985). Creating therapeutic rituals in the psychotherapy of the bereaved. *Psychotherapy, 22*, 236–240.

Rando, T.A. (1993). *Treatment of complicated mourning.* Champaign, IL: Research Press.

Rando, T.A. (1996). Complications in mourning traumatic death. In K. Doka (Ed.), *Living with grief after sudden loss: Suicide, homicide, accident, heart attack, stroke* (pp. 139–159). Washington, DC: Hospice Foundation of America.

Rando, T.A., Doka, K.J., Fleming, S., Franco, M.H., Lobb, E.A., Parkes, C.M., & Steele, R. (2012). A call to the field: Complicated grief in the DSM-5. *Omega: Journal of Death and Dying, 65*, 251–255.

Raphael, B. (1983). *The anatomy of bereavement.* New York, NY: Basic Books.

Redmond, L.M. (1989). *Surviving: When someone you love was murdered.* Clearwater, FL: Psychological Consultation and Education Services.

Redmond, L.M. (1996). Sudden violent death. In K. Doka (Ed.), *Living with grief after sudden loss: Suicide, homicide, accident, heart attack, stroke* (pp. 53–71). Washington, DC: Hospice Foundation of America.

Reed, M.D., & Greenwald, T.Y. (1991) Survivor victim status, attachment, and sudden death bereavement. *Suicide and Life-Threatening Behavior, 21*, 311–332.

Rees, W.D. (1971). The hallucinations of widowhood. *British Medical Journal, 4*, 37–41.

Richardson, V.E. (2010). Length of caregiving and well-being among older widowers: Implications for the dual process model of bereavement. *Omega: Journal of Death and Dying, 61*, 333–356.

Richardson, V.E., & Balaswamy, S. (2001). Coping with bereavement among elderly widowers. *Omega: Journal of Death and Dying, 43*, 129–144.

Roberts, J. (2003). Setting the frame: Definition, functions, and typology of rituals. In E. Imber-Black, J. Roberts, & R.A. Whiting (Eds.), *Rituals in families and family therapy* (rev. ed., pp. 3–48). New York, NY: W.W. Norton.

Roberts, P. (2010). What now? Cremation without tradition. *Omega: Journal of Death and Dying, 62*, 1–30.

Robertson, J.M. (2001). Counseling men in college settings. In G. R. Brooks & G. E. Good (Eds.), *The new handbook of psychotherapy and counseling with men* (Vol. 1, pp. 146–169). San Francisco, CA: Jossey-Bass.

Robertson, J.M. (2006). Finding Joshua's soul: Working with religious men. In M. Englar-Carlson & M.A. Stevens (Eds.), *In the room with men: A casebook of therapeutic change* (pp. 109–127). Washington, DC: American Psychological Association.

Robertson, J.M. (2012). *Tough guys and true believers: Managing authoritarian men in the psychotherapy room.* New York, NY: Routledge.

Robertson, J.M., & Fitzgerald, L.F. (1992). Overcoming the masculine mystique: Preferences for alternative forms of assistance among men who avoid counseling. *Journal of Counseling Psychology, 39*, 240–246.

Robson, P., & Walter, T. (2012–13). Hierarchies of loss: A critique of disenfranchised grief. *Omega: Journal of Death and Dying, 66*, 97–119.

REFERENCES

Rogers, C. (1951). *Client-centered therapy: Its current practice, implications, and theory*. Boston, MA: Houghton Mifflin.

Rognlie, C. (1989). Perceived short- and long-term effects of bereavement support group participation at the hospice of Petaluma. *Hospice Journal, 5*, 39–53.

Romanoff, B. D., & Terenzio, M. (1998). Rituals and the grieving process. *Death Studies, 22*, 697–711.

Rosenblatt, P., & Wallace, B. (2005). *African American grief*. New York, NY: Routledge.

Rosenblatt, P., Walsh, R., & Jackson, D. (1976). *Grief and mourning in cross-cultural perspective*. Washington, DC: HRAF Press.

Rosik, C. H. (1989). The impact of religious orientation on conjugal bereavement among older adults. *International Journal of Aging and Human Development, 28*, 251–260.

Rubin, S. S. (1999). The two-track model of bereavement: Overview, retrospect, and prospect. *Death Studies, 23*, 681–714.

Rubinstein, R. L. (1986). *Singular paths: Old men living alone*. New York, NY: Columbia University Press.

Russell, R. (2004). Social networks among elderly men caregivers. *Journal of Men's Studies, 13*, 121–142.

Rynearson, E. K. (1994). Psychotherapy of bereavement after homicide. *Journal of Psychotherapy Practice and Research, 3*, 341–347.

Rynearson, E. K. (2012). The narrative dynamics of grief after homicide. *Omega: Journal of Death and Dying, 65*, 239–249.

Sabar, S. (2000). Bereavement, grief, and mourning: A Gestalt perspective. *Gestalt Review, 4*, 152–168.

Sanders, C. M. (1983). Effects of sudden vs. chronic illness death in bereavement outcome. *Omega: Journal of Death and Dying, 13*, 227–241.

Sanders, C. M. (1999). *Grief: The mourning after* (2nd ed.). New York, NY: John Wiley & Sons.

Sanfelix, J., Palop, V., Pereiro, I., Rubio, E., Gosalbes, V., & Martinez-Mir, I. (2008). Gender influence in the quantity of drugs used in primary care. *Gaceta Sanitaria, 22*, 11–19.

Schaefer, C., Quesenberry, C. P., & Wi, S. (1995). Mortality following conjugal bereavement and the effects of shared environment. *American Journal of Epidemiology, 141*, 1142–1152.

Schaefer, G. J., & Bekkers, T. (2010). *The widower's toolbox*. Far Hills, NJ: New Horizon Press.

Schneider, R. M. (2006). Group bereavement support for spouses who are grieving the loss of a partner to cancer. *Social Work with Groups, 29*, 259–278.

Schut, H., & Stroebe, M. S. (2005). Interventions to enhance adaptation to bereavement. *Journal of Palliative Medicine, 8*, S140–147.

Schut, H. A. W., Stroebe, M. S., van den Bout, J., & de Keijser, J. (1997). Intervention for the bereaved: Gender differences in the efficacy of grief counseling. *British Journal of Clinical Psychology, 36*, 63–72.

Scott, S. (1987). Grief reactions to the death of a divorced spouse. In C. Corr & R. Pacholski (Eds.), *Death: Completion and discovery* (pp. 107–116). Lakewood, OH: ADEC.

Scott, S. (2000). Grief reactions to the death of a divorced spouse revisited. *Omega: Journal of Death and Dying, 41*, 207–219.

Servaty-Seib, H. L. (2004). Connections between counseling theories and current theories of grief and mourning. *Journal of Mental Health Counseling, 26*, 125–145.

Shernoff, M. (Ed.). (1997a). *Gay widowers: Life after the death of a partner*. Binghamton, NY: Haworth Press.

Shernoff, M. (1997b). Conclusion: Mental health considerations of gay widowers. In M. Shernoff (Ed.), *Gay widowers: Life after the death of a partner* (pp. 137–155). Binghamton, NY: Haworth Press.

REFERENCES

Shuchter, S. R., & Zisook, S. (1993). The course of normal grief. In M. S. Stroebe, W. Stroebe, & R. O. Hansson (Eds.), *Handbook of bereavement: Theory, research, and intervention* (pp. 23–43). New York, NY: Cambridge University Press.

Sieber, S. D. (1974). Toward a theory of role accumulation. *American Sociological Review, 39*, 567–578.

Silverman, P. R., & Klass, D. (1996). Introduction: What's the problem? In D. Klass, P. R. Silverman, & S. L. Nickman (Eds.), *Continuing bonds: New understandings of grief* (pp. 3–27). Washington, DC: Taylor & Francis.

Silverman, P. R., & Nickman, S. L. (1996). Concluding thoughts. In D. Klass, P. R. Silverman, & S. L. Nickman (Eds.), *Continuing bonds: New understandings of grief* (pp. 349–355). Washington, DC: Taylor & Francis.

Silverman, P. R., Nickman, S., & Worden, J. W. (1992). Detachment revisited: The child's reconstruction of a dead parent. *American Journal of Orthopsychiatry, 62*, 494–503.

Silverman, P. R., & Worden, J. W. (1992). Children's reactions in the early months after the death of a parent. *American Journal of Orthopsychiatry, 62*, 93–104.

Simon-Buller, S., Christopherson, V. A., & Jones, R. A. (1988). Correlates of sensing the presence of a deceased spouse. *Omega: Journal of Death and Dying, 19*, 21–30.

Skulason, B., Jonsdottir, L. S., Sigurdardottir, V., & Helgason, A. R. (2012). Assessing survival in widowers, and controls—A nationwide, six- to nine-year follow-up. *BMC Public Health, 12*, 96–104.

Smilansky, S. (1987). *On death: Helping children understand and cope*. New York, NY: Guilford Press.

Snyder, C. R., Lopez, S. J., & Pedrotti, J. T. (2011). *Positive psychology: The scientific and practical explorations of human strengths*. Thousand Oaks, CA: Sage.

Staudacher, C. (1991). *Men and grief*. Oakland, CA: New Harbinger.

Steiner, C. S. (2006). Grief support groups used by few—Are bereaved needs being met? *Journal of Social Work in End-of-Life and Palliative Care, 2*, 29–53.

Stelle, C. D., & Uchida, M. (2004). The stability and change in the social support networks of widowers following spousal bereavement. *Journal of Men's Studies, 13*, 85–105.

Sternbach, J. (1990). The men's seminar: An educational and support group for men. *Social Work with Groups, 13*, 23–39.

Stevens, M. A., & Englar-Carlson, M. (2006). An invitation: Bringing the reader into the book. In M. Englar-Carlson & M. A. Stevens (Eds.), *In the room with men: A casebook of therapeutic change* (pp. 3–11). Washington, DC: American Psychological Association.

Stillion, J. M. (1996). Survivors of suicide. In K. Doka (Ed.), *Living with grief after sudden loss: Suicide, homicide, accident, heart attack, stroke* (pp. 41–51). Washington, DC: Hospice Foundation of America.

Stroebe, M. S. (1992). Coping with bereavement: A review of the grief work hypothesis. *Omega: Journal of Death and Dying, 26*, 19–42.

Stroebe, M. S. (1998). New directions in bereavement research: Exploration of gender differences. *Palliative Medicine, 12*, 5–12.

Stroebe, M. S., Gergen, M., Gergen, K., & Stroebe, W. (1992). Broken hearts or broken bonds: Love and death in historical perspective. *American Psychologist, 47*, 1205–1212.

Stroebe, M. S., Hansson, R. O., Stroebe, W., & Schut, H. (2001). Introduction: Concepts and issues in contemporary research on bereavement. In M. S. Stroebe, R. O. Hansson, W. Stroebe, & H. Schut (Eds.), *Handbook of bereavement research: Consequences, coping, and care* (pp. 3–22). Washington, DC: American Psychological Association.

Stroebe, M. S., & Schut, H. (1999). Dual process model of coping with bereavement: Rationale and description. *Death Studies, 23*, 197–224.

Stroebe, M. S., & Schut, H. (2005). To continue or relinquish bonds: A review of consequences for the bereaved. *Death Studies, 29*, 477–494.

Stroebe, M. S., & Schut, H. (2010). The dual process model of coping with bereavement: A decade on. *Omega: Journal of Death and Dying, 61*, 273–289.

Stroebe, M. S., & Stroebe, W. (1989). Who participates in bereavement research? A review and empirical study. *Omega: Journal of Death and Dying, 20*, 1–29.

Stroebe, M. S., & Stroebe, W. (1991). Does "grief work" work? *Journal of Consulting and Clinical Psychology, 59*, 479–482.

Stroebe, M. S., & Stroebe, W. (1993). The mortality of bereavement: A review. In M. S. Stroebe, W. Stroebe, & R. O. Hansson (Eds.), *Handbook of bereavement: Theory, research, and intervention* (pp. 175–195). New York, NY: Cambridge University Press.

Stroebe, M. S., Stroebe, W., & Schut, H. (2001). Gender differences in adjustment to bereavement: An empirical and theoretical review. *Review of General Psychology, 5*, 62–83.

Stroebe, M. S., Stroebe, W., Schut, H., Zech, E., & van den Bout, J. (2002). Does disclosure of emotion facilitate recovery from bereavement? Evidence from two prospective studies. *Journal of Consulting and Clinical Psychology, 70,* 169–178.

Stroebe, W., & Schut, H. (2001). Risk factors in bereavement outcome: A methodological and empirical review. In M. S. Stroebe, R. O. Hansson, W. Stroebe, & H. Schut (Eds.), *Handbook of bereavement research: Consequences, coping, and care* (pp. 349–371). Washington, DC: American Psychological Association.

Stroebe, W., Schut, H., & Stroebe, M. S. (2005). Grief work, disclosure and counseling: Do they help the bereaved? *Clinical Psychology Review, 25*, 395–414.

Stroebe, W., & Stroebe, M. S. (1987). *Bereavement and health: The psychological and physical consequences of partner loss*. Cambridge, England: Cambridge University Press.

Stroebe, W., Stroebe, M. S., & Abakoumkin, G. (1999). Does differential social support cause sex differences in bereavement outcome? *Journal of Community and Applied Social Psychology, 9*, 1–12.

Sue, D. W., & Sue, D. (2013). *Counseling the culturally diverse: Theory and practice* (6th ed.). New York, NY: John Wiley & Sons.

Sullivan, E. M., Annest, J. L., Luo, F., Simon, T. R., & Dahlberg, L. L. (2013). Suicide among adults aged 35–64 years. *Morbidity and Mortality Weekly Report, 62*(17), 321–325.

Sweet, H. (2006). Finding the person behind the persona: Engaging men as a female therapist. In M. Englar-Carlson & M. A. Stevens (Eds.), *In the room with men: A casebook of therapeutic change* (pp. 69–90). Washington, DC: American Psychological Association.

Tatelbaum, J. (1984). *The courage to grieve*. New York, NY: Perennial Library.

Tedeschi, R. G., & Calhoun, L. G. (1993). Using the support group to respond to the isolation of bereavement. *Journal of Mental Health Counseling, 15*, 47–54.

Thompson, E. H. (1998). Older men as invisible in contemporary society. In M. S. Kimmel & M. A. Messner (Eds.), *Men's lives* (pp. 68–83). Needham Heights, MA: Allyn & Bacon.

Tolle, S. W., Bascom, P. B., Hickam, D. H., & Benson, J. A. (1986). Communication between physicians and surviving spouses following patient deaths. *Journal of General Internal Medicine, 1*, 309–314.

Troyer, J. M. (2011, June). *Action-oriented grief: Widowers' use of rituals*. Research presentation at the Annual Meeting of the Association of Death Educators and Counselors (ADEC), Miami, FL.

Troyer, J. M. (in press). Older widowers and post-death encounters: A qualitative investigation. *Death Studies*.

Umberson, D. (1987). Family status and health behaviors: Social control as a dimension of social integration. *Journal of Health and Social Behavior, 28*, 306–319.

Umberson, D. (1992). Gender, marital status and the social control of health behavior. *Social Science and Medicine, 34*, 907–917.

Umberson, D., Wortman, C. B., & Kessler, R. C. (1992). Widowhood and depression: Explaining long-term gender differences in vulnerability. *Journal of Health and Social Behavior, 33*, 10–24.

US Census Bureau. (2004). *Marital history for people 15 years and over, by age and sex: 2004 (Table 3.)* Retrieved from www.census.gov

US Census Bureau. (2010). *Marital status of the population by sex and age: 2010*. Retrieved from www.census.gov

US Census Bureau. (2012). *State and county quickfacts*. Retrieved from quickfacts.census.gov

US Department of Transportation. (2011, April). *Early estimate of motor vehicle traffic fatalities in 2010* (DOT HS 811 451). Retrieved from www-nrd.nhtsa.dot.gov/Pubs/811451.pdf

Utz, R. L. (2006). Economic and practical adjustments to late life spousal loss. In D. Carr, R. Nesse, & C. B. Wortman (Eds.), *Spousal bereavement in late life* (pp. 167–192). New York, NY: Springer.

Vale-Taylor, P. (2009). "We will remember them": A mixed-method study to explore which post-funeral remembrance activities are most significant and important to bereaved people living with loss, and why those particular activities are chosen. *Palliative Medicine, 23*, 537–544.

van der Hart, O. (1983). *Rituals in psychotherapy: Transition and continuity*. New York, NY: Irvington.

van der Hart, O. (1988a). Transition rituals. In O. van der Hart (Ed.), *Coping with loss: The therapeutic use of leave-taking rituals* (pp. 3–6). New York, NY: Irvington. [translated from Dutch by Carol L. Stennes]

van der Hart, O. (1988b). Myths and rituals: Their use in psychotherapy. In O. van der Hart (Ed.), *Coping with loss: The therapeutic use of leave-taking rituals* (pp. 7–22). New York, NY: Irvington. [translated from Dutch by Carol L. Stennes]

van der Hart, O. (1988c). Symbols in leave-taking rituals. In O. van der Hart (Ed.), *Coping with loss: The therapeutic use of leave-taking rituals* (pp. 23–33). New York, NY: Irvington. [translated from Dutch by Carol L. Stennes]

van Grootheest, D. S., Beekman, A.T. F., Broese van Groenou, M. I., & Deeg, D. J. H. (1999). Sex differences in depression after widowhood: Do men suffer more? *Social Psychiatry and Psychiatric Epidemiology, 34*, 391–398.

Vazquez, C. I., & Rosa, D. (2011). *Grief therapy with Latinos*. New York, NY: Springer.

Waskowic, T. D., & Chartier, B. M. (2003). Attachment and the experience of grief following the loss of a spouse. *Omega: Journal of Death and Dying, 47*, 77–91.

Wass, H. (2004). A perspective on the current state of death education. *Death Studies, 28*, 289–308.

Wayment, H. A., & Vierthaler, J. (2002). Attachment style and bereavement reactions. *Journal of Loss and Trauma, 7*, 129–149.

Weeks, O. D. (1996). Using funerals rituals to help survivors. In K. J. Doka (Ed.), *Living with grief after sudden loss: Suicide, homicide, accident, heart attack, stroke* (pp. 127–138). Washington, DC: Hospice Foundation of America.

Weiss, R. S. (1993). Loss and recovery. In M. S. Stroebe, W. Stroebe, & R. O. Hansson (Eds.), *Handbook of bereavement: Theory, research, and intervention* (pp. 271–284). New York, NY: Cambridge University Press.

Whiting, R. A. (2003). Guidelines to designing therapeutic rituals. In E. Imber-Black, J. Roberts, & R. A. Whiting (Eds.), *Rituals in families and family therapy* (rev. ed., pp. 88–119). New York, NY: W.W. Norton.

Wilde, W. (1997). No return. In M. Shernoff (Ed.), *Gay widowers: Life after the death of a partner* (pp. 43–58). Binghamton, NY: Haworth Press.

REFERENCES

Wilder, G. (2005). *Kiss me like a stranger: My search for love and art*. New York, NY: St. Martin's Press.

Winokuer, H. R., & Harris, D. L. (2012). *Principles and practice of grief counseling*. New York, NY: Springer.

Wisocki, P. A., & Skowron, J. (2000). The effects of gender and culture on adjustment to widowhood. In R. M. Eisler & M. Hersen (Eds.), *Handbook of gender, culture, and health* (pp. 429–447). Mahwah, NJ: Lawrence Erlbaum.

Wolfelt, A. (1990). Gender roles and grief: Why men's grief is naturally complicated. *Thanatos, 15*(3), 20–24.

Wolfelt, A. D. (2006). *Companioning the bereaved: A soulful guide for caregivers*. Fort Collins, CO: Companion Press.

Wolin, S., & Wolin, S. (1993). *The resilient self: How survivors of troubled families rise above adversity*. New York, NY: Villard.

Worden, J. W. (1982). *Grief counseling and grief therapy: A handbook for the mental health practitioner* (1st ed.). New York, NY: Springer.

Worden, J. W. (1996a). *Children and grief: When a parent dies*. New York, NY: Guilford Press.

Worden, J. W. (1996b). *Grief counseling and grief therapy: A handbook for the mental health practitioner* (2nd ed.). New York, NY: Springer.

Worden, J. W. (2002). *Grief counseling and grief therapy: A handbook for the mental health practitioner* (3rd ed.). New York, NY: Springer.

Worden, J. W. (2009). *Grief counseling and grief therapy: A handbook for the mental health practitioner* (4th ed.). New York, NY: Springer.

Worden, J. W., & Silverman, P. R. (1993). Grief and depression in newly widowed parents with school-age children. *Omega: Journal of Death and Dying, 27*, 251–260.

Worden, J. W., & Silverman, P. R. (1996). Parental death and the adjustment of school-age children. *Omega: Journal of Death and Dying, 33*, 91–102.

Wortman, C. B., & Boerner, K. (2011). Beyond the myths of coping with loss: Prevailing assumptions versus scientific evidence. In H. S. Friedman (Ed.), *Oxford handbook of health psychology* (pp. 438–476). Oxford: Oxford University Press.

Wortman, C. B., & Silver, R. C. (1989). The myths of coping with loss. *Journal of Consulting and Clinical Psychology, 57*, 349–357.

Wortman, C. B., & Silver, R. C. (2001). The myths of coping with loss revisited. In M. S. Stroebe, R. O. Hansson, W. Stroebe, & H. Schut (Eds.), *Handbook of bereavement research: Consequences, coping, and care* (pp. 405–430). Washington, DC: American Psychological Association.

Wright, P. H. (1982). Men's friendships, women's friendships, and the alleged inferiority of the latter. *Sex Roles, 8*, 1–20.

Yalom, I. D. (1980). *Existential psychotherapy*. New York, NY: Basic Books.

Yalom, I. D. (1989). *Love's executioner*. New York, NY: HarperCollins.

Yalom, I. D. (2002). *The gift of therapy: An open letter to a new generation of therapists and their patients*. New York, NY: HarperCollins.

Yalom, I. D., & Leszcz, M. (2005). *The theory and practice of group psychotherapy* (5th ed.). New York, NY: Basics Books.

Yalom, I. D., & Vinogradov, S. (1988). Bereavement groups: Techniques and themes. *International Journal of Group Psychotherapy, 38*, 419–446.

Zernike, K. (2007, November 18). Love in the time of dementia. *The New York Times*. Retrieved from www.nytimes.com/2007/11/18/weekinreview/18zernike.html?pagewanted=all&_r=0

REFERENCES

Zhang, B., El-Jawahri, A., & Prigerson, H. G. (2006). Update on bereavement research: Evidence-based guidelines for the diagnosis and treatment of complicated bereavement. *Journal of Palliative Medicine, 9*, 1188–1203.

Zinner, E. (2000). Being a man about it: The marginalization of men and grief. *Illness, Crisis, and Loss, 8*, 181–188.

Zisook, S., Chentsova-Dutton, Y., & Shuchter, S. R. (1998). PTSD following bereavement. *Annals of Clinical Psychiatry, 10*, 157–163.

Zisook, S., & DeVaul, R. (1985). Unresolved grief. *American Journal of Psychoanalysis, 45*, 370–379.

Zisook, S., & Shear, K. (2009). Grief and bereavement: What psychiatrists need to know. *World Psychiatry, 8*, 67–74.

Zisook, S., & Shuchter, S. R. (1985). Time course of spousal bereavement. *General Hospital Psychiatry, 7*, 95–100.

INDEX

absent grief 129–30
affective counseling strategies 144–5
African American widowers 191–3; importance of funeral 191; strengths 192
after-death communication *see* post-death encounters
alcohol abuse 10, 89–90
ambiguous losses 67, 85, 113
anger xx, 25, 56, 112, 117–19; all-male groups 166–7; attachment 73; divorced widowers 187–8; guilt and 115; inappropriate use of 165; preventable deaths 84; psychotherapists fear of 37; stages of grief 56; suicide and 81–2; tasks of mourning 60–1; traumatic death 80; unfinished business 162
Asian American widowers 194–6; expression of emotion 195; length of death rituals 195; losing face 195
assessment 138–40; benefits post-loss 140; continuing bonds 139; death-related factors 138; early grief experiences 138; grief reactions 138; health behaviors 138; pre-loss factors 138; rituals 138; social support 140; spiritual/religious reactions 140; strengths 140

bereavement: conjugal bereavement 41; *see also* grief
bibliotherapy 153
blended grieving style 105

caregiving husbands 2; guilt 83–4, 116; relief 123–5
client-centered counseling 143–4
closure 51, 55; as goal of counseling 135–6
cognitive and cognitive-behavioral counseling 145–7
cohabitating widowers 188–9; disenfranchised grief 189; social support 189
complicated grief 126–30; conceptualization of 126–7; distorted or traumatic grief 129; factors related to 127–8; inhibited or absent grief 129–30; masked grief 130; prolonged grief 126, 127–8; time and 127
connections to the deceased *see* continuing bonds
continuing bonds 46–7, 51–5, 64; assessment 139–40; counseling 54–5; grief outcome 53–4; harmful 52–3; tasks of mourning 61–2; transforming 54; types of 52
coping strategies: alcohol abuse 10, 89–90; Dual Process Model 62–4; emotion-focused and problem focused 63; finances 15; focus on practical problems 7; household tasks 8, 74, 108, 181–2; masculinity 75–6; religiosity 77; social support 4; substance abuse 10–11, 89–90; suicide 13; tasks performed by the deceased 74
counseling: assessment 138–40; avoidance of 34–6; closure and 135–6; common factors in 133–4; common mistakes 141–2; efficacy of 132–3; empathy 30–4; gender-aware perspective 36–7; gender roles

INDEX

108–10; goals of 134–6; grief counseling vs grief therapy 131; grieving styles and 107–10; group counseling 164–77; masculinity 108–10; multi-cultural process 37–8; phases of 137–42, 142–63; resolution and 135–6; use of metaphor 45; welcoming men to 36–8; *see also* counseling techniques; counseling theories; group counseling

counseling techniques 152–63; bibliotherapy 153; creative methods 155–6; empty chair 154–5, 162; exercise 153; experiments and 140–1; journaling & letter writing 152–3; rituals 156–63; *see also* rituals

counseling theories 142–52; affective strategies 144–5; client-centered 143–4; cognitive & cognitive behavioral 145–7; constructivist 147–50; existential 147–50; meaning reconstruction 147–50; spiritually focused 151–2;

course of grief 90–1; *see also* length of grief

creative counseling methods 155–6

cutting ties to the deceased 50–1, 54–5, 146; closure and 135–6; cognitive therapy 146; men's grief 94; tasks of mourning 58–9; *see also* closure

denial 56, 59–60, 80, 111–14, 120, 142, 157

depression 8–9, 72, 73, 125, 129

disenfranchised grief 66–9; age and 181; circumstances of death 67; divorced widowers 187; funerals 69; gay widowers 184–6; griever is not recognized 67; grieving styles 106–7; loss is not recognized 67; older widowers 181; post-funeral rituals 158; relationship is not recognized 66–7; relief and 124; self-disenfranchisement 69, 188, 189; spiritually 152; stigmatized deaths 86; use in grief counseling 69; ways individuals grieve 67

dissonant grieving style *see* grieving styles, dissonant response

distorted grief 129

divorced widowers 186–8; disenfranchised grief 187; social support 187–8

dosing emotions 63, 100, 101, 104, 115, 153

DPM *see* Dual Process Model of Coping with Bereavement

Dual Process Model of Coping with Bereavement 57, 62–4; loss-oriented stressors 62, 63; oscillation 62–3; restoration-oriented stressors 62, 63

emotions xx–xxi; affective strategies 144–5; coping strategies 7; dosing 63, 100, 101, 104, 115, 153; Dual Process Model 63; empty chair 155; grief work assumption 47–9, 93–4; grieving styles 97–9, 102, 104–5; groups 173, 174–5; male norms 19, 21–2, 23, 25, 26–7, 33–5; men's grief 94, 96; reluctance to express 7; rituals 158

empathy 30–4; action-oriented 75–6, 146; client-centered approach 143–4; fear and 120–1; minority widowers 197

empty chair 154–5, 162

engaged widowers 2, 190

ethnic minority widowers *see* African American widowers; Asian American widowers; Latino widowers

existential counseling 147–50

expectation to die before partner xx, 14–15, 75, 148

fear 120–1; breaking down emotionally 170; exposure techniques and 146

financial stressors 15; finances as mediator of grief 88–9

forgetting the deceased *see* cutting ties to the deceased

Four Injunctions 20–2; groups 173, 174–5; influence on widowers 24–6, 75, 113, 128; machismo and 193–4; modern influence 24; role of shame 23; *see also* male gender roles

Freud, Sigmund 47, 50, 91

gay widowers 183–6; disenfranchised grief 184; HIV/AIDS 185–6; homosexual identity 183–4; positive role models 184; recognition of relationship 185; social support 184

gender identity model 18

gender norms *see* male gender roles, gender norms

INDEX

gender role conflict 19–20
gender role discrepancy 19
gender role dysfunction 19
gender role strain paradigm 18–20
gender role trauma 19
ghosts *see* post-death encounters
goals of counseling 134–6
grief: containers and 158; course of 90–1; definition 40; length of 91–2; manifestations of 42–4; men's 93–6; metaphors for 44–6; secondary losses 41, 90, 113, 121, 172; *see also* closure; grief counseling; grief reactions; mediators of grief
grief counseling *see* counseling
grief reactions: anger 117–19; common responses 112–26; deification 125–6; denial 111–14; fear 120–1; guilt 115–17; helplessness 121–2; loneliness 122–3; meaninglessness 122; relief 123–5; shame 119–20; shock and numbness 114–15; symptoms 42–4; *see also* mediators of grief
grief theories 46–64; *see also* models of grief
grief therapy *see* counseling
grief work hypothesis xxi, 47–51; criticisms of 48–9
grieving styles xxi, 96–110; adaptive strategies 99–100; blended style 105; disenfranchised grief and 106–7; dissonant response 105–6; emotions and 99; grief counseling and 107–10; instrumental 97–104; intuitive 97–100; limitations of 110
group counseling 164–77; advertising 176; benefits of 169–70; characteristics of effective groups 172–5; Dual Process Model 170–1; emotional expression 174; grieving styles 170–1; pre-screening members 176–7; problem-solving 173–4; reluctance to join 170–2; rituals 175; safety and acceptance in 173; self-help vs. professionally led groups 164; single-sex vs. mixed groups 166–7; social groups 168–9; socializing outside of 177; specific loss vs. multiple loss groups 167–8; starting a group 175–7; structured vs. unstructured groups 165–6; time-limited vs. open-ended groups 168; widowed group leaders 164–5
guilt 53, 60–1, 115–17; attachment and 73; cohabitating widowers and 189; continuing bonds and 53; divorced widowers and 187; HIV/AIDS and 186; positive reframe for 34; prolonged illnesses 83–4; relief and 123; shame and 119; suicide and 81–2; survivor guilt 8; tasks of mourning and 60–1; traumatic death and 80; traumatic grief and 129; unexpected death and 79; unfinished business and 162

health behaviors 9–10; influence of diet 9–10
heart attack or stroke 79
Hispanic widowers *see* Latino widowers
homicide or violent death 80–1, 83, 85–6, 115, 117, 121, 196–7
household tasks 8, 74, 108, 181–2
humor: dual-process model and 75; instrumental style 100; in groups 166, 169; positive aspect of traditional masculinity 29

inhibited grief 72, 129–30
instrumental grieving style *see* grieving styles, instrumental
intuitive grieving style *see* grieving styles, intuitive

journaling 64, 152–3

Kübler-Ross, Elisabeth 46, 55–7, 59; stage model of grief 55–7, 65, 112

lack of grief expertise; funeral directors 66; nurses 66; physicians 66; psychotherapists 1, 65–6
Latino widowers 193–4; machismo 193, 194; orgullo 193, 194; tradicionalismo 193–4
length of grief 91–2; *see also* course of grief
liberating losses 115, 123–5
loneliness 5–6, 122–3; substance abuse and 10; tasks of mourning and 60
loss 40–1; secondary losses 41, 90, 113, 121, 172; *see also* grief

male gender roles 18–29; avoidance of femininity 21–2, 25; development of 20;

INDEX

gender norms 106, 109, 119, 144; gender role conflict 19–20; gender role strain paradigm 18–20; gender stereotypes 18; help-seeking 34–6; impermanence of masculinity 23; impossible standards 22–3; positive aspects 27–9; unclear standards 21–2

marriage: benefits for men 4

masculinity scripts 32–4; reframing empathically 33–4

masculinity: action-oriented empathy and 75–6, 146; conflict with counseling 34–6; coping strategies 7–8; dual process model 63–4; four injunctions 20–2; impermanence of 23; impossible standards 22–3; modern influence 24; positive aspects of 27–9, 75–6; recognizing strengths and weaknesses of 17–18; unclear standards 21–2; *see also* male gender roles

masked grief 130

meaning reconstruction 147–50

mediators of grief 70–92; characteristics of the bereaved 75–6, 77, 85; characteristics of the loss 78–82, 83–6; concurrent stressors 73, 88–90; relationship with the deceased 71–2, 73–4; social factors 86–8

men's grief 93–6; emphasis on grief work 94; historical perspective 93–6; influence of gender roles 95

models of grief: benefits 64–5; Dual Process Model 57, 62–4; Integrative Theory of Bereavement 57; limitations 64–5; Meaning-Making Model 57; process of mourning 57; psychotherapists outdated views of 65–6; stage models of grief 55–7; tasks of mourning 57–62, 112, 121, 143; Two-Track Model 46, 57, 65

mortality rates 11

mourning 40, 41; *see also* grief; tasks of mourning

multiple losses 84–5

new psychology of men perspective xix, 17–18

parenting 88, 108, 180, 189

patterns of grief *see* grieving styles

personal items of deceased 145, 159–60

Positive Psychology/Positive Masculinity (PPPM) perspective xix, 17–18; use with widowers 30–4

post-death encounters 46

preventable deaths 84

prolonged grief 126, 127–8

prolonged illnesses 83–4

pseudoautonomy of husbands xx, 26–7

relief 123–5; caregiving and 116; HIV/AIDS and 186; liberating losses and 123–4; suicide and 82

remarriage 167, 178, 181

rituals 156–63; containers and 158; counseling groups 175; disenfranchised grief 158; examples of 102–3, 104, 156–7, 158, 159–60, 161, 162, 175, 181, 190, 195, 196–7; expressing feelings 160; funerals 69, 85, 146, 157; gravesite visitation 158, 159–60, 175, 181; group recognition 160–2; honoring the deceased 159–60; letting go 160, 161; moments of significance 156–7; performing 159; pondering 159; preparation for 159; process of 159; purposes of 159–62; recognizing milestones 162–3; recognizing transitions 160; threshold experiences 156–7; unfinished business 162

shame 119–20; disenfranchised grief 68–9; female influence 27; gender norms 21–3; stigmatizing deaths 86; suicide and 82

shock and numbness 90, 111, 112, 114–15, 142; grieving style 100, 106; groups 177; suicide 81–2; unexpected death 78

social support xix, 86–7; gay widowers 184; offered less 4; reluctance to seek 4–5; social role involvement 87–8; widowers viewed as threat 5–6

spirituality: African American widowers 195; Asian American widowers 192; assessment 140; existential perspective 149; questioning 151–2; religiosity 77; rituals and 150, 156; tasks of mourning 60–1

spiritually focused counseling 151–2

INDEX

stage models of grief 55–7; criticisms of 56–7; misuse of 57, 65; *see also* Kübler-Ross, Elisabeth
substance abuse 10–11, 89–90
sudden and unexpected deaths 78–80
suicide 11–14; anger and 81–2; grief and 78, 81–2; guilt and 81–2; relief and 82; shame and 82; shock and numbness 81–2; widowers committing 12, 13–14

tasks of mourning 57–62, 112, 121, 143; evolution of fourth task 58–9, 61–2; use in counseling 64
tasks performed by the deceased 74
therapy *see* counseling
ties to the deceased *see* continuing bonds
traumatic deaths 80–2, 114, 121
traumatic grief 129

unmarried widowers 2

vehicle accidents 79–80

wedding rings 160, 161
widowers: challenges 2–15; children and 178–80; cohabitating widowers 188–9; definition 2; demographics 2–3; divorced widowers 2, 186–8; engaged widowers 2, 190; expectation to die before partner 14–15; forgotten population 3; gay widowers 2; oldest widowers 180–2; participation in research 3; research limitations 15–16; unmarried widowers 2
witnessing the death 82–3
Worden, William 57–62 *see also* tasks of mourning